What Happened to Fairbanks?

Social Impact Assessment Series

Charles P. Wolf, General Editor

What Happened to Fairbanks?
The Effects of the Trans-Alaska Oil Pipeline
on the Community of Fairbanks, Alaska

Mim Dixon

When the Alaska pipeline was planned, it was generally assumed that Fairbanks--serving as a transportation, employment,
and supply center--would reap many benefits. *What Happened to
Fairbanks?*, the result of a two-year research project, is a
close look at the actual effects of the pipeline construction
on the community.

Mim Dixon worked with the unique community-directed Impact
Information Center for two years and discovered that many of
the expected changes never materialized. Dixon describes what
Fairbanks was like during pipeline construction and how the
community responded to the project, and she assesses the un-
planned negative effects that, in many cases, outweighed the
positive ones. The influx of outsiders who came seeking pipeline jobs drastically affected the city's ability to provide
such vital services as housing, transportation, telephones,
and electricity. Increases in prostitution and street fighting,
decreasing family cohesiveness, and inflation caused by the
high wages of pipeline workers contributed to Fairbanks'
problems.

Dixon's conclusion is that official policy must require
that resource development projects take responsibility for
social effects and involve affected communities in planning
for their futures. The author not only analyzes the failure of
current planning models, but also offers a more comprehensive,
more viable model. The book closes with discussion of the lessons that can be learned from Fairbanks' experience and their
application to social science research.

Mim Dixon holds a Ph.D. in anthropology from Northwestern
University. She has served as a consultant to the Joint
Federal State Land Use Planning Commission and the State of
Alaska Office of the Attorney General, and most recently as
director of the community-directed research organization in
Fairbanks established to monitor, study, and report the local
effects of pipeline construction on the community.

Charles P. Wolf, general editor of the Social Impact Assessment Series, is associate professor in the environmental psychology program at the City University of New York. He was formerly AAAS Congressional Science Fellow in the U.S. Office of Technology Assessment and worked for two years as a sociologist with the U.S. Army Engineers Institute for Water Resources.

What Happened to Fairbanks?

The Effects of the Trans-Alaska Oil Pipeline on the Community of Fairbanks, Alaska

Mim Dixon

Westview Press ● Boulder, Colorado

Social Impact Assessment Series

Copyright © 1978 by Westview Press, Inc.

Published in 1978 in the United States of America by

Westview Press, Inc.
5500 Central Avenue
Boulder, Colorado 80301
Frederick A. Praeger, Publisher and Editorial Director

Library of Congress Number: 77-94011
ISBN: 0-89158-071-9

Printed and bound in the United States of America

CONTENTS

LIST OF TABLES

LIST OF FIGURES

FOREWORD

Social impact assessment (SIA) is a newly-emerging field of interdisciplinary social science knowledge and application. The analytic problem addressed by SIA is that of establishing and appraising the condition of a society organized and changed by large-scale applications of high technology. Its task is anticipatory research: to predict and evaluate the social effects of a policy, program, or project still in the planning stage, *before* these effects have occurred. It seeks to base expectations of legislative enactment, program operation, and project development on a rational and reliable basis.

The growing professional and scholarly interest in this field has created a demand for substantial treatment of its significant cases and salient dimensions. The Social Impact Assessment Series is designed to meet this need.

Charles P. Wolf

PREFACE

Two years of research preceded writing this monograph. From 1974 to 1976 I worked with the Fairbanks North Star Borough Impact Information Center, first as a research assistant and then as director. During that time, we produced for the local citizenry and other interested persons monthly reports and some special reports about changes in the community. To prepare these reports, we drew upon data collected by other agencies (such as traffic volume from the Alaska Department of Highways, arrests from the Fairbanks Police Department, and revenues from the Borough Comptroller). When figures were not available, we developed methods for obtaining them--using court records for the number of divorce complaints filed, surveying Senior Citizens and local pipeline employees, conducting regular food, fuel and rental housing price comparisons. To complement the quantitative data, we interviewed scores of people, attended public hearings and other meetings, and relied upon the news media.

Most research methods have been explained in the chapter notes. One very important component of the research method, however, requires additional explanation for those nct familiar with the Impact Information Center. Each of the Impact Information Center reports was reviewed by the Impact Advisory Committee, a group of Fairbanks residents representing the Chamber of Commerce, the Social Concerns Committee, the Borough Assembly, organized labor, Natives, Blacks, women--just about every interest group in the community. The meetings were open to the public and the press, and reports were available to all who wanted them free of charge. Data collected by the Impact Information Center were subjected to public scrutiny and improved by public criticism. Because the program was funded through local revenues, there was tremendous public participation, particularly at budget time. In this monograph, I have only referenced the Impact Information Center Reports in the chapter notes when I did not conduct the research myself or when I felt that an Impact Information Center report would provide additional relevant information.

As an applied anthropologist, I believe that this unique community-directed program (which incidentally received an Outstanding Achievement Award from the National Association of Counties) provided an ideal research setting. However, political constraints prohibited interpreting the data in the Impact Information Center reports. While the data presented in the manuscript has undergone broad public review, the interpretations of that data have not benefited by that process. Interpretations and analysis reflect not only my experiences with the Impact Information Center, but also my training as an anthropologist and my participation and observations of Fairbanks during the past seven years.

Readers may be confused by one point of style. Titles of persons are sometimes capitalized and sometimes in lower case. The lower case refers to the position in a generic sense, while the capitalized title refers to a specific person occupying the position. For example, "commissioner of labor" refers to the position of director of the Alaska Department of Labor and/or anybody occupying that position, while "Commissioner of Labor" refers to Edmund Orbeck, the person who occupied that position at the time referenced. A further point of style, I have elected to use "he" instead of "s/he" and "man" instead of "human." This decision was made to enhance readability and bears no sexist intent.

To assist readers with nomenclature, a few of the more commonly used abbreviations are given below:

AFL-CIO	American Federation of Labor-Congress of Industrial Organizations
AGC	Associated General Contractors
ASMUS	Alaska State Manpower Utilization System
BLS	U.S. Department of Labor Bureau of Labor Statistics
CETA	Comprehensive Employment and Training Act
CPI	Consumer Price Index
EIS	Environmental Impact Statement
GVEA	Golden Valley Electric Association
FMUS	Fairbanks Municipal Utilities System
FY	fiscal year (July 1 to June 30)
HUD	U.S. Department of Housing and Urban Development
NEPA	National Environmental Policy Act of 1969 (P.L. 91-190)
NLRB	National Labor Relations Board
OCS	Outer Continental Shelf
OMBE	Office of Minority Business Enterprises
SSI	Supplemental Security Income

ACKNOWLEDGMENTS

        While I bear the sole responsibility for the inter-
pretations on the following pages, those interpretations are
based on the observations and insights of many Fairbanksans
to whom I am indebted. Most of the research for this book
was conducted as part of my work for the Fairbanks North Star
Borough Impact Information Center. In this unique community-
directed research program, I received guidance from the Impact Advisory Committee whose dedicated members over the two-
year period included Larry Carpenter, David Crockett, Claude
Demientieff, Georgina Herron, Sam Kito, Leslye Korvola, Tom
Packer, Charles Parr, Gene Straatmeyer, James C. Thomas,
Jeanne Wilson, George Wise, and Phil Younker. I would also
like to thank the Borough Mayor John Carlson and his administration, members of the Borough Assembly, Joe LaRocca,
Sue Fison, Cindy Quisenberry, and others who have worked
with the Impact Information Center for their assistance and
support.

        When I suggested that data from Impact Information
Center reports ought to be consolidated and interpreted, I
received enthusiastic response from Kevin Waring, Director
of the Division of Community Planning, Alaska Department
of Community and Regional Affairs. The Department of Community and Regional Affairs provided financial support for
preparation of this manuscript.

        Through the generosity of Wayne Meyers, Director of
the Washington-Alaska-Montana-Idaho Regional Medical Education Program (WAMI) in Fairbanks, office space was arranged;
and WAMI-staffers Annie Roggasch, Kathy Driscoll, Joyce
Shoulders, and Bonnie Dinkel good-naturedly conveyed messages
and answered my needs during the period in which this manuscript was written.

        Participants in preparation of the manuscript included:
Cindy Lippincott, Pam Wyman, Cindy Quisenberry, and Dixie
Brown. Judy Vick, Bob Clemen and Don Arthur served as research assistants. Photographs are by Paul Helmar and
graphics by Andrea Fein.

        My colleagues who have been actively engaged in re-
search related to the impacts of the trans Alaska oil pipeline on Fairbanks have openly shared their information,
ideas, and research findings. I would like especially to
thank Sue Fison, John A. Kruse, Tim Normington, Jean Straatmeyer, and Monica Thomas.

Several very busy people have read the manuscript and provided editorial comments. Their knowledge and talents made a tremendous contribution to the final product. Suzanne Iudicello, Natalia Krawetz, Edmund Orbeck, Jerry Smetzer, Gene Straatmeyer, and Judy Vick were my critics.

I am particularly indebted to C. P. Wolf, who not only drew me into his network of social impact assessment professionals, but also served as a sensible and exceedingly helpful editor and arranged for publication in this monograph series.

Finally, I would like to express my appreciation to my husband, E. James Dixon, Jr., for his encouragement and to our son Bryan who very considerately awaited arrival until after the first draft of the manuscript was completed.

Mim Dixon

Fairbanks, Alaska
May 30, 1977

Chapter 1
WHAT HAPPENED TO FAIRBANKS?

Longer and larger pipelines had been built before. But the trans Alaska oil pipeline was different. The proposed 800 mile hot oil pipeline from Prudhoe Bay to Valdez was to cross territory both romantic and largely unknown to Western Civilization. The tundra on the North Slope of the Brooks Range to the Arctic Ocean, the remote mountains of the Brooks Range, the Yukon River memorialized from the earlier Gold Rushes, the forests of Interior Alaska, the statuesque Chugach Mountains, the Copper River valley with its salmon runs famed for sport fishing--all represented vital images of America's last frontier. As with other frontiers at other times, the United States was plunged into a national debate between whether to preserve the frontier's qualities or to develop its rich resources.

Discovery of commercial quantities of oil at Prudhoe Bay in July, 1968, came at a time when the nation was becoming more introspective. The economic materialism of the Fifties and the unpopular Vietnam War of the Sixties led to a questioning of national values in the late Sixties and early Seventies. The questioning began on college campuses among those who were most affected by the draft for the Vietnam War. The post-World-War-II baby boom led to a larger segment of the population in this age group, and the prosperity of the Fifties enabled a broader cross-section of the American population to attend college. As the national voting age dropped from 21 years to 18, the demands of the better educated young people spread into the national political arena.

Political rhetoric reflected changes in national goals from "prosperity" to "quality of life," from the Cold War emphasis on capitalism to a more equitable distribution

1

2

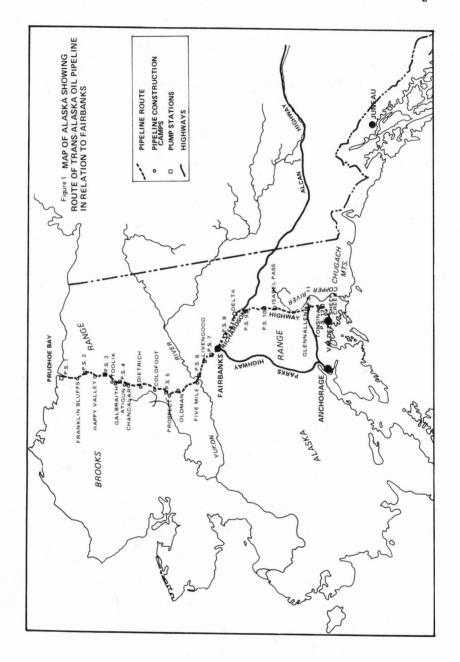

Figure 1 MAP OF ALASKA SHOWING
ROUTE OF TRANS-ALASKA OIL PIPELINE
IN RELATION TO FAIRBANKS

of national wealth through the civil rights movements and growing concern for the power of monopolies, and from a wholesale utilization of national resources to conservation. The emphasis on "quality of life" was accompanied by reversing the migration of folks from rural areas to urban areas. This led to an exodus from the cities and a growing vision of the American dream as living in places which were less populated and "closer to nature." One of those places was Alaska.

Against this backdrop, the trans Alaska oil pipeline came into national prominence as a test case of the emerging national values which were embodied in the conservation movement of that time. In 1969, the same year that the oil companies applied to the federal government for a right-of-way permit to build the trans Alaska pipeline, the 91st Congress was formulating Public Law 91-190, the National Environmental Policy Act of 1969 (NEPA). Formulated in recognition of "the profound impact of man's activity on the interrelations of all components of the natural environment, particularly the profound influences of population growth, high-density urbanization, industrial expansion, resource exploitation, and new and expanding technological advances," NEPA established the high priority national goal of "restoring and maintaining environmental quality."[1] The mechanism designated by NEPA for realizing that goal is that for every proposal for major federal action, the responsible official must prepare a detailed environmental impact statement (EIS). NEPA was signed into law on January 1, 1970. By March 20, 1970, the Department of the Interior had prepared an eight-page environmental impact statement on the trans Alaska oil pipeline right-of-way application.[2] Six days later the Wilderness Society, Friends of the Earth, and the Environmental Defense Fund sued the Department of the Interior for violating NEPA and the 1920 Mineral Leasing Act. An injunction against building the pipeline was in effect from April 13, 1970, throughout the course of the suit by the environmentalists until August 15, 1972, when the case was appealed to the Supreme Court.

Environmental objections were not the only barrier to pipeline construction. Before the right-of-way permit could be issued, questions of land ownership had to be resolved. From the time the United States purchased Alaska from Russia in 1867, Alaska's original inhabitants had not been compensated for their land and granted title to a portion of it. Commonly referred to as "Alaskan Natives" or "Natives," these people of Athabascan, Eskimo, Aleut, Tlingit and/or Haida cultural heritage were claiming ownership to some of the land which the proposed pipeline was to cross. It was clear that Native claims would have to be settled before a pipeline right-of-way permit could be issued. The problem of land ownership was further complicated by the fact that the State of Alaska had yet to choose some of the more than 102 million acres to which it became entitled at the time of statehood in 1958. These land ownership problems were remedied with respect to the pipeline with the passage of the Alaska Native Claims Settlement Act, which was signed into law December 18, 1971. Conflict between the pipeline developers and the environmentalists persisted after the problems of land ownership had been resolved, however.

Political pressure and legal action by the environmental groups served to clarify the NEPA process and expectations. For example, a ruling by the Appeals Court of the District of Columbia required the Department of the Interior to consider alternatives to the trans Alaska oil pipeline route to comply with NEPA. On March 20, 1972, nearly two years after the environmental groups sued the Department of the Interior for failure to comply with NEPA requirements

in its eight-page environmental impact statement, the Department of the Interior issued a nine-volume environmental
impact statement on the trans Alaska pipeline. This EIS was
a revised version of an earlier 196-page draft issued in
January 1971 and subjected to extensive public hearings in
Washington, D.C., and Anchorage, Alaska. By the time the
environmental groups had appealed their case to the Supreme
Court, the final EIS had been released and the court failed
to rule on the NEPA issue. In its February 9, 1973, ruling,
the Supreme Court decided that the proposed right-of-way for
the trans Alaska pipeline violated the Mineral Leasing Act
of 1920 and suggested that only Congress could remedy the
situation.

When the 91st Congress met in 1969, its members
passed the National Environmental Policy Act. The following year, the 92nd Congress devoted so much attention to
environmental issues that nearly one-third of the legislation enacted related to environmental policy.[3] By 1973,
however, there had been a dramatic change in public attitude
which was reflected in Congressional action with regard to
the pipeline right-of-way. The increasing political and
economic power of the Organization of Petroleum Exporting
Countries (OPEC) led to the increased price of Arabian
crude from $1.80 per barrel in 1970 to $5.12 per barrel in
1973, and by January 1974, the price skyrocketed to $11.65
per barrel.[4] At the same time, dependence on oil imports as
a percentage of consumption in the United States was increasing, from 19 percent in 1967 to 35.5 percent in 1973.[5] The
impending "energy crisis" in America led to a greater emphasis on domestic oil production to achieve greater independence, which in turn resulted in a realignment of national
values with respect to conservation. Congress debated a
bill to approve the pipeline EIS and relieve the Department
of the Interior of any further NEPA obligations with respect

to the trans Alaska oil pipeline in August 1973. Representative Morris Udall characterized the discussion as
"environmental backlash."[6] "This action would have been
laughed out of the chamber a year ago," Udall observed.
"Tonight a lot of those who helped write the National Environmental Policy Act into law are preparing to gut it."[7]
The bill passed and was signed into law on November 16,
1973. Pipeline construction officially began in April 1974.

During the five-year span in which the merits and
problems of the pipeline were debated, concern for the environment generally focused on the natural environment. Would
the pipeline obstruct caribou migrations? How would the
construction of the pipeline across streams and rivers affect fish spawning? How could the pipeline be engineered
to withstand the inevitable earthquakes in the areas where
it crossed fault zones? How would hot oil in the pipeline
be prevented from thawing permafrost? What would be the
effect of oil spills on migratory bird populations? These
and many other questions were virtually unanswered at the
time that the pipeline company applied for right-of-way permission in 1969. By the time the final environmental impact
statement of the Department of the Interior was issued, all
of these questions had been considered.

Although NEPA clearly addresses the issue of the
human environment, little attention was given to this aspect
of pipeline construction. Among NEPA's stated goals are to
"assure for all Americans safe, healthful, productive, and
esthetically and culturally pleasing surroundings."[8] During
hearings on the draft EIS, only Native leaders raised questions about the human environment. "The draft report essentially contains no study of the impact on the human environment," said Eskimo activist Charles Edwardson, Jr. "Why is
it that Western Civilization worries about things and does
not worry about people?"[9] Comments by Native leaders about

the "glaring deficiency"[10] of the EIS in relation to the
human environment were interpreted as a mandate to consider
only the social impact on Natives whose lifestyles were so
closely related to the land that degradation of the natural
environment could threaten their cultural survival.

Aside from negative impact on Alaska Native people
whose dependence on the land for subsistence might be jeop-
ardized by oil spills, it was generally assumed that the
social impacts of the pipeline would be positive. For the
nation as a whole, it was assumed that an increased supply
of oil would have a positive impact on the energy-starved
cities and create greater political and economic independence for the country, as well as stimulating the economy.
For the State of Alaska, the major positive social impacts
were thought to be (1) more jobs and, therefore, lower unemployment; (2) more economic stability through a lesser
dependence on the federal government; and (3) greater state
and local tax revenues which would both provide more services and reduce or retard the growth of the individual's
tax burden.

Each of these assumptions about the positive socioeconomic benefits of the proposed pipeline was challenged.
The North Slope oil would probably go to Japan rather than
oil-needy U.S. cities and the price of oil and oil products
would not drop, said economist Charles J. Cicchetti.[11] Although there would be more jobs in Alaska, in-migration of
job seekers would sustain high unemployment rates, concluded
the University of Alaska's Institute of Social, Economic and
Government Research.[12] Other economists said that the pipeline construction would trigger a boom/bust cycle which
would not lead to long-term stability for the state. While
state and local revenues would increase, said others, the
demand for services would keep pace with the growing revenues and therefore the individual's tax burden would not be

reduced. Furthermore, the structure of state taxes on the Prudhoe Bay oil meant that as the cost of the pipeline increased, the state oil revenues decreased. Even before pipeline construction began the estimated cost of the project increased from $1.5 billion to $4.5 billion, and has since been periodically adjusted upward to more than $10 billion. Also, some predicted that inflation would increase faster than revenues.

Unlike the natural environment, the social environment had no strong advocates. The most logical group of people to be concerned about the adverse effects of the pipeline on the social environment would be those people who would be most directly affected, the residents of towns located in the pipeline corridor. However, these were the people who thought they had the most to gain in terms of jobs, economic opportunities, and wealth. Located at the mid-point of the pipeline, Fairbanks sought to become the administrative, supply, and transportation center for the project. At the Department of the Interior hearings on the draft EIS for the pipeline, a Fairbanks Chamber of Commerce representative strongly urged immediate construction "for the social good it will make possible."[13] The political and economic leaders of Fairbanks advocated pipeline construction with a near-religious fervor. Acknowledging that he borrowed his ideas from the president of the University of Alaska, the Mayor of Fairbanks testified at the Department of the Interior hearing that pipeline opponents were "anti-God, they're anti-man, and they're anti-mind."[14]

Shortly after the oil discovery at Prudhoe Bay had been announced, Fairbanksans sought to learn from the Canadian experience with oil development by soliciting advice from the Calgary Chamber of Commerce. The advice which they received was to plan for oil development. This advice was reinforced by an editorial in the Fairbanks Daily News-

Miner on August 12, 1968:

> What we do in the months ahead will de-
> termine our future for years to come.
>   We have a choice now. We can, in the next
> decade, grow into a beautiful city of some
> 40,000 residents with broad streets, row upon
> row of attractive homes, a large business
> section offering everything we need to keep our
> money at home, and an industrial area close to
> but separate from the rest of the city.
>   Or we can grow like Topsy, unplanned, with
> small industrial plants fouling the air and
> homes around it; a town we have to apologize
> for to every visitor who comes, not because he
> wants to, but because business forces him to.

While the newspaper editorial emphasized zoning as the approach to planning, it was clear that planning was needed
for nearly every segment of community life.

However, from 1968 to 1974 the emphasis of state
and local leadership in business and government was to overcome the obstacles to the trans Alaska pipeline and assure
that it would be constructed. The goal of securing the pipeline superseded the goal of planning for the pipeline. To
these leaders it seemed a premature and inappropriate expenditure of energy and resources to plan for the pipeline
before it was certain that the pipeline would become a reality. To some extent, this attitude also prevailed in the
oil industry, which insisted that problems of engineering
and management could be resolved as the project progressed
rather than in planning prior to the issuance of a permit.
Indeed, the lack of information about the management of the
pipeline inhibited local planning efforts.

The people of Fairbanks hardly knew what to expect
when pipeline construction began in 1974. The magnitude of
the pipeline was overwhelming. First, a 361-mile long grav-
el road would be built from the Yukon River to Prudhoe Bay,
including bridges over 20 major streams and rivers and the

construction of a 2,300-foot bridge over the Yukon River.
Other preliminary construction included three permanent airfields, eight temporary airfields, 15 permanent access
roads, numerous temporary access roads, and 19 construction
camps. The second phase of the project, scheduled for completion in mid-1977, included construction of a 798-mile
long, 48-inch diameter steel pipeline from Prudhoe Bay to
Valdez. The final stage of the project was to construct
four additional pipeline pump stations and more oil storage
and tanker docking facilities at Valdez. The whole project
was to be completed in four years.

All of the people who were to work on the portion of
the pipeline from Prudhoe Bay to Glennallen were to have
been dispatched from union halls located in Fairbanks.
Originally, it was estimated that 14,000 persons were to be
employed on the pipeline during the peak construction period
in 1975. Later that figure was adjusted upward to a peak of
22,000 pipeline workers, 16,000 of them hired out of Fairbanks union halls. Most unions negotiated contracts stip-
ulating work cycles of nine or twelve work weeks, working
seven days per week as much as 12 hours per day, followed
by a rest and recreation period of one or two weeks. In
exchange for a no-strike clause, the unions negotiated high
wages. The combination of high base pay and much overtime
yielded paychecks of $1,000 to $1,500 per week for laborers
and skilled craftsmen. Because Fairbanks was both the
hiring and job termination point, it had the dual charge of
accommodating people who were seeking jobs and those who
were returning from work with hefty paychecks.

Fairbanks also became a management center for the
pipeline project. Surplus buildings on the North Post of
Ft. Wainwright Army Base were converted into construction
headquarters for the pipeline project. More than 500 project management personnel who worked there lived in the

Fairbanks community. In addition, a pipeline construction camp was located on Ft. Wainwright to accommodate workers at the Fairbanks pipeyard and along the segment of the pipeline near Fairbanks. The construction camp housed 1,164 workers.

Until the road to Prudhoe Bay was completed, both the railroad and highway systems terminated in Fairbanks. Supplies for the northern segment of the pipeline project were freighted to Fairbanks and then sent north by cargo airplanes. Fairbanks became a transportation and supply center, dispatching both people and materials for the pipeline project.

In response to these roles, Fairbanks also became a service center. Alyeska Pipeline Service Company, the consortium of eight oil companies which was formed to build the pipeline, employed contractors and subcontractors to execute the project. In turn, many of these companies established administrative centers in Fairbanks. This further expanded the demand for such services as banking, office supplies, equipment repair, warehousing, and office space.

Injection of all these activities into the 7,361 square mile Fairbanks North Star Borough, whose population numbered 45,864 in 1970,[15] was bound to have some rather traumatic effects, although nobody was sure just what they would be. Since this was a construction project of unprecedented magnitude, the usefulness of studies of social impacts on other communities experiencing booms was limited. They did, however, offer some clues about what to expect. For example, Robert Engler's analysis of the national and international politics of oil begins with a case study of changes in values and institutions of rural North Dakota when oil was discovered and developed there.[16] He reports some of the complaints by the people of North Dakota: land was bought from them cheaply, roads were damaged by heavy equipment, highway traffic increased, hotel and restaurant facilities were crowded, needs increased for law enforcement and school facilities, and rents increased particularly hurting people on fixed incomes. Engler reports that the press was not helpful in providing information about oil development to the people of North Dakota:

> It became difficult for the hired scribe to be unaware of the social and business relationship developing between his editors, publishers, radio station owners, and the new oilmen. Press coverage of oil tended to consist of handouts and statistical data, or where there were hearings, factual reporting with a minimum of critical interpretation as to the broader implications for the state.[17]

Perhaps even more directly related to the Fairbanks experience were the previous Alaskan experiences of gold rushes and oil development. Communities involved in those booms experienced massive influx of outsiders, housing shortages, lawlessness, increases in prostitution and gambling, and a variety of other problems. While these conditions comprise some of the romantic appeal of a boom town, they also pose threats to the stability of the community and its residents.

A few reports were written projecting various social and economic impacts of the pipeline, but the information was usually couched in general terms. Consultants preparing them tended to hedge on any definitive projections which might later be proven false. Like others, the consultants did not have experience with similar situations to draw upon and did not know what kinds of processes would occur to change the community. Their reports were based upon a series of assumptions, and each succeeding report drew upon the assumptions of the previous reports. The reports were not detailed enough to serve as planning documents. For the most part, they were ignored.

Fairbanksans were concerned with questions of whether there would be a pipeline, when there would be a pipeline, and what part of the pipeline action Fairbanks would get. It was not until February 28, 1974, less than one month before the official pipeline construction began, that the local citizenry sat down to discuss the potential effects of the pipeline on their community. On that Saturday, a group of Fairbanksans gathered for a public forum organized by the Social Concerns Committee of the Fairbanks Council of Churches. Various pipeline officials were invited to explain what the community could expect. Perhaps for the first time, local persons publicly expressed their fears about the impending project.

Two major concerns emerged from that meeting: rumors could get out of hand and there would be no way to control them; and while Alyeska would have an extensive public relations program to provide information about the pipeline, there would be no independent source of information about what was happening in the community. A rather novel approach was suggested for solving these two potential problems: an impact information center sponsored by local government. The concept of this unique, community-directed research project was further refined by the Presiding Officer of the Borough Assembly, who limited its purpose to collecting and disseminating information: "it does not forecast, predict, project, extrapolate, or otherwise attempt to indicate the shape of the future."[18] An advisory committee was appointed from various segments of the community, and a veteran political journalist with much experience reporting oil development in Alaska was hired to direct the operation. In June, 1974, the Fairbanks North Star Borough's Impact Information Center set about the immense task of monitoring the impacts of the pipeline on the Fairbanks community.

Unfortunately, the carefully prepared data in the reports issued regularly by the Impact Information Center were not always used by the scores of traveling journalists who filtered through the street-front office. Perhaps because much of the pipeline construction project was closed to journalists except on carefully prepared company tours, or because environmental stipulations and regulations on the pipeline project averted the types of environmental degradation of catastrophic proportions which would attract a national readership, most of the journalists coming through Alaska since the beginning of pipeline construction entertained their readership with sensational stories about the human impact.

While there was probably a grain of truth in the story about prostitution in Fairbanks in The New York Times Sunday Magazine,[19] and an element of fact in the series about organized crime in Fairbanks in the Los Angeles Times,[20] and some basis for the interpretation that Fairbanks was consumed by greed as reported in the Edmonton Journal,[21] what happened to Fairbanks is more complex than what was recorded in these popular accounts. These complexities are important to understand, because Fairbanks may be conceptualized as part of America in several contexts. Fairbanks embodies both the history and the spirit of the American frontier; it is a microcosm of the conflicts in contemporary American values; it is a fairly remote outpost of Euro-American culture which has developed its own idiosyncrasies; and it is typical of a small town in the process of rapid growth and change.

After six years of prominent coverage in newspapers and national magazines, the dimensions of the trans Alaska oil pipeline no longer seem staggering. It may no longer be the largest private construction project in history, as it was when first proposed. Only time will tell whether

technology was able to overcome the obstacles of trying to
transport hot oil over frozen and unstable earth without
endangering the vegetation and animals in the vicinity.
The shrill debate between developers and conservationists,
which has characterized this nation's westward expansion
and contributed to the delay in pipeline construction from
the discovery of commercial supplies of oil at Prudhoe Bay
in 1968 until the construction permit was issued in 1973,
has nearly subsided. Concern for the victims of resource
development in the North has shifted from caribou to humans.

Emphasis on understanding human impacts of the trans
Alaska pipeline is not just a response to the interest stim-
ulated by the national news media; it is also a response to
some fairly subtle changes in national values. Recently,
NEPA regulations have been revised to give more attention
to what are commonly called "socioeconomic" impacts of federal projects and decisions. There is a need for more information about this subject which has generally been neglected by social scientists. While the trans Alaska oil
pipeline was perhaps the first project proposed to give the
nation greater energy independence, development of the Outer
Continental Shelf (OCS) areas represents an even greater
undertaking. Impending OCS development in the United States
has led to a closer examination of OCS development in the
North Sea, where planning has emphasized human environmental
protection rather than conservation of the natural environment.[22] At the same time, in the United States there has
been a rise in the consumer protection movement and a growing distrust of large corporate conglomerates, such as the
oil industry, which have fostered greater advocacy for assessing the human consequences of resource development.

Fairbanks' experiences with the pipeline have not
ended. At the time this book was written, pipeline construction had not been completed and there was no way to

assess the long-term effects of the project on the community. Writing this story before it has an end is inevitable--
the interweaving of events through time makes it impossible
to define the beginnings and ends except through artificial
means. Time seems to blunt perceptions and the vitality of
the moment gives way to the leveling processes of intro-
spection and historical perspective. While the long-term
effects of the pipeline on Fairbanks will have to be left
to the interpretation of future historians, there is an
immediate need for a better understanding of this community's experience with a contemporary "gold rush."

Chapter 2
GOLD IN THE STREETS

"Gold in the streets!" is the image evoked by boom-
towns. Fairbanks had its share of gold in the streets,
quite literally, as a fleet of shiny, new yellow trucks em-
blazoned with the emblem of the Alyeska Pipeline Service
Company descended upon the town. In a town where people
drove dusty old trucks that were about to require the parts
of the salvaged vehicles rusting in their backyards, the
spiffy Alyeska fleet stood out on the roads like so many
gold nuggets in a time-worn stream bed. To the townspeople,
the yellow trucks became a symbol of Alyeska, of the rich
and powerful force from "Outside" which was moving into
Fairbanks.

Jokes about the yellow trucks peppered people's
conversations. A familiar edict to avoid snow which had
been urinated upon was transformed into, "Don't eat yellow
snow, it may be an Alyeska truck!" In reference to the
numerous workers who were moving from the oil-rich South to
Alaska, the riddle emerged: "Do you know why Texans wear
hats which turn up on the sides? So three of them can sit
in the front of a yellow truck." It became a contest among
youngsters to see how many gas caps they could steal from
the yellow trucks. Their collections became so extensive
that Alyeska had to switch from yellow to black gas caps.

Rumors about the yellow trucks began to emerge. It
was rumored that Alyeska "lost" 30 to 50 of the 700 project
vehicles estimated to be in the Fairbanks area. The "lost"
yellow trucks were said to have been sighted in nearly every
state of the union. Other rumors reflected a fear that
Alyeska might be receiving some types of privileged treatment. It was rumored that the "exempt carrier" sign on the
side of Alyeska trucks meant that those vehicles were exempt

17

from paying gasoline tax. In reality, "exempt carrier" is
a kind of identification required by law and has no bearing
on gasoline tax. It merely distinguished vehicles belonging
to general contractors from "contract carriers," "common
carriers," and "private carriers."

Yellow trucks became a symbol of the increased traffic, the congestion and irritation resulting from the population increases brought about by pipeline construction.
People who came to Fairbanks to escape urbanized areas resented having to wait in long lines at intersections, in
grocery stores, at restaurants, in hardware stores, at the
post office, at banks, at laundromats, and just about every-
place in the downtown area. They were irritated by having
to drive blocks to find a parking place, and going from
store to store to find a simple commodity. Residents used
to driving on icy streets were worried that the newcomers
from the South would create traffic hazards in the winter,
and that even under the best of driving conditions, more
traffic would mean more accidents. These fears were not unfounded. There was more traffic, especially in areas most
used in pipeline construction (see Figures 2 and 3), and
there were more accidents (see Table 1).

Traffic in Fairbanks is more closely related to
quality of life than in many small towns because, despite
its image as a frontier town, Fairbanks has severe air quality problems. Located in a basin surrounded on three sides
by hills and ridges, Fairbanks has such a stable air mass
that temperature inversions are roughly three times more intense than those in Los Angeles.[1] Fairbanks has temperature
inversions on 60 percent of all evenings and 80 percent of
the time during the extreme winter months.[2] The two requirements for air pollution are: (1) the availability of
pollutants, and (2) a restriction in the volume of air containing pollutants. The second requirement is usually

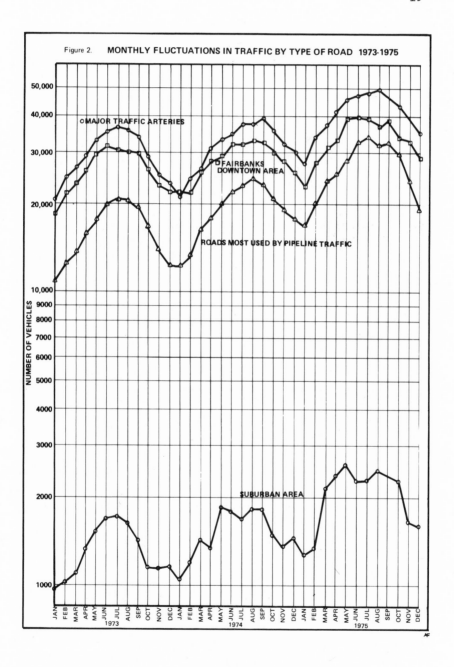

Figure 2.   MONTHLY FLUCTUATIONS IN TRAFFIC BY TYPE OF ROAD 1973-1975

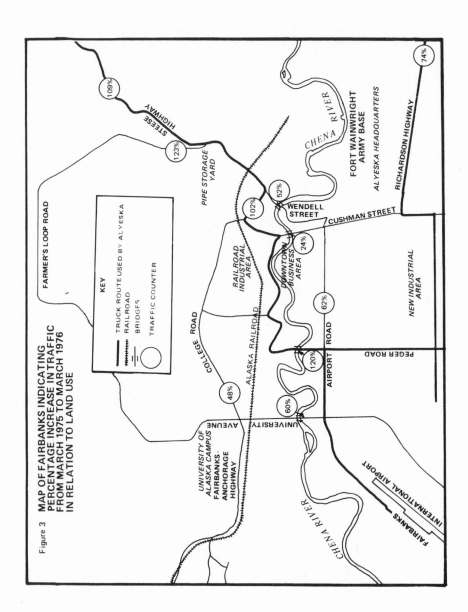

Figure 3 MAP OF FAIRBANKS INDICATING
PERCENTAGE INCREASE IN TRAFFIC
FROM MARCH 1975 TO MARCH 1976
IN RELATION TO LAND USE

KEY

TRUCK ROUTE USED BY ALYESKA
RAILROAD
BRIDGES
TRAFFIC COUNTER

FARMER'S LOOP ROAD

STEESE HIGHWAY

109%
123%

PIPE STORAGE YARD

102%
52%

WENDELL STREET

CUSHMAN STREET

CHENA RIVER

FORT WAINWRIGHT ARMY BASE

ALYESKA HEADQUARTERS

RICHARDSON HIGHWAY

74%

RAILROAD INDUSTRIAL AREA

DOWNTOWN BUSINESS AREA

24%

62%

NEW INDUSTRIAL AREA

PEGER ROAD

120%

AIRPORT ROAD

COLLEGE ROAD

ALASKA RAILROAD

48%

UNIVERSITY OF ALASKA CAMPUS

FAIRBANKS-ANCHORAGE HIGHWAY

UNIVERSITY AVENUE

60%

CHENA RIVER

FAIRBANKS INTERNATIONAL AIRPORT

Table 1

Auto Accidents in Fairbanks, 1973-1975[*]

	1973	1974	1975	Percent Change 1973-1975
Number of Accidents	1,149	1,366	1,906	+66%
Number of Vehicles Involved	2,125	2,389	3,640	+71%
Number of Persons Injured	179	203	353	+97%
Number of Persons Killed	3	1	1	-66%
Total Dollar Loss	$493,244	$857,737	$1,999,555	+305%
Average Dollar Loss Per Vehicle	$232	$359	$549	+137%

[*]Figures taken from Fairbanks Police Department reports.

satisfied by the stable air conditions in Fairbanks, particularly at low temperatures. The availability of pollutants depends upon human activity.

The automobile has been labeled the worst source of
pollution in Fairbanks because, "it moves about, is concentrated where people concentrate, discharges essentially
at ground level, and, as well as water vapor, it contains
products which are health hazards."[3] The two by-products
of automobiles which most concern Fairbanksans are carbon
monoxide and water vapor. When Fairbanks has winter cold
temperatures of 30 to 70 degrees below zero (Fahrenheit),
the water vapor from automobile exhaust and other sources
crystallizes into a dense ice fog. During long periods of

intense ice fog, visibility is so poor that driving is
hazardous, schools and businesses close, planes can't land
at the airport, and community activities generally come to
a halt.

Yellow trucks not only symbolized corporate power,
outsiders moving into Fairbanks, and the congestion and
hassles of the increased population, but also the life-
threatening traffic increases contributing to carbon monoxide, ice fog, and accidents. Recognizing the problems with
the image of the yellow trucks, Alyeska moved most of the
vehicles out of Fairbanks and ordered new trucks in a variety of more subdued colors. Alyeska also attempted to become the model citizen by announcing a plan to reduce their
contribution to the carbon monoxide problem by limiting
operation of project vehicles in Fairbanks during air quality alerts; forbidding employees from leaving unattended
vehicles idling; instituting an inspection and maintenance
program for project vehicles; providing engine heater plug-
in facilities at all project locations so that it would not
be necessary to warm vehicles by idling them; and providing
bus service for transporting employees to and from project
headquarters.

As the yellow trucks faded from the Fairbanks scene,
Alyeska introduced with much fanfare a new type of truck
especially designed to haul pipe for the pipeline. Alyeska
had planned to start construction of the pipeline in September 1969, long before the trans Alaska oil pipeline permit was issued. Anticipating early approval, they ordered
40-foot lengths of 48-inch diameter steel pipe from companies
in Japan. After the pipe was delivered to Alaska, a portion
of it was shipped via railroad to Fairbanks. A pipe storage
yard was located on the north side of the town, just outside
the city limits with access from the Steese Highway. During
the intervening years, the pipe was coated with a chemical

to keep it from corroding. When the pipeline permit was issued, it was necessary to transport the lengths of pipe to temporary storage nearer locations where it would be put into place to form the pipeline.

Alyeska sought special permission from the State Highway Department to weld the pipe into 80-foot lengths before transporting it. Special trailers were designed to carry three 80-foot pipe lengths. Since the pipe weighed 240 to 290 pounds per linear foot, the truck loads could vary from 13,600 to 17,400 pounds. The 95-foot long trailer rigs were designed so that the rear wheels of the trailer followed the pulling tractor's rear wheels to stay on Alaska's narrow, winding roads. In considering issuing a special permit, the Highway Department was faced with a trade-off. The double-pipe loads would be heavier and probably cause more damage to the roads. However, if Alyeska were refused permission to weld the pipe sections before transporting them, it would be necessary to make more trips, thereby increasing the safety hazards. The Highway Department issued a special permit to allow Alyeska to transport 80-foot sections.

Soon 125 of the specially designed trailers were on the Alaska roads. The rigs did not actually go through the City of Fairbanks but were routed instead through Ft. Wainwright Army Base. They did travel through the Fairbanks North Star Borough on the Richardson Highway south of the city and from the pipeyard north on the Steese Highway to the Elliott Highway and the Livengood and Yukon Roads (see Figure 4). Other large trucks carrying equipment and supplies to the pipeline camps also followed these routes.

By May 1975, the State Commissioner of Highways noted extensive highway deterioration caused by the pipeline traffic. The agreement between the state and Alyeska contained no stipulations about the repair of existing roads,

24

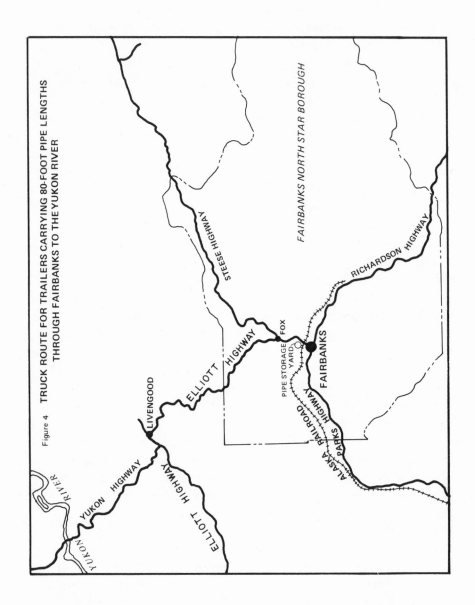

Figure 4   TRUCK ROUTE FOR TRAILERS CARRYING 80-FOOT PIPE LENGTHS THROUGH FAIRBANKS TO THE YUKON RIVER

which at that time was estimated to cost about $150 million.[4]
"One thing that we have learned from the Alyeska project,"
said State Commissioner of Highways Walter B. Parker, "is
that future major resource developments will require an
adequate road structure to support them."[5] In the meantime,
the state turned to the federal government for assistance.
In January 1976, Congress voted to appropriate $70 million
for the repair of highways damaged by trans Alaska pipeline
construction. The Secretary of Transportation was directed
by Congress to study the problems of road deterioration
caused by the pipeline construction and to investigate the
feasibility of Alaska repaying the highway repair funds.
According to the proposal, at least half, and possibly a
greater proportion, of the funds needed to repair roads
damaged by pipeline construction would be taken from state
coffers.

Safety problems and state responsibility for road
maintenance were focused on the 80-mile stretch of partial-
ly-paved, 28-foot wide road north of Fairbanks from Fox to
Livengood, known as the Elliott Highway (see Figure 4).
During the first winter of pipeline construction, there were
numerous serious accidents along this road, resulting in
five fatalities. One trucking company official estimated
that his firm averaged an accident a day on the road.[6] The
road became known among truckers as the "kamikaze" trail.

All trucking on the Elliott Highway and throughout
much of the state was halted for five days in February 1976
while Teamsters, trucking officials, Alyeska Pipeline Service
Company, and the State Department of Highways conducted
"safety meetings" (the Teamsters emphasized that it was not
a strike) to determine the source of the safety problem and
to find solutions. Teamsters Union officials and trucking
company executives blamed the Department of Highways for inadequate maintenance. The Highway Commissioner countered

that the Elliott Highway was maintained at higher levels than any in the state. At the time, 10 men were assigned to the maintenance route from Fairbanks to the Yukon River and provided with four graders, two four-by-four trucks, three Caterpillar tractors, two small trucks, and a rotary snowblower. "No professional driver who is competent to handle arctic roads in mountainous terrain should have trouble with the road," the Highway Commissioner stated following an inspection trip.[7]

State Trooper investigations of fatalities on the Elliott Highway determined that most of the accidents were due to driver error, which seemed to confirm the Highway Commissioner's assessment of the situation. "It's the damned Texans and Okies," said one trucker with more than 10 years of experience in Alaska, "those guys with pointed-toe alligator cowboy boots, they are the ones raising all the hell. The ones of us who are used to driving Alaska roads know how to drive these arctic conditions."[8] Many of the Teamsters hired to haul pipe and equipment for the pipeline were inexperienced with arctic conditions, the specific roads they were using, the rigs they were driving, and the oversized loads.

Alyeska and the trucking firms assumed some responsibility for improving the safety of the Elliott Highway. Alyeska agreed to provide funds for six additional highway maintenance personnel, graders and four-wheel-drive vehicles to augment the state's effort. To surmount the problems of steep curves, poor grading and narrow passages, the trucking companies agreed to station flagmen at dangerous areas along the highway and to make periodic inspections of the road.

The following summer, Alyeska also engaged in an expensive radio and newspaper advertising campaign to promote safety on the Elliott Highway and road to the Yukon

River. Typical of the campaign, one ad read:[9]

> ATTENTION MOTORISTS!
> This summer, more than 300 trans
> Alaska pipeline-related vehicles will be
> traveling the Elliott and Yukon Highways
> EACH DAY. In addition to the heavy truck
> traffic, dust conditions have resulted in
> extremely poor visibility--even though
> the highway will be oiled. For your
> safety, Alyeska Pipeline Service Company
> urges you to avoid driving the Elliott
> and Yukon Highways if at all possible.
> And if you must drive these highways,
> please . . . exercise extreme caution on
> the road. Thank you.

Some Fairbanksans viewed the wording of the advertisements
as presumptuous. A local attorney responded by writing his
own advertisement satirizing Alyeska:[10]

> ATTENTION ALYESKA!
> This summer, more than 30,000 Alaskan
> taxpayers will be traveling the Elliott and
> Richardson highways, highways that have
> been built and paid for by them. Because
> of heavy truck traffic, these highways have
> become extremely dangerous to these Alaskan
> taxpayers.
> Therefore, for the protection of these
> Alaskan taxpayers, I urge Alyeska to avoid
> driving Interior Alaska highways if at all
> possible, and if Alyeska must drive these
> highways, please don't take your half out
> of the middle.

After the ad ridiculing Alyeska's posture was played on the
radio for a week, Alyeska withdrew its advertisements from
radio coverage. The ads remained in the newspaper.

Controversy over highway safety in relation to pipeline construction did not end when the last 80-foot section
of pipe was delivered to its ultimate destination. In February 1976, Teamsters went to court to protest the State
Highway Department's issuance of special permits to allow
Alyeska to haul extra-wide loads of pre-formed insulation
units for the pipeline. The units, dubbed "bathtubs," were

loaded side-by-side on flatbed trucks, a load 12½ feet wide overhanging the left side of the truck by 18 inches and right side by three feet. The maximum legal width of loads hauled on state highways is eight feet, but Highway Department regulations enable them to issue special permits for wider loads that cannot reasonably be dismantled to conform to regulations.

Truckers maintained that there was no reason to stack the "bathtubs" side by side and that they presented a safety hazard. "Every time I meet a school bus, they've got to get out about as far as I do," testified one trucker, "This is one thing that really makes me shudder."[11] Attorneys for the state Department of Highways maintained that in the eight months in which 1,100 special permits had been issued for the "bathtub" loads, there had been no serious accidents.[12] The court's decision allowed the Highway Department to continue issuing the special permits. One trucker said that whether or not he would refuse to haul the extra-wide load would depend "on how long I've been out of work."[13]

Although safety was the focal issue in controversies about unusually large truck loads, it would seem that the Teamsters, trucking companies, Alyeska and the state also were motivated by economic interests. Smaller loads meant more trips and higher incomes for Teamsters and trucking companies. Truckers did not get hazard pay for hauling the extra-wide or extra-long loads. More trips meant that the pipeline would cost more to build; and the costlier the pipeline, the lower the revenues for the state. Trucks bearing oversized loads symbolized the dominant values in which expediency was given preference to safety. Yet, except for the tax burden, little attention was given to the issue of money in all of the public discussions of the "kamikaze" trail.

According to the president of Alaska Truck Transport, the real reason for the Teamster's safety meetings in

February 1976 was to pressure Alyeska into not using his company whose drivers were represented by the Retail Clerks union.[14] After the "safety" meetings, Alyeska did not do business with Alaska Truck Transport again, in spite of the fact that it was a minority enterprise--Bering Straits Native Corporation owned two-thirds of its stock. According to the Commissioner of Labor, "what actually happened" was that members of the Fairbanks Retail Clerks Union had formed a 'Transport Unit' to bypass the Teamsters Union. When Alyeska removed members of the Retail Clerks Union, which was not party to the project agreement, the "safety talks" ended.[15]

Without doubt, the safety meetings were one way that the Teamsters Union could flex its muscles. "I've got the hammer to shut it down," Teamster leader Jesse Carr told a reporter, "and I have."[16] Carr came to Alaska as a truck driver in 1949, and became business agent for Teamster's Union Local 959 in 1951. At that time the organization had 500 members and $600 worth of debts. Carr consolidated all the Teamsters in the state into one state-wide Local 959 and established the union's relative autonomy from control by the International Union. As Secretary-Treasurer of the union during the two decades before pipeline construction, Carr built Local 959's assets to $500,000 and the union membership to encompass nearly 80 crafts and trades, including the construction and communications industry and some state and local government employees. By contributing to campaigns, delivering votes, and hiring an effective lobbyist in Juneau, the Teamsters became the most politically powerful group in Alaska.

At the end of 1975, the peak of pipeline construction, Teamsters Local 959 claimed 23,000 members in a state whose total population numbered about 406,000--one out of every 10 working persons. At that time $1 million a week

was flowing into Teamster trust funds in Alaska and the
trusts had assets of nearly $100 million, all of which was
invested in Alaska. "It has to be one of the biggest union
success stories in the nation," said an Alaskan banker.[17]

To the union members, success was measured in terms
of their own well-being. Teamsters working on the pipeline
earned $9.98 to $10.88 an hour, plus time-and-half for
everything over eight hours a day. Truck drivers working
on the pipeline north of Fairbanks were guaranteed eight
hours of straight time and 10 hours of overtime each day,
even though they were prohibited by state and federal regulations from driving more than 10 hours in a 24-hour period.[18]
It was not unusual for drivers north of Fairbanks to take
home paychecks of $2,000 every two weeks. In addition, em-
ployers contributed $2-3 per hour in fringe benefits, pro-
viding Teamsters with prepaid medical, dental, optical, and
legal care; $25,000 in life insurance; and a pension aver-
aging more than $600 per month, for which a Teamster is eli-
gible after 10 years of work or at the age of 45. In addition, the Teamsters Union was constructing recreational complexes for its membership in Anchorage and Fairbanks.

Jesse Carr became something of a patron saint to the
Teamsters, and the Teamsters became standard bearers of the
working men and women of Alaska. According to the union,
90 percent of its new members approach the union about affiliation, rather than being recruited.[19] Acknowledging
the success of the Teamsters Union at the bargaining table,
Fairbanks school principals voted to have the Teamsters represent them in negotiations with the Fairbanks North Star
Borough School Board in February 1976.

Concentration of power in a single organization with
a single leader led some to speculate about the potential
abuse of that power. The reputation of the International
Brotherhood of Teamsters, Chauffeurs, Warehousemen and

Helpers of America to which Local 959 is affiliated led some
to suspect that the local union was subject to corruption,
illegal use of pension trust funds and organized crime.[20]
There is some evidence that the Alyeska warehouse in the
Fairbanks North Star Terminal complex was run by Teamsters
with extensive criminal records.[21] Carr himself was indicted
on six criminal charges by a federal grand jury, though he
was acquitted on four counts, and two were dropped.

Thus, while Jesse Carr became a folk hero to the
working people and the Teamsters were one of the success
stories of the pipeline boom, the union was feared for both
its power and the potential abuse of that power. The reaction of Fairbanksans to Alyeska's trucks was not separable
from their reaction to the Teamsters who drove them.

What started as gold in the streets ended as gold in
many people's pockets, not the least of whom were the businessmen who ran Alaska's trucking industry. In spite of
high union wages, which comprised 63 percent of the cost of
doing business in the trucking industry,[22] local businesses
were able to make handsome profits during the pipeline period. Their success may be attributed to several factors.
First, they were able to project the demand for their services over the short run and to respond with flexibility.
Alyeska's in-house figures called for a rapid escalation in
trucking needs to a peak average of 149 loads a day in October 1975, and then a rapid decline to an average of 15.8
loads a day by October 1976.[23] Rather than making heavy investments to meet this short-term demand, the local businesses were able to hire owner-operators who brought their
own trucks with them from the relatively depressed "Lower
48" states.

A second factor in their success was the introduction
of new technology. A large ship was built to haul cargo from
Seattle to the port of Anchorage and was designed so that

independent truckers and small businesses could roll their trailers on and off the ship. Previously, Sea Land Freight Service, Inc., was the only company providing sea-borne cargo service between Seattle and Anchorage, and the Sea Land ships were designed to handle only their own particular brand of cargo units. The introduction of the new ship, called the "Great Land," made smaller trucking businesses more competitive.

Fate also provided a boost to the trucking business. Alyeska had planned to use a flotilla of barges to haul materials from Seattle to Prudhoe Bay during the summer of 1975. However, ice conditions prevented 22 of the large barges from landing at Prudhoe Bay and they had to return to ports along the southern coast of Alaska to unload their wares, which were then trucked north.

Perhaps the most significant trend in the trucking industry during the pipeline period was that every major privately-owned trucking company in the state was sold to another larger company or partnership. Undoubtedly, the original owners benefited economically from the transaction. The trucking industry became to the Fairbanks business community a symbol of the wealth and success brought about by the trans Alaska oil pipeline construction project. At the same time, it symbolized a change in the structure of the business community--from a small town with small, local businesses in a tightly knit power structure to a growing community shifting control to businesses with "outside" interests and resources.

Chapter 3
$$$

For each individual and group in the Fairbanks community there were both benefits and costs associated with
construction of the trans Alaska oil pipeline. Specific
changes in the community harmed some and at the same time
helped others. It is difficult to assess the balance between
collective costs and benefits, because so many aspects of
pipeline impact are intangible and do not lend themselves
to quantitative measures. The ultimate assessment of where
the balance lies becomes a matter of value judgments which
vary from person to person depending upon the individual's
experiences, goals, philosophy, and world view.

Perhaps it was inevitable that money became a yard-
stick for measuring costs and benefits of pipeline construction in Fairbanks. Money is the most common denomi-
nator in American society as a measure of worth and status.
It is tangible and quantitative. And money was one of the
prime motivations for the pipeline in the Fairbanks community.

Using an economic approach, benefits are measured
as monetary income and costs are measured as monetary expenditures. While this method can be applied to both groups
and individuals, different factors affected the economic benefits and costs to businesses, local government, and individuals, as summarized below.

	Benefits	Costs
Businesses	Alyeska expenditures more customers greater demand for goods higher prices sustained increased value of assets increased loan opportunities	higher wages to employees higher overhead higher taxes employee turnover inflation

	Benefits	Costs
Local Government	higher tax revenues special impact funds	inflation need for more public services
Individual	greater job opportunities increased income	inflation higher taxes

It may be seen from the preceding table that benefits to one component of the community may result in costs to another. More customers and a greater demand for goods enable businesses to sustain higher prices which benefit the businesses, but at the same time contribute to inflationary pressures on other businesses, local government and individuals. Similarly, while local government benefits from higher tax revenues, both businesses and individuals pay the added costs of higher taxes. While individuals benefit from greater job opportunities, this creates greater employee turnover for businesses and agencies.

Inflation is a general theme which runs throughout the cost column. To the consumer, inflation means reduced purchasing power of the dollar. While economists cannot explain or control inflation very well, they have developed sophisticated methods for measuring it. The most widely accepted measure of retail price inflation is the consumer price index (CPI) conducted quarterly by the U.S. Department of Labor's Bureau of Labor Statistics (BLS) in 44 cities around the country, including Anchorage, Alaska. Until 1970, the BLS conducted an annual CPI in Fairbanks. The program was discontinued because measurements were based on an outdated consumer expenditure survey and therefore weighted inaccurately.

Estimated costs for reinstituting the consumer price index in Fairbanks were $150,000 for the initial consumer expenditure survey and $50,000 each year to conduct a quarterly CPI. Despite vigorous attempts by persons in the

Fairbanks community and members of the Alaska congressional
delegation to persuade the BLS to measure inflation in Fairbanks during the unusual conditions of pipeline construction,
funds for the needed studies did not materialize during the
pipeline period.

When pipeline construction commenced, the nation as
a whole was experiencing an annual inflation rate of 11.7
percent. Due to shortages of consumer goods and services
to meet the increased demand generated by pipeline construction, it was assumed that Fairbanks would experience "inflation on top of inflation." According to the BLS consumer
price index, the cost of living in Anchorage increased 13.8
percent in 1974, and 13.7 percent in 1975. For a number of
reasons, Fairbanksans believed that the Anchorage CPI could
not be used as a measure of inflation in their community.
Even before pipeline construction began, the cost of living
in Fairbanks was significantly higher than in Anchorage.
The cost of living differential between Fairbanks and Anchorage was estimated at 12 percent, based on 1970 data.[1] Data
from 1972 indicated that housing costs in Fairbanks were
9-18 percent greater than Anchorage, and food costs were 7-8
percent higher.[2] Weighting used in the Anchorage CPI would
not necessarily reflect the Fairbanks situation. For example, it is likely that Fairbanksans spend a greater percentage of their income on housing than do residents of
Anchorage.

Another reason for not applying the Anchorage CPI
to Fairbanks is that economists do not fully understand the
causes of higher prices in Fairbanks. Only a portion of the
added cost of commodities can be attributed to greater transportation costs and more extreme climate. Fairbanks is
roughly one-fifth the size of Anchorage and, therefore, unable to achieve the same economies of scale. Instability
of the Fairbanks economy and workforce may also contribute

to higher prices. Although there are no accurate data on
profit margins in Fairbanks, some economists speculate that
the relative lack of competition has led to higher profit
margins. All of these factors affecting prices in Fairbanks
make the use of Anchorage data speculative.

Perhaps the greatest deterrent to using the Anchorage CPI to approximate the rate of inflation in Fairbanks
during the pipeline construction period is that Anchorage
had a type of pipeline impact different from that which
Fairbanks experienced. Since Anchorage was a larger city,
it could absorb the impact of pipeline construction with
less trauma. Its expanding, self-sustaining economy encour-
aged investments in housing, businesses and public utilities
without the hesitation experienced in Fairbanks. In short,
it appears that Anchorage was better prepared to accommodate
the demands of pipeline construction and did not experience
the degree of impact which would account for intensified
inflation in Fairbanks.

While no accurate measure of inflation exists for
Fairbanks during the pipeline period, there are some indications
that consumer prices increased significantly. From October
1974 to October 1975, the price per gallon of heating oil
from some distributors increased as much as 20 percent.[3]
From the last six months of 1973 (prior to pipeline construction) to the last six months of 1974 (after pipeline
construction had begun), the dollar costs of automobile repairs in Fairbanks increased 52.4 percent; between 1974 and
1975 there was another 53 percent increase.[4] One consumer
complained in a letter to the editor of the Fairbanks Daily
News-Miner that the cost of having a local tax service prepare the federal income tax short form tripled from $26.25
in 1975 to $78.75 in 1976.[5] A food price survey conducted
by the Impact Information Center showed a 12.3 percent increase in food prices in Fairbanks from January 1975 to

January 1976, a period in which the nation as a whole experienced a 6.5 percent increase in food prices and Anchorage had a 4.2 percent increase.[6]

Not only did consumers feel the pinch of inflation,
but there were also higher costs to government. In 1974,
the state planned to build a four-story parking garage in
Fairbanks at an estimated cost of $3,648,550. Problems with
land acquisition delayed the project until 1975. By that
time the garage had been reduced to a two-story structure
and the cost had escalated to $4,165,550. A report by the
Budget and Audit Committee of the Alaska State Legislature
revealed that the reasons for the increased costs and decreased size were a change from steel to concrete construction and pipeline impact. By delaying the project until
after pipeline construction began, the cost of materials increased 15 percent and the cost of labor increased nearly
100 percent.[7]

Increased land values and other inflationary costs
attributed to pipeline construction activities were cited
by the Borough Mayor as reasons why the original funding for
the Fairbanks North Star Borough's Chena River Flood Control
Project was inadequate. During the two years after the
bonds were issued in November 1972, the project costs increased 64 percent.[8] Other examples of costs rising so rapidly that bonding became inadequate can be cited with regard
to new school construction and other government projects.

An even more visible aspect of inflation on government expenditures was cost of living adjustments to government employees. After three years without raises, state employees working in Fairbanks received wage increases total-
ling 39.3 percent over the two-year period from August 1973
to August 1975. Fairbanks city employees received 50-60 percent increases in wages in 1974 and a 15 percent increase
in 1975.

This wage spiral in Fairbanks, which occurred in both government and businesses, was related to the lack of accurate information about local inflation rates. As labor and management entered into wage negotiations, little was known about the norms for wages and changes in the costs of living. In the absence of norms, Alyeska and the pipeline workers became the standard against which wages were measured by non-pipeline workers and their employers. Pipeline wages were misleading, however, because the high paychecks were attributed in part to many hours of overtime. For non-union, non-management employees, such as clerical workers, the base pay for pipeline work was not very different from that of persons who did not work on the pipeline. At the end of 1974, clerk-typists working for Alyeska earned $4.50 an hour,[9] while their counterparts working at other jobs in the community earned $3.50 to $4.50 an hour.[10] However, a regular 40-hour work week at $4.50 an hour yielded a monthly paycheck of $780, while the Alyeska employee, working 60 to 70 hours a week with a base pay of $4.50, earned $1,365 each month. The greatest difference between pipeline and non-pipeline pay occurred in union wages. Some representative wages are given in Table 2.

Despite inflation and other factors contributing to higher costs in Fairbanks, the pipeline construction project brought to Fairbanks some monetary gains. The most obvious benefit to businesses in the Fairbanks community was the direct expenditures by Alyeska Pipeline Service Company and its contractors. Early in the construction period, the Chamber of Commerce was told by Alyeska officials that the pipeline company would spend $1 million each day in Fairbanks. Business persons in Fairbanks basked in the glow of this figure throughout most of the construction project.

Actually, Alyeska's average daily expenditures in Fairbanks were less than 80 percent of the "magic million."

Table 2

Representative Wages in Fairbanks, November 1974[1]

	Hourly Wage		Monthly Wage	
Job	Non-Pipeline	Pipeline	Non-Pipeline (40 hrs.)	Pipeline (60-70 hrs.)
Clerk	2.60-3.84	4.04	450-665	1,225
Intermediate Clerk - Clerk Typist	3.50-4.50	4.50	607-780	1,365
Senior Clerk- Secretary	3.50-4.68	4.79	607-811	1,452
Chief Clerk- Senior Secretary	4.04-5.59	5.42	700-969	1,644
Bookkeeper Jr. Accountant	4.04	5.42	700	1,644
Int. Accountant	4.61	6.52	800	1,977
Janitor[2]	3.87	8.31	671	3,061
Maid-Bullcook[2]	3.75	8.31	650	3,061
Cook[2]	5.87	9.12	1,017	3,359
Dishwasher[2]	3.68	8.31	638	3,061
Sales Person	2.60-4.65		4.50-806	
Laborer	4.00[3]- 9.60[4]	9.60[4]	693[3]- 1,664[4]	3,536[4]

[1] Wage rates have been obtained from Alaska State Employment Center Daily Job Demand Lists for October and November 1974; Alaska State Department of Labor survey of mean annual wages, 1974; 1974 starting wage schedule in Fairbanks for clerical employees of Bechtel, Inc., then management contractor for Alyeska Pipeline Service Company; and 1974 wage scales for the Laborer's Local No. 302 and the Culinary Workers Local No. 879.

[2] Union wage scale effective October 1, 1974 for pipeline jobs and July 1, 1974 for non-pipeline jobs.

[3] Non-union wages, jobs listed in Alaska State Employment Center Daily Job Demand List.

[4] Union wages.

Using projected expenditures for the peak period of May 1976, a senior cost engineer for Alyeska estimated that the pipeline company spent $800,000 in Fairbanks each day in the following way:[11]

Salaries in Fairbanks (taxes included)	$500,000
Freight, including trucking and aircraft rental	$150,000
Fairbanks services, including leases for housing and office space, catering and food, communications, and contract with McKlee-D.N.H. for maintenance (which accounted for approximately $25,000, or the largest portion of the $64,000)	$ 64,000
Fees to contractors and subcontractors, i.e., expenditures not including wages and salaries	$ 50,000
Local materials, the largest portion of which was purchased from N.C. Machinery which sells and services Caterpillar machines and parts	$ 30,000
Ft. Wainwright (about half for lease and half for utilities)	$ 6,000
Total daily expenditures in Fairbanks during peak	$800,000

Naturally, less than the estimated $800,000 was spent daily in Fairbanks during the months in which pipeline construction was not at its peak. Furthermore, the $800,000 figure was somewhat misleading because much of the money did not go directly into the local economy. The $6,000 paid for the use of the North Post of Ft. Wainwright Army Base went into the federal treasury, as did the portion of salaries withheld for federal income taxes. Because Alyeska provided housing, food and transportation for many pipeline employees in Fairbanks, their wages were not pumped into the community to pay for those necessities. Furthermore, it was estimated that at least 45 percent of the pipeline workforce were non-residents who took a large portion of their salaries out of

the state. Thus, if one conservatively subtracts 60 percent
of the salary figure to account for taxes and wages leaving
the community, and also subtracts expenditures for the use
of Ft. Wainwright, the amount of money Alyeska pumped into
the Fairbanks economy each day during the peak period was
approximately $494,000, or less than half of the "magic mil-
lion." The $494,000 figure is probably high, not only be-
cause the estimates used were conservative, but also because
a portion of the expenditures left the community since most
of the materials purchased were produced outside the state
and many of the companies receiving fees were headquartered
outside Fairbanks.

Even if one assumes that only $200,000 of Alyeska's
daily expenditures stayed in Fairbanks, this was a considerable boost to the local economy. In addition to Alyeska's
direct expenditures for goods and services to accomplish the
construction project, the pipeline activities generated a
greater population in Fairbanks, more wealth in the community, and greater demand for consumer goods and services.

Prosperity was probably most apparent as Fairbanksans
did their Christmas shopping in 1975. Three days before
Christmas, one of the two local department stores reported
that it was selling four to five microwave ovens each hour.
It had the best Christmas season in its lengthy history as
one of the oldest stores in Fairbanks.[12] The largest drug
and hardware store in Fairbanks also reported the busiest
season in its history.[13] Christmas comes but once a year,
as the well-worn saying goes, but Fairbanks' prosperity was
visible at other times and in other ways. Stores upgraded
their merchandise so that expensive stereo equipment was
available to Fairbanks consumers and cheaper record players
were difficult to find. Fancy sports cars dotted the
streets. A local furrier advertised that his wares were "so
affordable."

More spending in Fairbanks brought more sales tax
revenues to local government. The Fairbanks North Star Borough levied a two percent consumer sales tax, not to exceed
$50, and the City of Fairbanks levied a three percent sales
tax. Purchases made within the city limits were therefore
subject to a combined five percent sales tax. Borough sales
tax revenues, including penalties and interest, jumped 81
percent--from $2.497 million in fiscal year 1972-73, prior
to the pipeline, to $4.518 million in fiscal year 1974-75
when pipeline construction was well underway.[14] This dramatic increase is illustrated in Figure 5.

Even more significant as a source of local revenues
was the increase in property tax assessments. During the
three years from fiscal year 1973-74 through fiscal year
1975-76, the Borough's property tax levy remained at 6.5
mills. During this same period, the general property tax
revenues, including penalties and interest, increased 71
percent from $2.29 million to $3.914 million.[15] Since the
tax levy remained constant, increased revenues may be attributed to increased assessed valuations. Indeed, the January 1 total assessed value of property in the borough went
from $344,987,500 in 1973 to $610,249,995 in 1975, a 77 percent increase.[16] Higher property values were due in part to
new business and industrial buildings constructed in response
to the pipeline, and new housing and residential developments built to accommodate the increased population. Under
the boom conditions, market value of existing real estate
fluctuated in such a way that individual property and home
values escalated. In some residential areas, property values
increased between 30 and 40 percent in less than a year.[17]

A major source of taxable property emerged during
the pipeline construction period: the pipeline. Starting
in 1974, oil company properties contributed $50,497,430 to
Fairbanks North Star Borough's assessed valuation,[18] 12

43

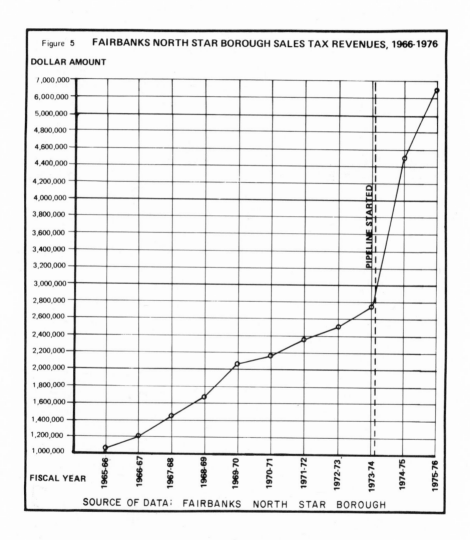

Figure 5 **FAIRBANKS NORTH STAR BOROUGH SALES TAX REVENUES, 1966-1976**

DOLLAR AMOUNT

7,000,000
6,000,000
5,000,000
4,800,000
4,600,000
4,400,000
4,200,000
4,000,000
3,800,000
3,600,000
3,400,000
3,200,000
3,000,000
2,800,000
2,600,000
2,400,000
2,200,000
2,000,000
1,800,000
1,600,000
1,400,000
1,200,000
1,000,000

PIPELINE STARTED

FISCAL YEAR

1965-66
1966-67
1967-68
1968-69
1969-70
1970-71
1971-72
1972-73
1973-74
1974-75
1975-76

SOURCE OF DATA: FAIRBANKS NORTH STAR BOROUGH

percent of the total property valuation. The following year,
oil company assessments totalled $64,804,820 in the borough.[19]
With the completion of an oil refinery in the City of North
Pole in 1978, the assessed value of oil properties in the
borough are expected to jump to $400,000,000.[20] Unlike
other taxpayers in the borough, oil companies are taxed for
personal property, as well as real property.[21] This accounts
for a considerable portion of local revenues from the oil
industry.

Local government not only experienced increased revenues, but also increased demand for services. The structure of the economy and the procedures for collecting taxes
caused the demand for services to precede the increased flow
of revenues. The state legislature recognized this problem
and, shortly before pipeline construction began in 1974, appropriated $10 million directly to local governments which
were expected to bear the burdens of pipeline impact. Under
this appropriation (Chapter 147, SLA 1974), referred to as
"impact funds," the Fairbanks North Star Borough received
$3,030,000, the City of Fairbanks received $606,000, and the
City of North Pole received $152,000. In total, the Fair-
banks area received $3,788,000 in direct grants which the
municipalities were free to use in the ways they decided
would best relieve problems created by pipeline construction.[22]

Later that year, the legislature was called into
special session. One of the bills passed during that session provided an additional $10 million appropriation for
emergency financial assistance to communities experiencing
pipeline impact. This legislation (Chapter 8, SLA1974SSS),
signed into law on July 15, 1974, stipulated that municipalities could not use impact funds either directly or indirectly to reduce municipal tax rates or to retire existing
bonded indebtedness. It directed the State Department of

Community and Regional Affairs to administer the "discretionary grants," and limited the purposes of the grants to
expenditures for extraordinary municipal and/or educational
operating expenses, the purchase of relocatable classrooms,
and the purchase of open spaces which were threatened by
development. The limitations placed on discretionary impact funds forced the local governments to adopt different
strategies in spending their direct impact appropriations
to qualify for funds under Chapter 8.

Local governments in the Fairbanks area received
considerably less funding under Chapter 8 than requested in
their grant applications. The Fairbanks North Star Borough
requested $3,628,174 and received $1,665,800. The City of
Fairbanks requested $2,398,249 and was granted $2,070,000.
And the City of North Pole received only $35,000 of the
$1,414,075 it requested. After the 1974 gubernatorial elec-
tion, the new governor brought to his office a philosophy
of fiscal conservatism and eliminated impact funds from the
state budget, declaring that the benefits of pipeline construction would outweigh the costs to local governments.
Before the appropriation under Chapter 8 was depleted, however, the Fairbanks North Star Borough received an additional
$30,000.[23]

How the local governments spent their impact funds
was largely dependent upon their jurisdictional powers. The
powers of local government are defined both in terms of territory and services. The Fairbanks North Star Borough, which
encompasses 7,361 square miles, functions somewhat like a
county in other states. It provides to this entire area
such services as education, libraries, planning and zoning,
environmental services, flood control, animal control, and
parks and recreation. In addition, the Borough collects
taxes both for itself and for the cities within its boundaries. Within the Fairbanks North Star Borough, there are

two cities: the City of Fairbanks (population 18,053 in
1970)[24] and the City of North Pole (population 265 in 1970).[25]
The cities encompass small areas in the Borough, and to the
residents of those areas they provide such services as police and fire protection, public utilities, inspection services to enforce building codes, ambulance, sanitation, and
health services. Each of these governmental units has its
own mayor and administrative body, and its own council or
assembly to perform legislative functions. The elected
council or assembly determines the levels and types of taxation, expenditures, and services.

It was expected that impact funds would be used to
beef up the existing services offered by local governments.
In general, that is what happened. Local governments added
one or two positions to the staffs of existing departments
and bought the equipment needed to support the additional
staff. In addition, the Borough made capital improvements
on its school facilities, purchased relocatable classrooms,
and acquired some land to serve as a green belt. A summary
of impact fund appropriations is given in Table 3 for the
Fairbanks North Star Borough, Table 4 for the City of Fairbanks, and Table 5 for the City of North Pole.

The only new or innovative programs in the Fairbanks
area funded by local governments through state impact monies
were the Fairbanks North Star Borough's Impact Information
Center, a recreation program conducted by the Fairbanks Native Association in conjunction with the Borough's Department of Parks and Recreation, and an emergency service patrol and sleep-off shelter for the alcoholism program
administered by the Fairbanks Native Association under contract with the City of Fairbanks. The total amount allocated
for these programs designed especially to address specific
problems created by pipeline impact was $301,048, or 3.97
percent of the total $7,588,900 impact funds received in

Table 3

Fairbanks North Star Borough Impact Funds

	Direct Grant (Ch. 147)	Discretionary Grant (Ch. 8)	Total
Total Appropriations	$3,030,000	$1,665,900	$4,695,900
Itemized Appropriations			
Operating Expenditures	1,093,700	1,147,500	2,241,200
Capital Expenditures	1,885,950	400,000	2,285,950
Green Belt Purchase	50,350	118,400	168,750
Appropriations Itemized by Government Activity			
Education			
Operating Expenditures	500,000	1,004,300	1,504,300
Capital Expenditures	1,885,950	400,000	2,285,950
Total	2,385,950	1,404,300	3,790,250
Parks and Recreation			
Operating Expenditures			
Regular Programs	39,859	0	39,859
Fbks Native Association	0	113,100	113,100
Acquisition of Green Belts	50,350	118,400	168,750
Total	90,209	231,500	321,709
Assessing, Taxation, Finance	241,163	0	241,163
Planning and Zoning	83,984	20,000	103,984
Impact Information Center	49,198	10,100	59,298
Environmental Services	44,300	0	44,300
Animal Control	39,478	0	39,478
Engineering	29,713	0	29,713
Mayor's Office	21,743	0	21,743
Libraries	17,530	0	17,530
Election Office	13,750	0	13,750
Borough Assembly	12,982	0	12,982

Table 4
City of Fairbanks Impact Funds

	Direct Grant (Ch. 147)	Discretionary Grant (Ch. 8)	Total
Total Appropriations	$606,000	$2,070,000	$2,676,000
Itemized Appropriations			
Operating Expenditures	424,894	1,986,345	2,411,239
Capital Expenditures	181,106	83,655	264,761
Appropriations Itemized by Government Activity			
Public Works & General Govt.			
Dept. of Public Works	323,847	217,464	541,311
Street Maintenance	101,047	150,000	251,047
General Government	0	117,024	117,024
Engineering	0	62,296	62,296
Building Inspection	0	55,536	55,536
Capital Expenditures	0	18,700	18,700
Total	424,894	621,020	1,045,914
Municipal Utilities System			
Telephone Department	0	443,390	443,390
Water & Steam Department	0	99,000	99,000
Electric Department	0	30,000	30,000
Total	0	570,390	570,390
Fire Department			
Operating Expenditures	0	229,905	229,905
Capital Expenditures	140,000	64,955	204,955
Total	140,000	294,860	434,860
Police Department			
Operating Expenditures	0	154,640	154,640
Capital Expenditures	41,106	0	41,106
Total	41,106	154,640	195,746
Alcoholism Program			
Detoxification Program	0	242,730	242,730
Emergency Shelter	0	113,730	113,730
Emergency Service Patrol	0	14,920	14,920
Outreach Services	0	21,060	21,060
Total	0	392,440	392,440
Health and Sanitation	0	36,650	36,650

Table 5

City of North Pole Impact Funds

	Direct Grant (Ch. 147)	Discretionary Grant (Ch. 8)	Total
Total Appropriations	$152,000	$35,000	$187,000
Appropriations Itemized by Government Activities			
Salaries for City Employees	33,579	35,000	68,579
Street Improvement	42,100	0	42,100
Water Plant Contract	20,000	0	20,000
Attorney Fees for Annexation	12,500	0	12,500
Surveying for Streets	4,185	0	4,185
General Fund (item not identifiable)	39,636	0	39,636

the Fairbanks area.[26]

Due to the political climate, increased sources of local revenue, and the availability of impact funds, local governments in the Fairbanks area attempted to refrain from raising the mill rate by avoiding the introduction of new services. In fiscal year 1974-75, mill rates were lowered by the City of Fairbanks from 12.0 to 11.0 mills and by the City of North Pole from 5.8 to 2.0 mills. At the same time that the political leadership was trying to reduce the tax rate, voters were demanding more services from local government. In local elections, residents of the Fairbanks North Star Borough overwhelmingly voted in favor of a referendum to establish a public transportation system and approved bond issues for new schools and swimming pools.

Rather than reflecting a new wealth, local governments in the Fairbanks area went into belt-tightening

postures during the pipeline period. ⌈The attitude seemed to
be that individuals and businesses could profit from the pipeline, but not local government. It was felt that local government could best serve the collective good by minimizing taxes
and services and passing along the savings to taxpapers.⌉

  While rates of taxation did not increase appreciably,
individuals were faced with higher taxes resulting from increased assessed valuations. Even more significant in terms
of monetary costs to the individual were inflation and other
factors driving up the cost of living in Fairbanks. Using
1972 data, Arlon Tussing and Monica Thomas[27] found that the
higher cost of living in Alaska was offset by high wages in
the contract construction and mining industries, principally
petroleum and natural gas production. Earnings in other industries did not compensate for the higher cost of living.
Tussing and Thomas showed that not only were incomes in most
categories lower in proportion to cost of living in Alaska
than in the rest of the United States, but also that low income families in Alaska had a disproportionately higher cost
of living compared to the rest of the country, than did families with higher incomes. Assuming that the same mechanisms
were operating in the pipeline period, this meant that to
benefit from the pipeline construction, an individual had to
be employed at a pipeline job or related work.

  Not everybody living in Fairbanks desired pipeline
employment. Some people did not want to be separated from
their families, or to work the long hours required by construction companies, or to live in the construction camps.
For professional reasons, or just by personal preference, some
people did not want construction work. But there were many
Fairbanksans who did want to work on the pipeline, or felt
that they must do so to maintain the standard of living
they desired under conditions in which everything cost more.
Yet those who sought pipeline-related jobs did not always
have the opportunity.

Chapter 4
ALASKA HIRE AND MINORITY HIRE

After oil was discovered at Prudhoe Bay and before
pipeline construction began, the Alaska State Legislature
decided that,

> It is the policy of the state in the develop-
> ment of its natural resources to seek and
> accomplish the development of its human re-
> sources by providing maximum employment
> opportunities for its residents in con-
> junction with natural resources management.[1]

In 1972, this policy was incorporated in Title 38 of the
Alaska Statutes, the Public Land Laws. Section 38.40.030
provides that,

> In order to create, protect and preserve the
> right of Alaska residents to employment,
> the commissioner of natural resources shall
> incorporate into all oil and gas leases,
> easements or right-of-way permits for oil or
> gas pipeline purposes . . . a provision
> prohibiting discrimination against Alaska
> residents, and . . . a provision requiring
> compliance with the Alaska Plan . . .

Accordingly, the state pipeline right-of-way lease with
the oil companies building the trans Alaska oil pipeline
included provisions requiring the hiring of Alaska residents
in compliance with Title 38.[2]

Preferential hiring for Alaska residents was not
unique to the pipeline project. Chronic problems of high
unemployment in Alaska had long been recognized, and the
legislature sought to address those problems by ensuring
that when state resources were being used Alaskans would
benefit through increased employment opportunities. Since
1970, Title 36 of the Alaska Statutes, concerning public
contracts, has stipulated that when the state or a political
subdivision of the state lets a contract, the workforce employed to carry out that contract shall be 95 percent

residents when possible; and in all cases of public works
projects, preference in hiring shall be given to residents.[3]

Since the State of Alaska has a relatively small
workforce to draw upon, the legislature realized that it
might not be possible to build a pipeline with 95 percent
Alaska resident labor. Therefore, Title 38 provided that
the commissioner of labor determine the "maximum feasible
effort by employers to fill available jobs with qualified
Alaskans."[4] As the law was written, its provisions applied
not only to Alyeska Pipeline Service Company, but also to
its contractors, subcontractors, and suppliers located in
the state.[5] If the commissioner of natural resources found
that there was non-compliance with the law, penalties might
be imposed ranging from monetary fines to requiring that all
or a portion of the project be halted.

To further ensure that Alaskans received preferential
hiring, Title 38 provided a very specific definition of
"Alaska resident": person who

    (1) except for brief intervals or military
        service, has been physically present in
        the state for a period of one year im-
        mediately prior to the time he enters
        into a contract of employment; and

    (2) maintains a place of residence within
        the state; and

    (3) has established a residency for voting
        purposes within the state; and

    (4) has not, within the period of required
        residency, claimed residency in another
        state; and

    (5) shows by all attending circumstances that
        his intent is to make Alaska his perman-
        ent residence.[6]

Thus people who came to Alaska to seek pipeline employment
could not be considered Alaska residents unless or until
they resided in the state for a year prior to being employed
on the pipeline, and changed their voting registration and
legal residence.

Not only were there special laws which affected the
hiring of Alaskans for pipeline jobs, but there were also
state and federal laws and regulations which applied to the
hiring of minority persons and women. Title 7 of the 1964
Federal Civil Rights Act and Title 18 of the Alaska Statutes
prohibit discrimination in hiring, job promotion, labor organizations, and employment agencies. In keeping with the
1964 Federal Civil Rights Act, the Trans Alaska Pipeline
Authorization Act (U.S. Public Law 93-153, Title II) in
Section 403 established non-discrimination standards for the
project and required the oil companies building the pipeline
to submit an affirmative action plan for approval by the
Department of the Interior. However, specific regulations
for submission of the plan were not adopted until September 24, 1974, five months after the project had begun.[7] The
regulations called for two separate proposals, an employment
practices plan and a contracting practices plan.

On October 11, 1974, Chairman Henry Jackson of the
Senate Committee on Insular and Interior Affairs held a
meeting in Washington, D.C. At this meeting, which was
closed to the public, Black and Latino businessmen contended
that because the trans Alaska oil pipeline crosses federal
land, minority contractors from throughout the United States
should be brought into the project. They had the support of
the Department of Commerce's Office of Minority Business
Enterprise (OMBE). Alaska representatives, including U.S.
Senator Ted Stevens, maintained that Alaskans ought to come
first in minority participation in the pipeline construction.[8]

A second meeting, also closed to the press and the
public, was organized by Pat Mayo of the Department of the
Interior's Office for Equal Opportunity and was held in
Anchorage on November 13 and 14, 1974. It resulted in the
formation of the Ad Hoc Minority Business Enterprise Task
Force, composed of Alaskan and Outside minority groups and

individuals. Since minority business comprises 4.2 percent
of all business in the United States, the minority group
representatives at that meeting demanded that a minimum of
4.2 percent of the contract awards for the pipeline project,
$252 million, go to minority enterprises.[9] They recommended
a policy that "Alaskan natives and other Alaskan minority
groups will be given first right to bid on any and all contracts to be let by Alyeska Pipeline Service Company within
the boundaries of Alaska."[10] They also requested a task
force to establish assistance centers for reviewing bid
specifications, evaluation of bidding and awarding procedures, initiation of joint ventures between minority enterprises and major companies, and identification of minority
business resources available to Alyeska.

Following these meetings, Alyeska Pipeline Service
Company was required to file its affirmative action plans
by November 23, 1974. On November 22, Alyeska submitted a
plan which provided for $115 million worth of pipeline pro-
ject work to be contracted to minority firms, publication
of monthly forecasts of bidding opportunities to be made
available to minority contractors, and a plan for internal
hiring quotas. On December 10, Alyeska was notified by the
Department of the Interior's Office of Equal Opportunity
that the affirmative action plans which it had submitted
were unacceptable and therefore rejected on the grounds that
the goal for minority contracts was too low and Alyeska's
internal minority hire plan was deficient.

Rejection of the affirmative action plans precipitated further meetings between Alyeska and Department of the
Interior officials. A second plan, which increased the minority business goal to $150 million in contracts and busi-
ness orders, was submitted on January 12, 1975. This plan
met with disapproval from the Minority Business Enterprise
Task Force. Their spokesperson, Tom Evans of the Alaska

Federation of Natives, stated that $150 million in contracts
ought to be awarded starting at the time that the affirmative
action plan was accepted, rather than inclusive of all contracts awarded as Alyeska proposed.[11] Feeling they were not
getting an equitable share of the contracts, minority contractors and businessmen representing the Minority Business
Enterprise Task Force picketed the San Francisco headquarters of Alyeska's management contractor, the Bechtel Corporation; the Exxon headquarters in New York; and Pier 91 in
Seattle on January 24, 1975.

The third affirmative action plan which Alyeska submitted was accepted on February 4, 1975. It specified a
goal of offering at least $200 million in contract bidding
opportunities to minority businesses and $155 million in
contract awards. It also stipulated that Alyeska increase
its employment by 15 percent among Alaska Natives in the
office and clerical category, 14 percent minorities in the
technicians category, 10 percent minorities and four percent
females among professionals, and six percent minorities and
two percent females among officials and managers. While the
goals in the final affirmative action plan were more acceptable to minority people, the net effect of the process was
to delay the implementation of the plan until after the first
year of the three-year project had been completed.

Alyeska's employment practices affirmative action
plan applied only to its internal operations. Construction
contractors and subcontractors were required by Title 38 of
the Alaska Statutes, the state leases with Alyeska, and federal and state executive orders to comply with the goals
set forth by "The Alaska Plan to Provide Equal Employment
Opportunity in the Construction Industry," better known as
the "Alaska Plan." The Alaska Plan was originally formulated in response to Executive Order 11246 issued by President Lyndon B. Johnson on September 24, 1965, as an

elaboration on Title 7 of the 1964 Civil Rights Act. The
effect of Executive Order 11246 was to force participants
in the construction industry to show that they had not and
were not engaging in discriminatory practices by demonstra-
ting that the level of participation by minority group members in unions and contracting firms is the same as the level
of minority group persons in the population as a whole. If
this cannot be demonstrated, the unions and contractors are
subject to severe penalties unless they actively engage in
an affirmative action plan to meet the minority hire goals.

The Alaska Plan Policy Board was established in 1969
to formulate an affirmative action plan which would bring
unions and contractors in the state into compliance with the
federal anti-discrimination laws. The plan, approved by the
U.S. Department of Labor on March 31, 1972, called for recruitment, classification, and training of minority persons
in Alaska. Minority persons seeking employment or training
in the construction industry were to be classified by an Ad
Hoc Panel on Equivalency which determined whether the applicants had the skills of journeymen, apprentices, advanced
trainees or trainees. Persons who qualified were to be admitted to the appropriate union or training program. The
Plan established a schedule, or timetable, of minority participation goals over a seven-year period with the ultimate
goal of equalizing the percentage of minority participation
in the construction industry in Alaska with the percentage
of minorities in the local population.

The Alaska Plan was voluntary with no legal provisions for enforcement. More than 300 unions, contractors,
and governmental agencies signed the Plan, indicating their
intention to pursue this approach to affirmative action and
their willingness to comply with anti-discrimination laws.
If their voluntary actions did not significantly increase
minority participation in the construction industry, the

Office of Federal Contract Compliance could make the Alaska Plan mandatory rather than voluntary.

Although the legal basis for hiring Alaskan residents for pipeline work was quite different from the legal protection given to minorities, the two overlap in the area of Alaskan minorities. Alaska Natives originally claimed title to land which was used for pipeline right-of-way, and they were the most visible and well-organized minority group in Alaska. In January 1970, the first injunction against building the trans Alaska oil pipeline came as a result of a suit by five Native villages which had waived their claims to the pipeline right-of-way in exchange for a promise of pipeline jobs. After the pipeline company had selected its construction contractors, the villages sued for breach of contract because no Native contractors had been chosen and the contractors selected were not likely to give jobs to the Native residents of the villages. Because of this and actions by other minority groups according Alaska Natives priority in minority participation, several special provisions and programs were made for training and hiring Alaska Natives for pipeline jobs.

As early as September 30, 1969, the Department of the Interior issued a stipulation requiring the oil companies to recruit, test, train, place, employ, and counsel Alaskan Natives. This requirement, "Stipulation C," led Alyeska to develop "A Plan of Action--Native Utilization." Although the Alaska Native Claims Settlement Act became law in 1971, Stipulation C was retained in Section 29 of the Agreement and Grant of Right-of-Way for Trans-Alaska Pipeline which was signed January 23, 1974. In fulfillment of this section of the agreement, Alyeska Pipeline Service Company entered into a contract with the State of Alaska in which the oil companies agreed to subsidize training programs carried out by the state to prepare Alaska Natives for pipeline

employment. Alyeska also contracted with the Alaska Federation of Natives for recruitment of Native persons, and
hired counselors for each of the construction camps to resolve Native employment problems and foster the retention
of Native employees.

In spite of all the legal provisions and special
programs, not all Alaskans who desired pipeline jobs were
able to obtain them. This paradox resulted from a number
of complex factors including the timing of programs, funding, and decisions; the structure of various institutions
ranging from state agencies to labor unions; and social,
cultural, and personality traits creating informal structures which circumvented formal institutions.

When a project such as the trans Alaska oil pipeline has a duration of only three years, timing is critical
for the implementation of employment goals. The case of
Alyeska's affirmative action plans has been cited to illustrate this point. Alyeska employees comprised only a very
small percentage of the total number of people working on the
pipeline project, however. The Alaska Plan, which was the
affirmative action plan for the contractors and unions who
represented most of the pipeline employees, also suffered
from delays in implementation. Until 1974, the year that
pipeline construction began, the Alaska Plan remained un-
funded, and it was voluntary throughout the duration of the
project. Delay and noncompliance served to undermine its
goals. The Executive Director of the Alaska Plan resigned
on September 23, 1974, stating, "It's just to damn discour-
aging that no one wants to cooperate; no one ever works as
fast as they could for more minorities . . ."[12]

Effective enforcement of Alaska hire laws also was
delayed. Title 38 of the Alaska Statutes ordered the commissioner of labor to determine the amount of work to be
performed by qualified Alaskan residents under state oil and

gas leases. However, during the first year of pipeline construction, no such quota was set. At the end of 1974, the
newly-elected governor appointed a new commissioner of labor
who, for six months, wrestled with the problem of setting
an Alaska hire quota for the pipeline. Well into the second
season of pipeline construction, he decided that it was impossible to set such a quota and amended the regulations to
stipulate that all qualified Alaskans wanting pipeline work
receive preference in hiring. By that time winter layoffs
were looming near and Alaskans worried that no laws or regulations gave them preference in retaining employment. Again
a plan was not formulated until after the problem had presented itself. After winter layoffs had begun, the State
Department of Labor began working with Alyeska Pipeline Service Company to develop a policy of retaining Alaskans. A
letter dated September 4, 1975, was issued by Peter DeMay,
Vice President of Project Management for Alyeska, directing
contractors to retain Alaskans during the layoff period.
Observers claimed that the directive never filtered down to
the foremen who did the hiring and firing, and that the
letter was not backed up by any legal means of enforcement.
But, on October 6, 1975, the Commissioner of Labor issued an
order directing pipeline employers to give preference for
continued employment to Alaskan residents. It was not until
the legislature met in 1976 that Title 38 was amended to encompass "employment" rather than just "hiring."

Another problem of timing in issuing regulations to
carry out the Alaska hire law related to the definition of
"Alaskans." While Title 38 very clearly defined Alaskan
residency, it did not provide a mechanism for ensuring that
the people referred by unions and hired by contractors were
Alaskan residents. For the first year of pipeline construction, the prime evidence of Alaskan residency used by unions
and contractors was the possession of an Alaskan driver's

license. Unions and contractors told job seekers from out-
of-state to obtain driver's licenses to quality as Alaskan
residents.[13] Acquiring an Alaska driver's license requires
$5 and may be accomplished in one day, even the first day a
person arrives in Alaska.

It was not until March 29, 1975, nearly a year after
pipeline construction had begun, that the State Department of
Labor developed a procedure for identifying Alaskans according to the definition in Title 38. At that time, the Department of Labor instituted a program of certifying residency.
Persons seeking employment on the pipeline had to respond to
a questionnaire covering most of the points in the Title 38
definition of residency. If the applicant met the qualifi-
cations, the state issued a certificate of residence. These
"residence cards" then replaced driver's licenses for identifying residents in the hiring process.

Most pipeline jobs required particular skills. Regardless of any other circumstances, Alaskans could not find
employment in those jobs unless they had the requisite
skills. Skills such as plumbing, carpentry and ironwork
take years of training usually acquired through union apprenticeship programs. Other jobs, such as welder's helper or
oiler, only take a few weeks or months to learn. Few Alaskans possessed the skills for many of the pipeline jobs when
the construction project commenced. This enabled Alyeska
Pipeline Service Company President E. L. Patton to assert in
December 1974, "We have not been able to find a qualified
Alaskan who didn't get a job on the pipeline if he wanted
it."[14] Because of the timing and volume of training programs, there simply weren't many qualified Alaskans to be
hired.

Although the oil pipeline construction project had
been anticipated since 1968, it was not until March 1974,
just one month before the actual construction began, that

the State Department of Labor formulated a plan to train
Alaskans for pipeline jobs. This plan depended upon a $1.9
million two-year contract from Alyeska to the state to provide job training for Natives and $3.3 million in federal
impact funds. From Alyeska's perspective, it was not advis-
able to train prior to the time that jobs were available.
It was their feeling that people who were well-trained before
the need occured might "go home" and be "lost to the workforce."[15] Therefore, Alyeska did not provide funding for
job training until after pipeline construction actually
began.

 Although funding was potentially available from
state revenues, the state government did not fund training
for pipeline jobs until fiscal year 1975-76 when $1.6 mil-
lion was appropriated for that purpose. According to State
Senator John Sackett, the failure to train for pipeline jobs
was due to the state's "inability to prioritize the need for
recruitment, employment assistance, and training through the
past ten years."[16] Others charged that prior to the commencement of pipeline construction, the State Department of
Education spent disproportionately less on vocational education than on college education compared to the distribution of jobs for which training was needed.

 In 1973 the federal government consolidated its manpower programs into the Comprehensive Employment and Training Act (CETA). Under CETA, the federal government subsidized state training programs for minority people, female
heads of households, Vietnam era veterans, people under 22
years old, and poor and near-poor. In fiscal year 1974-75,
more than $3.4 million in federal funds was allocated for
job training to the Northern Region of Alaska. An estimated
400 to 500 persons were to be trained with those CETA funds
during that fiscal year. However, CETA funds were not released until October 1974, after the end of the first

construction season. By the end of 1974, the CETA funds
still had not been spent because there were no facilities
for housing trainees in Fairbanks. In January 1975, the
Department of Labor contracted with the University of Alaska
in Fairbanks to provide dormitory space in which to house 80
CETA trainees. The first CETA training class began on February 10, 1975, with 25 people enrolled to learn clerical
skills. The second of three pipeline construction seasons
started before any federal funds were used to train Alaskans
for pipeline jobs.

The Department of Education contracted to provide all
the institutional job training programs funded by the CETA
base grant, the CETA impact grant, and the Alyeska contract.
Record keeping for these programs was so fragmented that it
is not known how many people were trained, for what jobs,
during what time period and at what cost. The records which
are available do not specify how many people completed the
courses which were offered. Rather, there was a system of
classifying students into "positive" and "non-positive"
terminations. "Positive" terminations include trainees who
left the program to take a job or enter the military. Furthermore, there was no follow-up to determine how many people who were trained actually entered the pipeline workforce.
Perhaps because the job training started so late, the state's
philosophy about vocational education during the pipeline
period was to train people both for pipeline jobs and for
jobs which were vacated during the pipeline period due to
high turnover rates. Thus the CETA impact funds were used
to train people for clerical, maintenance, and other work
which was not necessarily preparatory for pipeline employment. Using a variety of different sources, the Department
of Education made a "best estimate" of the amount of money
spent and the number of people trained from July 1974 to
July 1976 in Table 6.

Table 6

Job Training Provided by State of Alaska Department of Education

Source of Funds	FY 1974-1975*			FY 1975-1976	
	Amount Obligated	Amount Spent	Number Trained	Amount Obligated	Estimated Number Trained[K]
CETA Base Grant	$219,285.24	$149,575.52	181	$383,467.44	388
CETA Impact Grant	$704,505.93	$659,973.28	459	$797,079.20	496
Alyeska Pipeline Service Company	$1,339,088.60[σ]	$1,114,045.07	660[ψ]	$407,274.00	287
Total All Funds	$2,262,879.77	$1,923,593.87	1300	$1,587,820.64	1171

*From Report dated January 9, 1975 - may include programs which ended after July 1, 1975, as late as January 1, 1976.

[K]Estimates for period January 1, 1976 through October 30, 1976 for people entering training programs; this number is higher than those actually enrolled and approximately 23% higher than those having positive terminations from training programs.

[σ]Includes $168,981 obligated from April 1, 1974, to July 30, 1974.

[ψ]Some people trained with funds obligated in FY 1975-76 are included in figure for FY 1974-75 as they began training in that period (FY 1974-75 includes people trained by Alyeska from April 1, 1974, through October 31, 1976.)

Those who did not qualify for subsidized training programs
and were able to pay for their training were faced with the
same problem of no training programs in which to enroll. It
was not until October 15, 1975, that the Tanana Valley Community College began its Winter Studies program in Fairbanks
to prepare people for jobs in construction, food service,
and other industries related to pipeline work. Before pipeline construction began, each union had only one apprenticeship class per year, and sometimes not that often. It was
only after pipeline work began and Alyeska and CETA funds
were used to subsidize union apprenticeship programs that
unions stepped up their training programs to two or three
classes per year. Most apprenticeship programs required
three to five years of training, and there was usually a one
or two year delay from the time an application for admittance
was submitted until a person began an apprenticeship program.
During the pipeline period, the demand for job training made
apprenticeship programs more competitive than college entrance. For example, the electricians union received approximately 1,000 applications for its 1976 training program.
Approximately 375 of the applications were complete and from
those 60 persons were selected for apprenticeship.[17]

Training for pipeline jobs was clearly a case of
"too little too late." But training and timing were not the
only factors which worked against the effective implementation of laws to give perference to Alaskans and to integrate
minorities into the pipeline workforce. There were also
problems with the structure of the systems which were responsible for enforcement of the laws, job training, and job
placement. Each system was characterized by the participation
of many institutions, each with its own organization and set
of rules. In most cases, there was minimal coordination between institutions, making the resultant system complex and
fragmented.

No less than 11 different agencies were responsible
for the protection of minority rights in hiring for pipeline
jobs. These included six federal agencies (U.S. Equal Employment Opportunity Commission, U.S. Department of Labor,
U.S. Department of the Interior's Office for Equal Opportunity, Office of Federal Contract Compliance, National
Labor Relations Board, and the Federal Authorized Officer
for the Trans Alaska Pipeline Project) and five state agencies (Alaska State Human Rights Commission, Alaska Department of Labor, The Alaska Plan, the State Pipeline Coordinator's Office, and the Alaska Attorney General's Office).
In addition, four state agencies had enforcement responsibilities with regard to the Alaskan hire laws (Alaska Department of Labor, Alaska Department of Natural Resources,
State Pipeline Coordinator's Office, and the Alaska Attorney
General's Office). Each of the agencies was responsible for
the enforcement of different parts of different laws, contracts, or administrative orders.

While the State Department of Labor was given most
of the responsibility for enforcing Alaska hire laws, there
was no single agency in a leadership role with regard to
effecting the hiring of minorities and women. When the Executive Director of the Alaska Plan resigned in September 1974,
he complained, "No one agency has taken the bull by the
horns to fend for minority hire."[18] Many of the agencies
designated to enforce the laws were either inaccessible or
understaffed. During the first year of pipeline construction, the Alaska Plan had only one grievance brought before
it; the Human Rights Commission had a backlog of 204 complaints, two-thirds of them pipeline-related, and had brought
only one case to court;[19] and the U.S. Equal Employment Opportunity Commission had a backlog of 100,000 cases of which
20,000 had been on file more than two years.[20] The National
Labor Relations Board and the Department of the Interior's

Office for Equal Opportunity had offices located only in Anchorage, hence inaccessible to most Fairbanksans. None of the agencies was able to make independent audits of the levels of hiring of minorities or Alaskans on the pipeline project. Most figures on the percentages of minorities and Alaskans in the workforce were prepared by Alyeska and its contractors, the very companies which the agencies were supposed to monitor.

In 1974, a plan was formulated to consolidate state hiring enforcement activities related to the pipeline by establishing yet another hiring enforcement agency under the auspices of the State Pipeline Coordinator's Office. According to this plan, a six-person staff would work with Alyeska and its contractors on problems in meeting hiring quotas. On October 14, 1974, the legislature's Budget and Audit Committee approved $148,000 to hire the six field investigators for two years, with the understanding that Alyeska would reimburse the state according to Section 18(a) of the right-of-way lease which provides that the lessees reimburse the state for costs of monitoring the project.

Appointment of the field representatives was delayed, first due to the resignation of the Executive Director of the Human Rights Commission and then to await the appointment of a new Commissioner of Labor by the newly-elected Governor. By the end of the year, the number of proposed positions was cut by half and the funding was cut. The Human Rights Commission and the Department of Labor refused to relinquish their jurisdictions and agreement on operational procedures was never reached. The plan for consolidation of responsibility and resources never materialized, and each of the enforcement agencies continued operating in its own fragmented way.

Similar to the enforcement situation, job training in Alaska involved more than 13 different agencies

administering more than 19 different programs. The different
agencies received their funding from federal, state, and local
governments, as well as private sources. Each agency and
program had its own administration, rules and organization.
In conjunction with "planning" for pipeline jobs, the State
Department of Labor instituted the Alaska State Manpower
Utilization System (ASMUS) to coordinate job training and
placement activities. The ASMUS plan is illustrated in
Figure 6.

As with enforcement, each of the job training agencies was struggling for funds, manpower to provide the necessary services, and power to accomplish its individual goals.
This type of fragmentation in enforcement and job training
activities had three effects. First, it served to confuse
both prospective employers, and especially, prospective employees. It made the task of seeking a pipeline job more
difficult for Alaskans who did not know how the systems
functioned and how to function within them. Second, existing
funds were scattered over such a broad spectrum of agencies
that none was capable of accomplishing the tasks at hand,
and much of the funding was allocated to administrative
costs in each agency. "Divide and conquer" appeared to be the
third effect of the fragmentation. The division of responsibilities between agencies meant that no agency knew what all
the other agencies were doing, and no agency could get a
firm grasp of the overall minority and local hire situations.
Without a knowledge of the existing situation, Alaska resident and minority hire could not be monitored and deficien-
cies could not be remedied. It was possible that some of
these complications could have been resolved in the long-run.
But for the trans Alaska oil pipeline construction there was
no "long-run."

Faulty timing of decisions and programs, and the inability of training and enforcement agencies to carry out

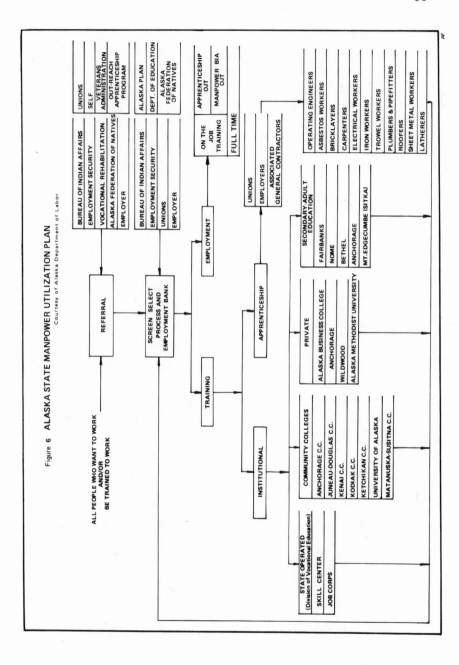

Figure 6   ALASKA STATE MANPOWER UTILIZATION PLAN

Courtesy of Alaska Department of Labor

their functions were not the only obstacles to implementation of Alaskan hire laws and minority participation in the
pipeline project. Fundamental to the implementation of hiring laws was the structure of the hiring process. The ground
rules for hiring persons for pipeline jobs were contained in
the Project Agreement between Alyeska Pipeline Service Company, 15 international labor unions affiliated with the
Building and Construction Trades Department of the AFL-CIO,
and 24 local labor unions affiliated with the Western Alaska
(Anchorage) and Fairbanks Building and Construction Trades
Councils. In exchange for a provision that there would be
no strikes or work stoppages on the trans Alaska oil pipeline project, Alyeska Pipeline Service Company agreed that
the construction project would employ only persons referred
directly to the contractors by the labor unions.

The Project Agreement, which became effective
April 29, 1974, stipulated that even though labor unions
were the exclusive referral agencies for pipeline employment,
"the selection of applicants for referral to jobs shall be
on a nondiscriminatory basis . . . and shall not be based
on, or in any way affected by union membership, or the lack
thereof."[21] However, the labor unions were structured to
refer union members first, providing a strong incentive to
join the union.

In Fairbanks, 11 labor union locals were the major
sources of referral for pipeline jobs:

Carpenters Union Local No. 1243
Culinary Workers Local 879
International Brotherhood of Electrical Workers
    Local No. 1547 (IBEW)
Iron Workers Local No. 751
Labor's International Union of North America
    Local 942 (Laborers)
Operating Engineers Local No. 302
Painters Union Local No. 1555
Plasterers and Cement Masons Local No. 912
Plumbers and Steamfitters Local 375
Sheet Metal Workers Union Local No. 72
Teamsters Union Local 959

Most of the pipeline workers were affiliated with the Teamsters, the Laborers, the Operating Engineers, or Culinary Workers. While pipewelders comprised a significant craft within the pipeline labor force, most pipewelders came from a very specialized union local in Oklahoma, Local 798, rather than the Fairbanks Plumbers and Steamfitters Local 375.

Each union had a separate hiring hall, organization procedures, wages, dues and benefits. In general, skilled trades distinguish two types of members: journeymen and apprentices. Unions which do not have those distinctions generally classify their members or prospective members according to job experience and union tenure on either "A," "B," or "C" lists, with "A" being the most experienced and/ or tenured and "C" the least. Traditionally, unions have functioned in accordance with their agreements with the Associated General Contractors (AGC). When contractors or subcontractors called the union with requests to fill available jobs, the more tenured union members were dispatched before the less tenured ones.

Local unions have varying relationships with union members residing in other areas. For example, the Teamsters local covers the entire state of Alaska. According to its established rules, "A" cards from anywhere in the state have been considered equal in bidding for jobs, as are "B" and "C" cards. Teamster cards from out of state have been ranked below Alaska cards, so that Alaskans will get first choice for jobs in the state. Operating Engineers Local 302, however, is based in Seattle; Alaska union halls are branches of the Seattle-based union, rather than independent locals. Although Alaska "A" and "B" list members were given first preference on Alaska jobs, according to AGC agreements, Alaska "C" list members came after Seattle "A" and "B" list members in assigning jobs. This procedure made it difficult for Alaskans to be recruited into the Operating Engineers

Union.

Union.

Depending upon the closeness of ties with national and/or international labor organizations, local affiliates might have preferred to assign jobs to union members from outside the state rather than recruit Alaskans into the organization. Since Alaska has been subject to extreme economic fluctuations, some locals have tried to keep their memberships small so that existing members have better opportunities when jobs are scarce. When jobs are plentiful, they have expanded their labor forces by bringing outside union members into the state for short periods, rather than expanding the Alaskan locals. Several unions discouraged nonmembers from registering for employment by charging monthly registration fees, usually $10.

Title 38 was carefully lobbied through the legislature by the unions so that contractors, not unions, were responsible for resident hiring. The state pipeline right-of-way lease holds the owner companies responsible for their contractors' compliance with Title 38. To protect the owner companies, Alyeska Pipeline Service Company in turn insisted on a resident hire clause in the project labor agreement with the unions. For nearly two years, that clause in the Project Agreement was ignored by the unions, which found themselves in a "damned-if-you-do-and-damned-if-you-don't" situation. If they complied with the residency hire clause in the pipeline Project Agreement, they could be sued by their non-Alaskan members; if they didn't comply, they could be sued by Alaskans seeking pipeline jobs. At least one powerful union considered going to court to challenge the constitutionality of Title 38. The union was dissuaded from such action when the legal counsel for the state pointed out that the union would still be subject to the terms of the Project Agreement unless the National Labor Relations Board (NLRB) ruled differently, and cautioned the union about adverse public relations ramifications of such a suit.[22]

After it was determined that the NLRB would decide whether unions could change their procedures to give preference to Alaskans for pipeline jobs, the Commissioner of Labor convinced the unions to adopt policies which would comply with the resident hire clause in the Project Agreement. Anticipating an angry response from their non-resident members, union officials asked the Commissioner to issue an official state order to help deflect the hostility.[23] Although he had no real power to do so, on March 1, 1976, the Commissioner of Labor issued an order to the unions to "cease and desist" dispatching non-residents when qualified residents were available to fill pipeline project jobs. As anticipated, action by the unions led to complaints by non-resident union members to the NLRB.[24] In keeping with previous NLRB decisions,[25] the National Labor Relations Board found, on May 18, 1976, that giving preference to Alaskans was lawful. It also found that the change in union hiring hall procedures did not violate the National Labor Relations Act, but rather brought the unions into compliance with the terms of the pipeline Project Agreement.

While the NLRB decision was a victory for the proponents of Alaska hire, it came in the midst of the third and final major construction season. By that time the workforce was relatively stable and few pipeline jobs remained to be filled by Alaskans. Pipeline workers realized that the employment opportunity was drawing to an end and were less likely to quit their jobs. Thus the change in union procedures came at a time when turnover rates were relatively low and did not jeopardize employment opportunity for non-Alaskan union members who had obtained pipeline jobs during the first two years of the project.

Changes in hiring hall procedures did not eliminate all the aspects of union structure hampering employment for

non-union members. Another obstacle to hiring Alaskans was
the stipulation in the Project Agreement that unions dispatch
workers within 48 hours of the time requested, excluding
weekends. If dispatches were not made within that time,
the contractors were free to hire non-union workers. This
48-hour limit, combined with a deficient communications
system and limited transportation, posed problems for rural
Alaskans. After a union received a job request, it usually
took more than 48 hours to notify a member residing in a
rural area and to make travel arrangements to Fairbanks.
This forced people to remain in Fairbanks while awaiting
jobs, a very costly strategy due to the housing shortage
and high cost of living. Few unemployed people from rural
areas could afford to wait in Fairbanks for jobs, which
meant that Fairbanksans and persons from outside the state
with greater financial resources had an edge in the hiring
process. The 48-hour limit was most detrimental to Alaskan
Natives who reside in the villages throughout Alaska.

There were also other problems with the union structure which affected minority hiring. While minority persons
might be assisted in the initial training stages by state or
federal agencies or the unions themselves, they were not
exempt from union rules. Even though contractors were required to hire a percentage of minority persons to comply
with federal standards, the unions did not always have enough
minority persons enrolled for referral to the contractors,
possibly because the Alaska Plan was voluntary and not subject to enforcement. According to agreements with the unions, a contractor or subcontractor might request minority
persons, or a percentage of minority persons, to be dispatched
from the union hall. If the union could not find enough
minority persons, the contractor was free to hire non-union
minority persons; however, it was difficult for contractors
to find trained individuals in that category.

The "catch-22" came when a minority person went directly to the contractor's office to solicit a job and then went to the union, alleging that the company wanted to hire him and expecting to be dispatched. According to Teamster rules, for example, the union could honor requests for specific individuals if they previously worked a specified number of hours for the company. However, dispatching a person who was not requested under those conditions was against the union rules. Thus, it appeared that the union was discriminating against minority persons when, in fact, the union was applying the rules in a non-discriminatory fashion.

Unions are very complex institutions designed to protect their members. To command high wages and other benefits, unions attempt to keep their supply of members small in relation to the demand for their specialized services. The major strategy for expansion is to incorporate more types of jobs into the union, thereby increasing the demand for services the union members provide. Thus, union structure is not conducive to recruitment of unemployed persons, and does not facilitate preferential treatment for non-union members, such as Alaskans and minority persons who have not belonged to the union previously. Not only is the formal structure of the unions complex, but there is also an informal structure which works to maintain the status quo. One aspect of the informal structure which is not well understood by outsiders is the system of favor by which persons gain preferential treatment within the union.

Bonding is another aspect of the informal structure. Most union members refer to their co-members as "brothers." Many long-time union members derive much of their identity from their union status. Union "brothers" tend to stick together and to consider non-union persons or persons belonging to other unions as adversaries. An air of superiority develops often taking on racist dimensions. This racism is maintained in the informal structure in spite of changes imposed on the formal structure by laws or plans intended to increase minority participation.

In the case of the pipeline, the overt racism of the 798ers, the pipewelders from Oklahoma, was tolerated by the pipeline contractors and state and federal officials whose highest priority was getting the pipeline built and who viewed the small group as essential to the process. Rather than incur the wrath of the tightly knit brotherhood of 798ers, the pipeline contractors attempted to isolate them and satisfy their demands. And, rather than see the pipeline delayed by union disturbances, the state and federal officials responsible for the enforcement of minority hire and Alaska hire laws simply ignored the 798ers.[26] This type of prima donna treatment was reinforced by periodic rampages of 798ers in the pipeline camps over such issues as wanting to cook steaks for lunch, wanting automatic washing machines rather than the wringer washers in the construction camps, wanting accommodations separate from the unions whose memberships were racially integrated, and wanting Black pipeline workers to ride in the backs of the buses.

Thus people hired in complicance with Alaska hire and minority hire laws sometimes found themselves objects of tokenism, subtle discrimination, or outright racism. The laws did not apply to management or supervisory personnel, many of whom were hired from "Outside" and were not sympathetic to the rights of Alaskans or minorities. They believed that they were being forced to comply with the letter of the law and often rebelled against the spirit of the law. Minority persons sometimes found themselves in "make-work" situations. For example, one crew of mostly Native Laborers was told to move sand bags from one side of the road to the other. When they finished the task, they were told to move the bags back to their original position. "I barely made it for a month and a half on the pipeline," said one Native person, "even though I once worked a camp job for nine months--for $250 a month. I couldn't make it for nine months in a pipeline camp because of the 'wall of hatred.'"

On September 26, 1974, just three days after the executive director of the Alaska Plan resigned, the executive director of Alaska's Human Rights Commission submitted his resignation. "Most unions, contractors and state people are just trying to protect themselves," he said. "They're not out to hire minorities."[27] The delays, the lack of funding, the lack of coordination, the complexity of systems, the underlying structures of organizations, all indicated that there was a lack of commitment to the goals of hiring Alaskans and minority persons for pipeline jobs. Officials at the highest levels of state government admitted that they were reluctant to enforce Title 38 because they feared that such a resident hire law would be found unconstitutional. In the case of minorities, where there was no question of constitutionality, federal and state officials were unable to perform their enforcement duties because of their positions in a power structure fundamentally opposed to changing the status quo.

In spite of all these obstacles, more Alaskans than anticipated worked on the pipeline project. Prior to the pipeline, Alaska construction union membership numbered about 9,000 people, less than 600 of whom were Natives.[28] Many Native and non-Native Alaskans who had never worked construction jobs before desired pipeline employment, either for the experience, or the economic opportunity, or because they needed the pipeline job to keep up with the cost of living. By May 21, 1976, 30,456 people had applied for Alaska residency cards and 24,507 cards had been granted.[29] During a peak period, 18,316 certified Alaskans were

hired to work on the pipeline.[30] The number and percentages
of Alaskans working on the pipeline each quarter are given
in Figure 7. The figures must be interpreted cautiously
because (1) the same person may have been hired more than
once during the quarter; (2) by 1976 many of the people
eligible for residency cards had come to Alaska specifically
to seek jobs after pipeline construction began; and (3) the
figures were prepared by the contractors, who are liable for
compliance with the law, and not by an independent auditing
agency. Nevertheless, the figures reflect two outstanding
concepts: many Alaskans who had never worked in construction
before actively sought pipeline jobs; and, if training and
enforcement programs had been initiated earlier, it is likely
that more Alaskans would have taken advantage of the pipeline
employment opportunities over a longer time span.

Minority and female hire rates were not nearly as
impressive. Most of the minority persons hired for pipeline
jobs were dispatched from a very few unions and most of the
women were hired for clerical positions. In Figure 8 the
numbers of minorities, females and Alaska Natives in the
pipeline workforce by month are shown; and Figure 9 percentages are indicated. Again, it may be noted that numbers
and percentages increased substantially over time. This
suggests that prior planning, training, and enforcement
could have enabled more minorities and women to take advantage of pipeline employment over a longer time span.

Prior to the commencement of pipeline construction,
Alyeska estimated that 2,000 Native Alaskans would be avail-
able for pipeline employment, and the Bureau of Indian
Affairs estimated 2,470.[31] Representatives of the Alaska
Federation of Natives believed that those estimates were low.
Alyeska's "Plan of Action--Native Utilization" made a com-
mitment that "a minimum of 2,470 individual Alaska Natives
will be utilized in fulfilling the overall 3,500 training or

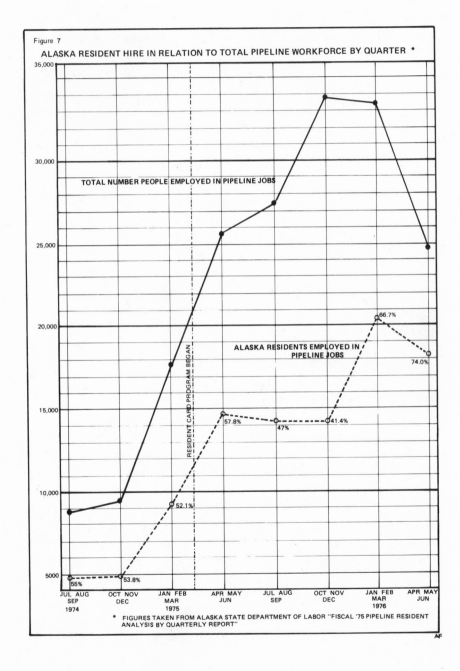

Figure 7

ALASKA RESIDENT HIRE IN RELATION TO TOTAL PIPELINE WORKFORCE BY QUARTER *

TOTAL NUMBER PEOPLE EMPLOYED IN PIPELINE JOBS

RESIDENT CARD PROGRAM BEGAN

ALASKA RESIDENTS EMPLOYED IN PIPELINE JOBS

66.7%
74.0%
57.8%
47%
41.4%
52.1%
55%
53.8%

JUL AUG SEP 1974 / OCT NOV DEC / JAN FEB MAR 1975 / APR MAY JUN / JUL AUG SEP / OCT NOV DEC / JAN FEB MAR 1976 / APR MAY JUN

* FIGURES TAKEN FROM ALASKA STATE DEPARTMENT OF LABOR "FISCAL '75 PIPELINE RESIDENT ANALYSIS BY QUARTERLY REPORT"

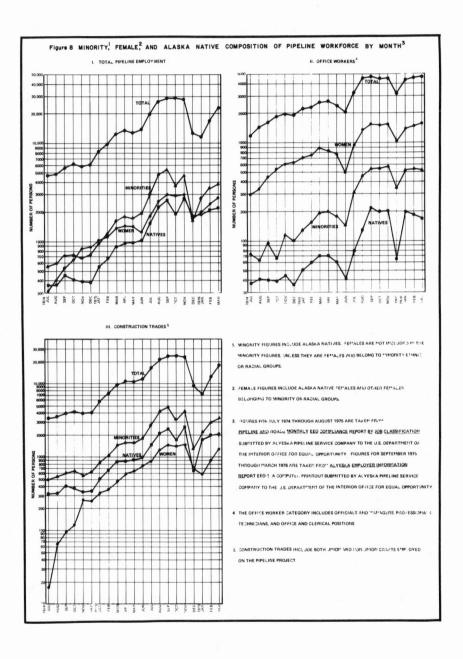

Figure 8 MINORITY, FEMALE, AND ALASKA NATIVE COMPOSITION OF PIPELINE WORKFORCE BY MONTH

I. TOTAL PIPELINE EMPLOYMENT

II. OFFICE WORKERS

III. CONSTRUCTION TRADES

1. MINORITY FIGURES INCLUDE ALASKA NATIVES. FEMALES ARE NOT INCLUDED IN THE MINORITY FIGURES, UNLESS THEY ARE FEMALES WHO BELONG TO MINORITY ETHNIC OR RACIAL GROUPS.

2. FEMALE FIGURES INCLUDE ALASKA NATIVE FEMALES AND OTHER FEMALES BELONGING TO MINORITY OR RACIAL GROUPS.

3. FIGURES FOR JULY 1974 THROUGH AUGUST 1975 ARE TAKEN FROM PIPELINE AND ROADS MONTHLY EEO COMPLIANCE REPORT BY JOB CLASSIFICATION SUBMITTED BY ALYESKA PIPELINE SERVICE COMPANY TO THE U.S. DEPARTMENT OF THE INTERIOR OFFICE FOR EQUAL OPPORTUNITY. FIGURES FOR SEPTEMBER 1975 THROUGH MARCH 1976 ARE TAKEN FROM ALYESKA EMPLOYER INFORMATION REPORT EEO-1. A COMPUTER PRINTOUT SUBMITTED BY ALYESKA PIPELINE SERVICE COMPANY TO THE U.S. DEPARTMENT OF THE INTERIOR OFFICE FOR EQUAL OPPORTUNITY.

4. THE OFFICE WORKER CATEGORY INCLUDES OFFICIALS AND MANAGERS, PROFESSIONALS, TECHNICIANS, AND OFFICE AND CLERICAL POSITIONS.

5. CONSTRUCTION TRADES INCLUDE BOTH UNION AND NON-UNION CRAFTS EMPLOYED ON THE PIPELINE PROJECT.

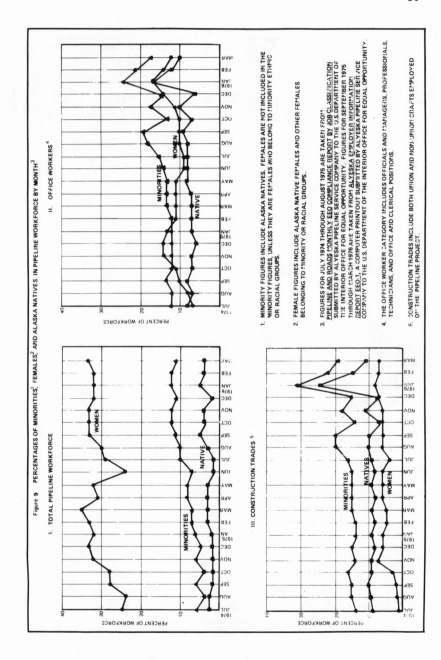

Figure 9 PERCENTAGES OF MINORITIES[1], FEMALES[2] AND ALASKA NATIVES IN PIPELINE WORKFORCE BY MONTH[3]

I. TOTAL PIPELINE WORKFORCE

II. OFFICE WORKERS[4]

III. CONSTRUCTION TRADES [5]

1. MINORITY FIGURES INCLUDE ALASKA NATIVES. FEMALES ARE NOT INCLUDED IN THE MINORITY FIGURES, UNLESS THEY ARE FEMALES WHO BELONG TO MINORITY ETHNIC OR RACIAL GROUPS.

2. FEMALE FIGURES INCLUDE ALASKA NATIVE FEMALES AND OTHER FEMALES BELONGING TO MINORITY OR RACIAL GROUPS.

3. FIGURES FOR JULY 1974 THROUGH AUGUST 1975 ARE TAKEN FROM PIPELINE AND ROADS MONTHLY EEO COMPLIANCE REPORT BY JOB CLASSIFICATION SUBMITTED BY ALYESKA PIPELINE SERVICE COMPANY TO THE U.S. DEPARTMENT OF THE INTERIOR OFFICE FOR EQUAL OPPORTUNITY. FIGURES FOR SEPTEMBER 1975 THROUGH MARCH 1976 ARE TAKEN FROM ALYESKA EMPLOYER INFORMATION REPORT EEO-1, A COMPUTER PRINTOUT SUBMITTED BY ALYESKA PIPELINE SERVICE COMPANY TO THE U.S. DEPARTMENT OF THE INTERIOR OFFICE FOR EQUAL OPPORTUNITY.

4. THE OFFICE WORKER CATEGORY INCLUDES OFFICIALS AND MANAGERS, PROFESSIONALS, TECHNICIANS, AND OFFICE AND CLERICAL POSITIONS.

5. CONSTRUCTION TRADES INCLUDE BOTH UNION AND NON-UNION CRAFTS EMPLOYED ON THE PIPELINE PROJECT.

employment opportunities."[32] By January 1976, the Alaska
Federation of Natives had referred 2,568 Native persons who
wanted pipeline jobs, and Alyeska had trained 1,324 Native
persons in institutional training programs and 1,320 on the
job.[33] From April 1974 to April 1976, a total of 5,147
Native Alaskans worked on the pipeline project.[34] Once
again, the figures express a need or desire for pipeline
employment which exceeded all expectations.

At the same time, it must be emphasized that the
number of pipeline jobs exceeded expectations. Before construction began, it was estimated that the peak workforce
would be 16,000. During the summer of 1975, the workforce
peaked at approximately 21,600,[35] 35 percent higher than
anticipated. While Alaskans were available to fill as many
as 50 percent of the jobs, this meant that the other 50 percent had to be filled by non-Alaskans.

During this period of relatively high unemployment
in the Lower 48 states, many people who lived outside Alaska
knew that there were a lot of jobs associated with pipeline
construction. While they might not have known that Alaskans
were to be given preference for the jobs, the high wages
provided strong incentives for them to travel to Alaska to
seek pipeline work. To Fairbanksans, these non-resident
job seekers were "Outsiders."

Chapter 5
OUTSIDERS

One bright June day in 1975, a young man bounded into my office full of energy and enthusiasm. His blue jeans,
T-shirt and backpack were typical garb of one type of people
newly arrived in Fairbanks. From outward appearances, he
looked like many of the young people who filtered through
the Impact Information Center in hopes that we could give
them the secret of how to get a pipeline job. By the time
they came to our office, most of them already realized that
they were being classified as Outsiders in the job market,
but they didn't know why that classification existed. I
usually gave them some literature about the Alaska hire law,
answered some questions, and offered some suggestions.

Most of the newcomers felt that being an Outsider
was a little like being a foreigner in a strange land. Similar to attitudes toward foreigners in many countries, including the United States, Fairbanksans ascribed a rough
classification system to the newcomers. As pipeline construction began, there were three general classes
of Outsiders in Fairbanks. Those with the highest status
were the managerial personnel associated with the pipeline
project, many of whom were "on loan" from parent oil companies. These persons were expected to bring their families
with them to Fairbanks. Alyeska sought out executive homes
and luxury apartments to house these higher echelon personnel and their families. These newcomers were welcomed into
the community by the Welcome Wagon, the Newcomers Club, the
Petroleum Wives Club, churches and other organizations
which expected them to become integrated into the social
fabric of Fairbanks life.

Experienced construction workers with skills that
assured them jobs on the pipeline comprised the second

group of Outsiders. These people from California, Texas and Oklahoma were expected to pass through Fairbanks every nine or 13 weeks as they commuted from their families in the Lower 48 states to their jobs in the pipeline construction camps. They posed no real problems to the community, but Alaskans harbored a certain amount of resentment toward them for taking jobs which many Alaskans believed were rightfully theirs.

Outsiders with the lowest status in Fairbanks were the unskilled and inexperienced persons coming to Alaska for "the big bucks." While it was anticipated that there would be a finite number of persons in the first two categories, it was feared that hordes of persons from depressed areas of the Lower 48 would descend on Fairbanks without jobs and without the resources to sustain themselves. It was assumed that they would form long lines, not only at the union halls, but also at the welfare and food stamp offices. In conversations, many Fairbanksans conjured the image of ruffians spilling out of the bars onto the streets where they would accost and rape the wives and daughters of upstanding Fairbanksans.

In the wake of a severe housing shortage, the community contemplated providing a campground to contain these persons, for it was feared that they might set up squatter communities which would pose health hazards. Although impact funds were available for the campground, the idea was rejected for two reasons: (1) the local leadership was of the opinion that campgrounds should be left to private enterprise and, therefore, should not be a government function; and (2) several Borough Assembly members believed that if they made it "easier" for these persons to survive in Fairbanks, they might stay longer when it was preferred that they depart immediately.

Fairbanksans decided to rely upon a campaign to

discourage people without jobs from coming to Alaska. The
Alaska Commissioner of Labor sent letters to commissioners
of labor in the other states to inform them of the job
situation in Alaska. Both the state and Alyeska Pipeline
Service Company engaged in a national news media campaign
to discourage people from coming to Alaska, unless they were
tourists or jobs had been assured to them. The national news
media made its own contribution by printing sensational
stories about pipeline impact in Fairbanks, Valdez and other
pipeline corridor communities.

Despite this discouragement, some people came to Fairbanks hoping to obtain pipeline jobs. One was Tim Normington,
the young man who walked into my office that bright June day.
He had read all the scare stories about Alaska, but somehow,
as he said, "The more I was discouraged, the greater became
my resolve. When people I told about my trip plans shook
their heads at me and laughed at my foolishness, I passed the
derision off as an expression of their own frustration in
life. I figured Alaska was a land of opportunity where a
person with will and enthusiasm could be successful." On
the ferry from Seattle to Alaska, he met a couple of Operating Engineers who told him about their experiences obtaining
union jobs without ever having seen the machines they were
hired to run. He pumped them for information about how the
heavy equipment worked and how one operated them. He was
convinced that if anybody could fake it, he could.

Tim had saved about $1,500 before he departed on
his trip to Alaska. He hoped to make more money, but
his real motive was different. He had just graduated
from the University of California at Berkeley with a Phi
Beta Kappa key and honors in anthropology. But his strongest
desire was to become a writer. Like surprisingly many others
who came to seek pipeline jobs, he anticipated that his Alaskan experience would provide the material for a novel.

We talked about the hiring hall experience and the people he had encountered. I told him that we didn't know very much about the people who were coming to Fairbanks to seek pipeline jobs. There was no sociological data on their ages, their places of origin, their family status, their experiences. I had spent a little time in the union halls, a hotel in which many people stayed while awaiting jobs, and a couple of construction camps. From talking to people in those places, I had some ideas about their needs in Fairbanks, but I didn't understand the whole social structure that surrounded this group of transient people. The Impact Information Center had compiled lists of the formal rules by which the unions operate, but we didn't have a good understanding of the informal rules that affected people seeking pipeline jobs.

An astute observer, Tim agreed to keep detailed notes of his experiences in the hiring hall. He attended daily union calls and fraternized with others in similar positions during the day. As he waited for a job, he worked nights as a janitor in a local inn and later drove a taxi. At first he lived in a state campground, but when it got too wet he moved into a dilapidated rooming house. After months of waiting his number was called and he was finally dispatched to a pipeline job. Before he left, he assembled his notes into a description of the hiring hall milieu. The rest of this chapter is Tim Normington's attempt to help us understand what it meant to be an Outsider seeking a pipeline job in Fairbanks.

On Call at the Operating Engineers Local 302

Acquiring a pipeline job through the Operators Union involves more than simple formal registration procedures. At the C Hall, men with common aims and grievances gather to wait for their jobs to materialize. During the wait men share with one another a wealth of information that enables them to successfully exploit their working and living environments.

By meeting regularly at the union hall and through the conversations which ensue, the men develop supportive relationships which will promote cooperation when they finally reach their work sites. In the interim, the relationships help to provide encouragement, dissipate grievances, cultivate a sense of opposition to agents who compete for or interfere with job opportunities, and affirm personal goals.

C Hall men are not union men. The C Hall is not, technically speaking, a union hall. It is a hall that the union rents. Men who patronize it are simply paying ten dollars a month to buy the privilege to wait in line for a job. While the men depend upon the union to supply them with jobs, the union depends upon a highly skilled and flexible labor force to maintain its credibility. Thus, the union absorbs people from the C Hall through an informal system which selects people with patience, resolve, and an ability to seek out information and withstand hardships.

Most of the men in the C Hall have left their families and friends to work machines on the Alaska pipeline. For a two to six month period, they experience the process of signing up, waiting, learning to survive in Fairbanks, and going on call, before they are sent out for a pipeline job. As they wait, they are all men without machines, exposed to the vagaries of contract needs and seasonal fluctuations in the workforce. It seems that the men who succeed at getting out "to the Slope" and into the union are those who use the informal social and communications network.

Signing Up

During the warm months in Fairbanks, groups of men dressed in work clothes and wearing shade caps linger in

front of the post office and the stores downtown when the
union halls are closed for lunch. A newcomer can ask any
one of them where the Operators Hall is and he will be directed to First Avenue, a few blocks west along the Chena
River.

One of the men on the post office steps will probably
mention that the Operators Union has three lists: the A list,
the B list, and the C list. The A list and the B list dispatchers are located in one building, and the C list dispatchers are located in another. A person from out-of-state
who is not a member of Local 302 must sign up at the C Hall.

C Hall is a small clapboard house, whitewashed but
so neglected that part of the building is about to be condemned. A wood sign hangs over the sidewalk with the words
"Odd Fellows Temple" and the insignia of three interlocking
links in a chain. A sign on the wall of the building announces that the hall is for rent. but the phone number has
been blacked out. In a small side yard, ten to fifteen men
can be seen milling about smoking cigarettes and drinking
coffee. A cement walkway leads from the yard the an entrance
at the back of the hall. The door is closed now because the
dispatchers go to lunch from twelve to two.

At two o'clock the door opens and the men file into
a small square room and line up in front of a half-door leading into the dispatchers' office. During the long wait there
is time to study the dark marbled linoleum and the flattened
cigarette butts on the floor. The air is heavy with sweat
and cigar smoke. There are no windows. A bare lightbulb
illuminates the pale green walls and gray molding.

A narrow writing bench lines the wall where various
notices have been pinned. An advertisement for a rooming
house with a downtown location announces: "kitchen, T.V.,
bath. Rent from $40.00 a week. Call Sam at 452-4594. No
drinking or smoking." Other notices include "Instructions

for Application," which nobody seems to read, and a letter
from the state explaining the priority classification given
to Natives.

The novice waits in line until his turn comes, then
he tells Elmer that he wants to sign up. Elmer is the dis-
patcher--he assigns jobs. Elmer moves nonchalantly to a
cabinet and brings back two forms to the doorway. He writes
the name and social security number of the applicant on one
card, and gives him the card and an application form to fill
out.

Each applicant pushes through the men to the bench
where he checks the boxes on the card that indicate which
machines he "runs": Crane, Dozer, Driller, Loader, Scraper,
Shovel, Sideboom, Mixer, Crusher, Compressor, Bump Cutter,
Piledriver, Stake Hopper, Drag line, Conveyor, Cement Hog,
Finishing Machine. The card also lists jobs such as mechanic,
welder, machinist, helper and oiler.

The application requires the usual personal information and work history. Most of the men come to Alaska
with experience running one or two of the machines. But
more than a few men sent out from the C Hall never before
worked as operators. Whether or not a novice is fired at the
job site depends on which machine he tells the dispatcher he
can operate, and whether or not the experienced men at the
site help him.

One young operator, named Al, got his start by tell-
ing the hall that he ran scraper, a large earth-moving
machine. When his date came up, he bid for a job and got
out on the Slope. The foreman at the work camp merely pointed to one of the scrapers and told him to run it to the sand
pit.

"I got in and fiddled with the levers," Al told me.
"I managed to drive it to the sand pit where the dozer man
immediately saw that I didn't know what the hell I was doing.

But this old guy took a liking to me and showed me how to run it."

According to talk among the men at the hall, some machines such as scraper, bulldozer, and loader can be learned quickly by relaxing, driving them hard, and having some coordination. Nevertheless, while some men, like Al, make a go of it, there are many who are sent right back. "We sent twelve men out the other day who claimed they ran sideboom," Elmer told the men in the room, "and they were back in here the next day. They didn't know what they were doing."

In the hall a novice can learn which machines he might be able to run without experience, and which machines demand expertise in order to ensure safe working conditions. An inexperienced operator could endanger a fellow worker's life with machines such as the sideboom, a long arm with straps which lowers sections of pipe into a ditch, or a driller, where a five thousand pound auger swings overhead, or a crane, which lifts enormous weights around construction crews. The experienced men in the hall let others know about these machines if they ask questions.

"No, that sideboom you can't mess around," one seasoned operator told me. "You drop that pipe in a ditch on top of a welder and you'll kill the son-of-a-gun. I got a buddy at Happy Valley who had a guy drop one on him and he's messed up. His back gets real sore when he walks out in cold weather."

Those who are inexperienced and have not asked any questions while waiting to sign up usually list themselves as unskilled workers, for jobs such as welder's helper, machinist's helper, driller's helper, or oiler. But most eventually discover that the opportunity for unskilled jobs is slim.

"We don't get many calls for helpers of any kind,"

Elmer told someone signing up, "because they don't want to do any work. The mechanic makes all the money and the operator-helper thinks all he has to do is hand him the tools. The contractors usually ask for a light mechanic." Elmer told another hopeful, "Afraid you'll have trouble getting an oiler job. We give most of those to Natives and Alaskan women. Minorities."

"Figures," said the young man at the window.

"We can't help that," Elmer said. "State law. We have to have twenty-eight percent Natives on the Slope by September."

Some machines are not necessarily dangerous, but demand expertise to insure product quality and the orderly progress of work schedules. After Elmer turned down an applicant for a crusher operator job because he had no experience, Elmer told the men in the hall, "The crusher operator can make the company money or lose it for them. If you lose money they get rid of you. Got to have the right screen size or the rocks just keep going around and around and clog the screen. The grade inspector will check the bed for three side crush which tends to pack like it should, for a solid bed. If you don't have a three side pack, he'll condemn the whole road. The crusher operator is in charge of ten to fifteen guys. I know, I ran one for Green for eight years."

"What do you run," one of the men asked me. He knew that I was just starting. "Front loader? Got to be good, cause you're at the front of the line and you'll hold everyone up. Scraper too? I guess scraper's good when you're young."

These matters are discovered in time, by asking people in the yard and in the hall while waiting. Now it's time to take the application back to the window. Elmer explains that there is a ten dollars a month hall fee and that the union will let fees fall delinquent for three months

before removing a name from the list. He gives the applicant a receipt with a number on it, and writes the date on
the receipt. He cautions not to lose the receipt, for the
date determines how long a person has to wait for a job.

The Wait

While Elmer assists the new men signing up, another
dispatcher named Bob calls out the jobs for the crowd of men
in the room. "How many winch cat operators we got out there?"
he says. Several men speak up. And then Bob asks them,
"What's your date?" Voices from the crowd say, "I got 5-15,"
"4-6," "6-5" . . . These are the months and days that the men
signed up. Bob listens to all the dates and then says, "Well,
I'll take the earliest date. That's the way we work."

Someone in the crowd speaks, "I think he's got it,
Bob." Bob gives the man with the April date his work orders
and tells him to go to the A and B hall to have the papers
processed. As the man leaves, everybody seems happy. "We
don't want to see you back here," someone tells him. After
he departs, another says, "Well, every guy who goes out,
that's one better."

Fellows in the hall or the dispatchers explain that
the length of the wait depends on the jobs a person is qualified to do, the unpredictable needs of special construction
projects, and the preferential policies of the union.

The union saves the unskilled jobs for Natives and
women who are residents of Alaska. Most men in the hall are
ambivalent about this policy. One day a Native walked up to
the window and left in five minutes with a job as oiler.
One of the men waiting for a job said, "That's the thing to
be, a Native. Get out right away. I say, if they're trained,
fine. But it's hard to find any trained. They're trying to
give the Natives oiler jobs. Which is fine. It's their
land. Of course, they got paid for it."

Another operator complained, "These Alaskans bitch about not getting a fair share of the pipeline jobs, but there isn't a single one of them that couldn't work. They think they've got a case. Maybe they do. But Alaska couldn't build the pipeline by themselves."

Most jobs are scarce because there is a low turnover. One man had been waiting five months for a power plant operator job. "It's a good job because during the winter the power plant is under cover," he said glumly.

Men who run more complex machines--sideboom, crane, grade-all, winch cat, ditcher, drag-line--or qualify as a heavy equipment or crusher mechanic, or a driller, are usually dispatched in ten to forty days. Opportunities for less skilled jobs, such as dozer, loader or scraper, depend upon whether a big unexpected construction project starts up, and whether the jobs can be filled by men in the A and B Hall.

When the pipeline contractors call and tell the union that they need, for example, fifteen to twenty dozer operators, the dispatcher in the A and B office offers the job first to the A card holders, then to the B card holders. Any jobs remaining are offered to men in the C Hall. During slow spells when no jobs filter down to the C Hall, the men in the C Hall start to grumble about the unfairness of the preferential policy.

One day as I was leaving the hall, I fell into step with an operator who was also leaving. There were no jobs early in the week. "Ain't a damn thing here Monday's and Tuesday's," he complained to me.

We encountered a couple of men headed for the hall. They asked us about the call. The fellow with me told them, "No call. There were three mechanic jobs and three guys just walk in right up to the window and give Elmer their sign-up receipts. The guy behind them didn't even hear the call because there was none. Sounds usual. The way they're coming in the back door."

One of the men replied, "I suppose there's guys come up here on the weekend from Seattle and make the A and B list." The Fairbanks Operators Local 302 has a sister office in Seattle. It was rumored that men travel to Washington, work 200 hours on a union job to earn their B cards, then come to Fairbanks where they are dispatched out of the B hall right away, even though they reside out-of-state.

The C Hall men in Fairbanks resent this loophole because they are told that even if they belong to the Operators union, if they are not Alaskans they have to sign up and wait on the C list. One man had traveled around the world as a union operator for twenty-five years, yet he was stuck in the C Hall for three months.

The C Hall men also complain about the requirements for proving Alaska residency. Some will stay in Alaska for more than a year. They want to be sure that, when the time comes, they can benefit from preferential hiring policies like other resident Alaskans.

A small group of operators talked about residency requirements. One said, "You got to have a card."

"What's that?"

"You fill out a whole batch of papers and then take them to a notary and send them off to Juneau."

"Yeh," growled a third man entering the conversation. "I just fought them bastards in Juneau for eight weeks. The guy down there is still checking on me but the fellow up here said 'to hell with him, here's your card.'"

"They're trying to get jobs for Alaskans but look how they're messing up."

A Louisianian joined the conversation: "They're flying in planeloads of operators every day and they'll tell you right off they don't care to be residents. They want to get their money and spend it in Oklahoma and Texas."

"Mostly Oklahoma. And we sit here waiting for jobs and there ain't a damn thing we can do."

"You'd think the union'd be upset," said another.

"The union is controlled by money. Damned politics. Perty near everything is controlled by money these days."

It is hard on the men who have been waiting for several months to watch an operator arrive from Texas and get dispatched three days later. After observing such a situation, one of the C Hall men in the group suggested that the Texan was a foreman.

"He's not a foreman," another retorted. "He's one of those cigar-smoking, cock-sucking Texans."

"Problem is," another man said, "is to get a few more ten dollar bills and flash them in front of these bigshots."

"They're playing politics, taking these people's ten bucks damn well knowing they'll never get out. I've been here since March, off and on, and I don't know if I'll get out."

"We ought to send some guys from here downtown to buy a Texas outfit and then stand in line. Boots. Hats."

"We ought to bug the union office over there by the window just like the Nixon men. Har har."

"Those men in the union office will tell us who these goldbrickers are. What their dates are so we can straighten things out."

"No they won't! The only way is to get a two-foot rubber pipe and the next time one of those son-of-a-bitches comes out of the A and B hall grinning we ask him his date and if he don't answer, then just lay it on top of his head!"

The men seem to be passing the time, rather than organizing any formal protest. Topics shift back and forth from union issues to information about how each man came to Fairbanks and how he survives during the long wait.

Surviving in Fairbanks

Fairbanks is a town that demands a degree of resource-fulness. Prices are high. Living quarters are hard to find. There are few recreation facilities outside of the bars and churches. Aside from a few notices for rooming houses posted in the union halls, there is no formal referral service available to newcomers. Most people keep their ears open around town, ask questions, and learn from the personal histories of others.

Some men simply return home after signing up at the hall. One example is a fellow who signed up in April, returned to Montana the next day and worked a crane for a couple of months. After quitting his job in Montana he drove back to Fairbanks in a little camper which he parks in the driveway of some friends. He takes his showers at his friend's house but eats in restaurants.

Jerry is a mechanic from New York City. Conspicuously unlike others at the C Hall, he dresses in a black plaid sportscoat and hard street shoes like he just stepped out of the Bronx. Jerry flew to Fairbanks last April and signed up, then flew back to New York City. He called Elmer (the dispatcher) three months later. Elmer told Jerry that "they're catching up on mechanics." So Jerry quit his job in New York City and returned to Fairbanks. Now he stays in a forty-dollars-a-night motel room. He doesn't mind spending so much money because he expects to get out on the pipeline in a few days.

Most union men come to Fairbanks, sign on, and live in and around town until their dates come up. Many have friends and relatives with space in their backyards for small campers or tents. Others pay for rooming houses and motels. Few remain idle very long, eventually finding a job in town that covers expenses and occupies time.

Jack flew up from South Dakota in March, got room in

a motel where he works odd jobs for the owner. He drives the owner's truck. His cousin and a few friends from Minnesota also came to Fairbanks. All the men work so much that they don't have much time to see one another.

Bob came from near Odessa, Texas. His date is March 20. He is young, slight, cut square. He was drafted, went to Vietnam as an infantryman, and returned home trained as a mechanic. He also studied at a radio broadcasting school in Texas. He drove to Fairbanks with his wife. They live with his sister-in-law outside of town in a trailer parked in the backyard of a house. The trailer is owned by his brother, who works on the Slope as a mechanic. Bob's wife works two jobs, one as a messenger and another as a security guard. Bob works nights as a disk jockey at a radio station in Fairbanks so that he can go to the union hall every day to make his face known.

Dave is another young Texan. He flew up to Fairbanks in February with his wife and they stayed in an apartment with his parents who live in Fairbanks. He drove a dozer and frame loader at a batch plant site in Texas. After arriving in Fairbanks, he was hired by the state to drive a dump truck. His wife works as a file clerk with a pipeline company. They now have an efficiency apartment which costs them three hundred dollars a month.

Joe lives in his van which he drove from Washington to Alaska in March. When he signed up at the union hall, he told the dispatcher he could run anything. He then got a non-union job with a contractor in Fairbanks and learned how to run loader and dozer. He works twelve hours a day, at seven dollars an hour, excavating basements. In his spare time he hustles girls at dances and bars.

Rob came to Fairbanks by bus as soon as he finished a college term in Idaho. He signed up in March and found a basement rooming house in which to keep warm during the cold spring. He found a job as a night janitor in a hotel and spends most of his free time sleeping or running errands. About the rooming house he said, "Six of us in a basement. Forty bucks a week each. Mrs. Smith runs the place. She's kind of religious. No drunks. No smoking or drinking. She's got a sink and a hot plate."

Al hitchhiked up from Minnesota and registered immediately with the Operators Union in June. "You can't get places to stay in Fairbanks, but then the bars never close," he told me. He said that he signed up at the Operators Union even though he had never run any big machines before. He spent the first two-and-a-half weeks sitting right under the dispatcher's eye, so that when time came to get work Bob would know that Al really wanted to work. Al slept in campgrounds. As soon as he was kicked out of one campground, he would move to another. He ran out of money in a month and ended up spending all his time in a particular bar bumming drinks. He found a job as a helper in a garage for five bucks an hour and worked until he was called by the union, four months after he came.

A man in his fifties brought his wife, daughter and grandson from Sun City where he has a home. They drove to Fairbanks in a camper and then moved into a thirty-five-dollar-a-night motel room. "I was clearing $500 a week in town as a mechanic," he told me, "but I quit when my date got closer."

A middle-aged man with a red face and dark wavy hair, cowboy boots, white slacks and a Delta Junction Caterpillar belt buckle is leaning against a wall next to the union hall yard drinking coffee from a styrofoam cup. He's short but stands very erect, almost cocky. There's a hint of bemusement in his eyes and a slight smile. According to the silver belt buckle, his name is Roger M. Brown. He lives in Delta Junction, a small settlement a hundred miles south of

Fairbanks. He drove dozer for small contractors down there.
He came from Louisiana in 1965 and homesteaded: "Worked for
myself for a couple of years," he drawls in that soft Southern lilt, "but all my equipment wore out." He came to Fairbanks and signed up in February. He has waited six months,
commuting back and forth between the Fairbanks union hall
and his home in Delta Junction. He is holding out for a job
in the Delta work camp where his wife now works.

Another regular in the hall is a middle-aged oyster
fisherman and mechanic from Virginia. He came to Fairbanks
last year and worked as a mechanic. He returned this year
to get a job on the pipeline, bringing with him a twenty-
eight foot trailer. He lives in a trailer park just outside
of town and spends most of his time gardening at his brother's
house in Fairbanks. He doesn't get a job because he is living
on his savings.

The backgrounds and circumstances of the men are diverse, but they all experience the equalizing force of the
passage of time. When first arriving in Fairbanks some feel
like the newcomer who told me that he was not homesick because there was too much excitement in town. The boomtown
atmosphere filled with Cadillac taxis, flashing gold jewelry,
twangs and lilts from all corners of the world, beguiles the
most intrepid traveler.

But men who have lived and worked in Fairbanks for
a few months tend to share the viewpoint of one union man
who said, "I'll tell you, if you live and work up here,
you'll think about going back home. All the novelty's worn
off now. I kind of expected the wait and the union lines,
but I've learned a lot. How to get by by myself."

A Sense of Purpose

Men in the halls complain of the inactivity, the
waiting, the boredom, the high summer and low winter

temperatures. But, many stay in Fairbanks until their date
come around and they can get out on the pipeline. In most
cases determination to withstand the inconveniences
and discouragements of the temporary stay in Fairbanks
may be attributed to an intensely personal sense of purpose.

Every man at the C Hall came to Fairbanks to work
on the pipeline. The pipeline offers extraordinary opportunity, not only because the pay is good, but also because
the workcamps provide free room and board. There are union
jobs available in and near Fairbanks but the C Hall men only
take them as a last resort. One day there was talk in the
union hall about a truck mechanic job in town--no free room
and board, a car was required, and there was little opportunity for overtime. After considering these conditions,
one man said, "Stand here in the union hall for a couple
of weeks, might as well be working for a couple of weeks."
Another answered, "Nah, I might as well stay home. I came
up here to work on the Slope, not in town."

To all these men the pipeline means money. "Where
else can a guy like me save five thousand dollars in nine
weeks?" I was told. Another man said, "I came up to see
what fourteen hundred a week looks like." The men at the
hall thread sums of money through their conversations with
a sense of wonderment. Two fellows argued for thirty minutes
about whether one day of work on the pipeline equals five
days or three days of pay back home. The three-day fellow
kept pointing to the higher cost of living in Alaska. The
five-day fellow cited the unpredictable work season in the
States.

For the majority of men the abstract sums of money
represent a stake in life--college tuition, land, a house,
a small business. In a few cases the pipeline money represents financial restitution. An operator from Connecticut
fretted because he had twenty thousand dollars worth of

gambling debts. Another operator planned to fix a fence
that burned on his ranch in Texas. An older truck driver
from Seattle told how his knee had been operated on a couple
of times for industrial accidents. After he was laid off,
two other employers told him that they didn't like knee dis-
abilities. The truck driver claimed that, since employers
can't legally discriminate against the aged, the companies
were using the disability issue to keep him out of the workforce. "I'm fifty years old," he told me. "They see my gray
hairs and they don't want anything to do with me. I can't
stand that. It's demoralizing. It's not right. I came up
to Alaska because I can save some money up here and work
casual in Seattle and maybe buy a little backhoe."

For others the money was not so important. One operator pointed out that the work camps are populated by two
kinds of people, the greedy newcomers who are after their
stake and the international crowd of veteran operators. A
veteran worker explained to me his reasons for not taking a
particular pipeline job. "I didn't just come up here to make
money," he said. "I want to do something that I like." A
college student told me, "I came up here for adventure. I
was getting bored."

Outside the hall one day, I casually asked a group
of men, "What do you think it is that draws people to Alaska?"

"Money," one fellow answered.

"Why do they all tell you they always wanted to come
up here anyway?" I persisted.

"Because all the people around here don't want to
hear that you're just after the big money."

Another union man disagreed. "I think it's more than
money," he said, "even though money might have been the first
attraction. I think they come up because of the opportunity.
A man can respect himself up here instead of having to kiss
ass back in the States for lousy jobs. Even in California

everything's buttoned up. You got to start out on the bottom
and work your way up. Even then the competition's rough."

On Call

A few months after signing up, men quit their jobs
and start "going on call" at the union hall. Some men with
night jobs manage to work and go on call during the day. If
a man has an advanced registration date and runs machines
which are in demand, his period on call may be less than a
week.

But many men can be seen lingering around the hall
every day for several weeks. "It gets to be a habit," one
man said of the process. "You go here in the morning and
then come back in the afternoon. The weekends get longer.
At first the weekend's short. Seemed like a day. Now it
seems like five."

The men come every day because there is no way to
predict what jobs the contractors will offer to the dispatcher at the hall, and whether or not there will be any jobs
left after the A and B Hall men pick them over. One C Hall
veteran observed, "It's mostly luck. Being here at the right
time."

In spite of their diverse backgrounds, the men at the
C Hall look similar. Almost all of them wear some kind of
work clothes, even if they are not working. Levi's. Flannel
shirts. Work boots or cowboy boots. Heavy belt buckles.
Shade caps with the insignias of various heavy equipment
companies: Caterpillar, Williams, International. There are
no women and few men who aren't white. There are some men
under thirty, and a few over forty, but most fall somewhere
in between. Most of the men are husky, particularly in the
upper parts of their bodies, thick, rounded shoulders and
calloused hands. They are not afraid of getting dirty by
crouching against the wall outside the hall, or by sitting on

a plywood sheet stretched across two garbage cans in the yard.
Conversations reveal accents from all over the United States.
The men talk about what they can share, the world of
machines and construction. A Louisianian in a group of
operators initiated a conversation after some small talk.
"Worked pipelines all throughout the south, never north of
Memphis. My dad, he's a pipeliner. Thought he could help
me out. My first job I worked the ditch and it was easy.
If I missed the grade I'd always run up to the bending machine and tell them to bend it a little." Everyone in the
group laughed.

"Now, I'd work road crossings or tie-ins. Dope gang.
Dope gang puts the preservative on the pipes. That's a
finger smashin' job."

Elmer, the dispatcher, called out a job for an operator running drag-line. A mechanic who was not interested in
the job said, "Yeh, I've run drag-line quite a bit. Hell,
I owned one myself. My brother and I bought a 392. First
job I ever had was on a drag-line. First thing they had me
loading rocks on a truck. That was over in southeastern
Montana. I was new at the thing and I didn't know why I was
getting only half of the rocks into the truck and half on the
ground. Hell, I had to throw the rocks at the old man (who
drove the load truck), he wouldn't come any closer." More
laughter.

Humor keeps the men's spirits up when the jobs coming
out of the C Hall are scarce. One day Elmer asked the crowd,
"Got any sidebooms out there." There was a pause, and then
a voice said, "No, no but you got a guy who wants to go up
to Ice Island." The men laughed. "Got any salt?" Elmer
parleyed. Then I asked the guy next to me, "What do you
operate?" "A.F.T. operator," he told me. I asked him what
the letters meant. "Any Fucking Thing," he answered with a
grin.

Some of the older men intersperse their talk of money
and the pipeline work camps with a perspective on life working in construction and the discouragement with which an age-
ing worker must somehow cope.

"Spain, Guam, Morocco, Iran. I been there," said a
tough-looking worker sitting on the steps outside the C Hall.
"I worked them all. Freelance mechanic. But there's no more
for me. M.K. (a construction company), their policies are
good for me. They sent me to that hydraulic school over
there (in Saudi Arabia).

"They got an advantage on us, those new guys," he
continued. "We can beat 'em out in the field," he said addressing another old-timer sitting next to him, "cuttin',
hammerin'. But them guys with the gauges have an advantage."
His voice trailed off.

And then, "That Morocco's the place to go. Spain,
too. Girls. Nightclubs. Exotic sites. All those camels
and donkeys. It was just like back in Christ's time . . .
That's the wonderful thing about construction. It's rough
and wild, but you see a lot of exciting sights."

The other old-timer told a story about some fellows
at one of the pipeline work camps who smuggled in a few
prostitutes and blew five thousand dollars in one night. I
shook my head and reapeated the sum in wonderment.

"Five thousand bucks ain't nothing," the old-timer
said to me. "It may be to you and me sitting here. But you
make it and five thousand dollars will just be like a fifty
dollar bill in your pocket."

I told the men that my friends tried to discourage
me from coming to Alaska, because of the high cost of living,
the scarcity of jobs, the harsh environment. They listened
and then one said, "I used to never let anything beat me, I
never let a job beat me until I was forty. Well, I don't
have the determination that I used to have. But it will get

to you eventually.

"I hope I get out," he said a little sadly. "Wouldn't hurt me if I put in forever."

Waiting at the hall has its ups and downs. When there are no jobs, some start complaining, others turn glum. But eventually the men who persist get out on the pipeline.

An older man who had worked twenty-five years as an operator finally got his orders to report for pipeline work. He walked into the yard where all the men congratulated him and told him they didn't want to see him back in the hall. With his head bent low, rocking almost inperceptibly from side to side, he half-addressed the group of men who were sending him off, and half-mumbled to himself: "God damnit! Son of a bitch! I'm at the end of the trail. Construction's something else. It really is. Eleventh grade education. I can barely write my own name. Make more money than doctors sometimes. It's some life. A lot of waiting. But it's worth it."

Chapter 6
IMPACTS THAT DIDN'T HAPPEN

Fairbanks was not besieged by rapists. The number of forcible rapes reported to the Fairbanks Police Department prior to the pipeline in 1973 was 10. During the first two years of pipeline construction the number of reported rapes was 14 in 1974 and 11 in 1975. Rape cases which received the most publicity did not involve men who were associated with the pipeline construction project, or people who were waiting for pipeline jobs.

Neither did the influx of Outsiders swell the lines at the food stamp and public assistance offices. After pipeline construction began, the number of people and families receiving food stamps declined dramatically. From January 1973 to January 1976 there was a 90 percent drop in food stamp recipients in Fairbanks, from 3,007 persons to 310 persons (see Figure 10). From 1972 to 1975, the number of public assistance cases in the Fairbanks area declined by 36 percent (see Figure 11).

Based upon impact statements and other available information, the Fairbanks North Star Borough School District anticipated 11,994 students during the 1974-75 school year.[1] To meet this anticipated demand, some of the schools handled students in double-shifts, the teaching and administrative staff was expanded, and modular, relocatable classrooms were acquired. The 11,994 students expected was 3,150 more than the 8,844 that had been projected without pipeline construction. In fall 1974, however, the total enrollment in the Fairbanks North Star Borough School District was 8,864, only 20 more than expected without the pipeline. In spite of preparations to cope with their impact on the school system, the other 3,130 students who were expected did not appear (see Figure 12). In fact, during the course of the 1974-75

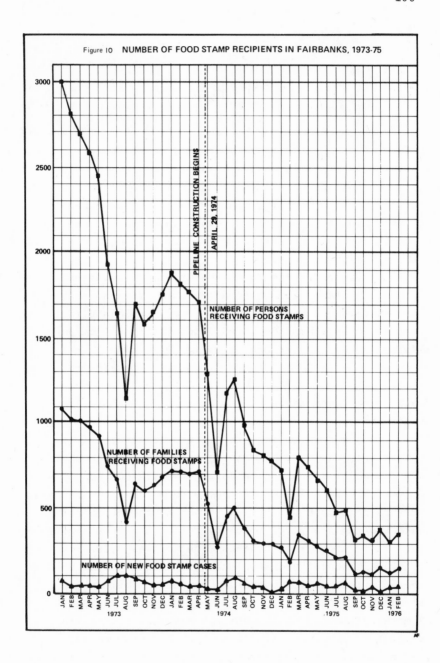

Figure 10   NUMBER OF FOOD STAMP RECIPIENTS IN FAIRBANKS, 1973-75

PIPELINE CONSTRUCTION BEGINS

APRIL 29, 1974

NUMBER OF PERSONS RECEIVING FOOD STAMPS

NUMBER OF FAMILIES RECEIVING FOOD STAMPS

NUMBER OF NEW FOOD STAMP CASES

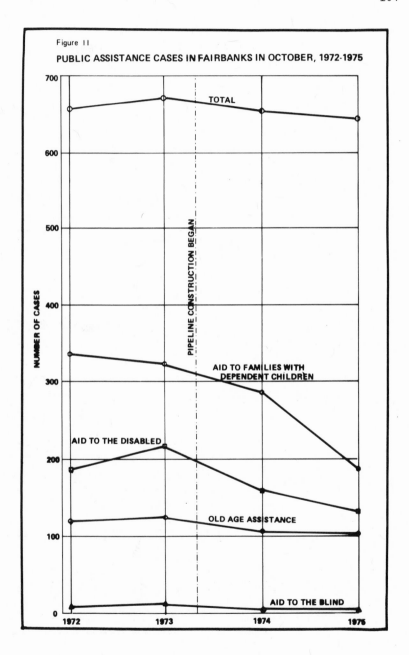

Figure II

PUBLIC ASSISTANCE CASES IN FAIRBANKS IN OCTOBER, 1972-1975

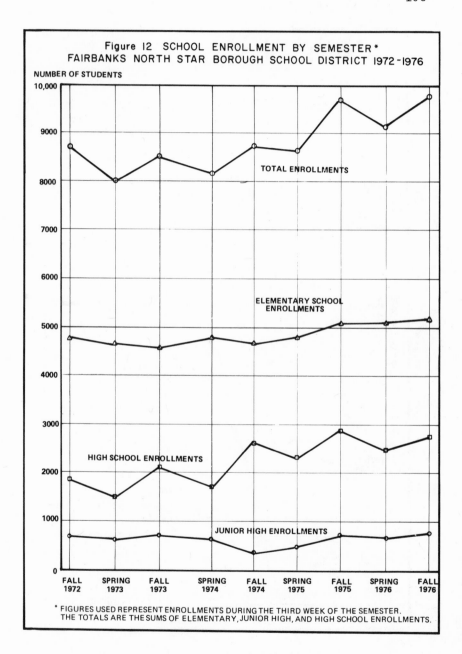

Figure 12 SCHOOL ENROLLMENT BY SEMESTER*
FAIRBANKS NORTH STAR BOROUGH SCHOOL DISTRICT 1972-1976

* FIGURES USED REPRESENT ENROLLMENTS DURING THE THIRD WEEK OF THE SEMESTER.
THE TOTALS ARE THE SUMS OF ELEMENTARY, JUNIOR HIGH, AND HIGH SCHOOL ENROLLMENTS.

school year, school enrollments actually declined.

Squatter communities which were expected did not materialize and there were no epidemics.

The absence of these anticipated impacts can be explained--not through the logic of numbers which were used to project impacts prior to the pipeline, but through an understanding of the structure of the community and the structure of in-migration. The combination of the campaigns by the state and Alyeska to discourage prospective job seekers and the sensational publicity of social conditions in pipeline corridor towns in the national news media may not have eliminated or reduced the influx of people, but it probably did have an effect on the type of people who came to Fairbanks.

Most of the people who came to Fairbanks to work on the pipeline were "working class" people--conservative, independent, proud. While they had access to unemployment compensation, they were not likely to use the social service system. Food stamps and public assistance had a "welfare" connotation which ran counter to their value systems. Most of the people who came to Fairbanks knew what to expect, in general, and came prepared. Few people sold all their possessions, packed up their families and moved to Alaska "lock-stock-and-barrel" under the false assumption that they could get pipeline jobs. In fact, during the period from August 18, 1974, to December 20, 1975, only one out of every 97 persons hired to work on the pipeline had brought a family or intended to bring a family to Fairbanks. This resulted in a ratio of one new child in the community for every 47 individuals hired to work on the pipeline. Approximately 82 percent of the pipeline workers' children anticipated were school age and 18 percent were pre-school.[2]

Three general strategies of preparedness were used by Outsiders. Some people came to Fairbanks with round-trip airplane tickets or other arrangements so that they could go home again if they ran out of money or job opportunities did not materialize. They viewed the trip to Alaska as a vacation in which they would explore the employment situation to see if they could get pipeline jobs. Others who were more familiar with the construction industry, more confident of their skills, and more assured of their job opportunities came to Fairbanks with enough resources to sustain themselves until they were hired for pipeline work. A third strategy, often used in combination with other strategies, was that people seeking pipeline jobs knew somebody residing in Fairbanks before they came. The friend, relative or other "connection" was expected to assist the newcomer in obtaining housing and a job.

During the pipeline construction period, Fairbanks had a severe rental housing shortage. In 1975 for the entire month of March, only 18 units were advertised for rent in the local newspaper. A postal vacancy survey conducted on May 21, 1975, indicated that .6 percent of the housing units were vacant on that day, the lowest vacancy rate in Fairbanks since 1954. A vacancy rate of less than 3 percent had been defined as a housing emergency by the state.[3]

Most of the hotel and motel rooms in Fairbanks were leased by Alyeska for pipeline employees, thereby creating a shortage of transient housing, which was expensive when available.

In response to the housing shortage and influx of Outsiders, it was not unreasonable to expect the emergence of squatter communities. The preparedness of in-migrants offers a partial explanation for the absence of shanty towns. Many of the people who came to Fairbanks to seek pipeline jobs brought their own housing accommodations with them in the form of campers and trailers. Perhaps an even greater number were absorbed into the community through the networks they had established before coming to Alaska. Fairbanks

acted like a sponge, as residents found themselves with
visitors, guests, and/or additional occupants of their
dwellings during the pipeline period. Increased occupancy
of rental units was a common complaint of landlords during
this period, since more people residing in the same units
meant greater consumption of water and electricity and
greater maintenance costs. While the number of residential
hook-ups for city water increased only 1 percent from July
1974 to July 1975, during that same period the gallons of
water consumed by residential customers increased by 25 percent. Similarly, the number of residential customers for
city electric services remained constant from 1971 to 1975,
while the amount of electricity consumed per residence increased by nearly 30 percent. A portion of these increases
may be attributed to greater affluence enabling people to
purchase appliances such as dishwashers and washing machines
which use more water and electricity. But the figures clearly
support the assumption that population density increased
within the existing housing units. Attempting to cut housing
costs, many new arrivals in Fairbanks shared their housing
with people whom they had not known previously.

To accommodate the increased demand for housing, an
institutionalized form of shared-housing emerged in Fairbanks.
These were commonly called "dormitories" or "rooming houses"
or "sleeping rooms." Approximately 25 of these lodgings
sprung up in Fairbanks during the pipeline period. In some
cases, a landlord would divide the basement of a house to
accommodate as many people as beds would fit into the space.
In some cases, there were no partitions between the beds,
and in some cases, there were not any beds. Most places
charged $10 per night. In one of the more publicized dormi-
tories, 45 people slept in a converted two-bedroom house.[4]
In defense of the living conditions, one of the occupants
of that rooming house wrote a letter to the editor:[5]

Dear Editor:

. . .Granted that zoning regulations, fire
codes, requirements of 400 cubic feet of
space per person, etc. are being violated
to various degrees by boarding and rooming
houses around the city, but let's not for-
get that these people are helping to alleviate a critical housing shortage.

Sure they're making money but so did
Ford, Rockefeller, Hunt, Lady Bird and a
lot of other people. Al Cannon charged
$40 a week and that's low in Fairbanks, it
sure beat $198.45 a week that I was paying
at Chena View . . .

During this rapid expansion of Fairbanks some bending of regulations is
necessary--within safe and sensible limits.

Fire is always a hazard and exits
and ample extinguishers should certainly be
available. Al Cannon has no alarm system
to my knowledge but there are two exits
from each level.

If you think I'm an alumnus of the Al
Cannon rooming house you're right, it
served me well and I enjoyed the company
of some interesting people while "bunking
with five other human sardines" in that
ex-living room.

Respectfully yours,
Len Will
c/o Alaska Constructors, Inc.
Crazyhorse Camp

While most people seeking pipeline jobs came to Fairbanks prepared for the housing shortage and high cost of
living, there were some who were not. During the pipeline
period, religious organizations provided shared-housing accommodations for those without resources or friends in Fairbanks. On February 15, 1974, the Rescue Mission opened a
50-bed rooming house in Fairbanks and on July 15, 1974, the
Salvation Army opened a 27-bed rooming house. Both groups
provided temporary housing accommodations and meals free of
charge, but the rooming houses had a religious component.

Persons staying at the Rescue Mission were required to attend religious services every morning and evening. In 1974, the Salvation Army provided 3,773 nights lodging and 9,890 meals, and the Rescue Mission provided 9,795 nights lodging and 17,624 meals. In 1975, the Rescue Mission provided 18,823 nights lodging and 30,627 meals. Monthly Rescue Mission activities are given in Figure 13.

Both the Rescue Mission and the Salvation Army reported that more than half the people they served were Outsiders seeking pipeline jobs. "We are now into the third month of 1976," the Superintendent of the Rescue Mission wrote in his March newsletter,

> and we here at the Rescue Mission find we are again running a full house. Many nights we have every bed full with as many as 20 men sleeping on the floor of the Chapel. We are seeing new faces here as more men arrive seeking employment in Fairbanks. . . Our dining hall seats 45 and we often have as many as 70 men crowded into it for a hot meal.[6]

The 50 percent or less who were not Outsiders seeking pipeline jobs were members of local families whom the director of the Salvation Army rooming house described as "marginal people pushed over the edge" by the economic situation created by the pipeline construction. He characterized them as people who were handicapped emotionally or socially, and could not hold jobs for long periods of time.

Housing structure in Fairbanks changed somewhat through the emergence of informal, commercial, and religious shared-housing arrangements. The absence of squatter communities, however, may be attributed in large part to aspects of the community housing structure which did not change during the pipeline period. More specifically, both before and during pipeline construction, community values of individualism, independence and a frontier lifestyle resulted in lax

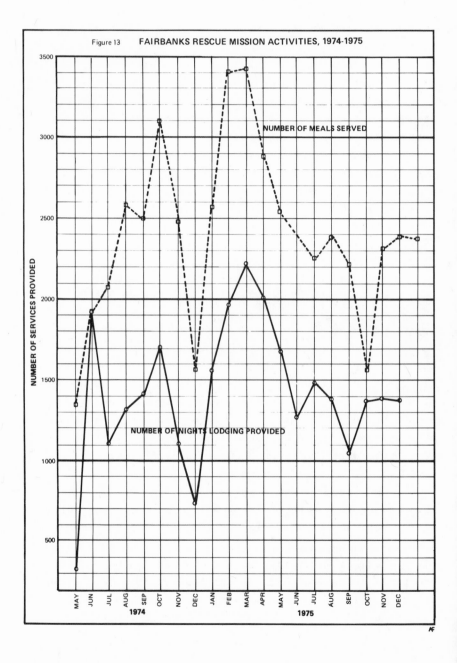

Figure 13   FAIRBANKS RESCUE MISSION ACTIVITIES, 1974-1975

NUMBER OF SERVICES PROVIDED

NUMBER OF MEALS SERVED

NUMBER OF NIGHTS LODGING PROVIDED

building and zoning codes and the existence of many dwellings which would be considered "substandard" in other parts
of the United States. Remoteness and high cost of materials
led Fairbanksans to save resources rather than destroy them.
Buildings, no matter how dilapidated, have been moved from
one location to another instead of being demolished. Furthermore, people who seek a "frontier lifestyle" are more
adaptable in their living conditions and tolerate more inconveniences, such as the lack of running water, plumbing,
electricity, and/or conventional sources of heating. Indeed,
to many Fairbanksans a rustic log cabin in the woods is considered ideal housing.

As a result of community values, many so-called
"substandard" structures were distributed throughout the
Fairbanks area prior to pipeline construction, although not
all of them were used as dwellings. As housing pressures
in Fairbanks intensified during the pipeline period, people
occupied more and more of the substandard types of structures.
Because these dwellings were distributed throughout the area,
people could live in them without being very visible and no
one section of town became identified as a "shanty town."
Since most Fairbanksans tolerate a diversity of lifestyles,
the community did not define the "substandard housing" as a
community problem and, thus, there was no reification of the
concept of "shanty town" or "squatter community."

Many of the people who lived in "substandard" housing
were long-time Fairbanksans, not Outsiders. It was often the
Fairbanksans who did not have pipeline jobs, who could not
afford rental housing, who were likely to have some land on
which to pitch a tent, and who were resourceful in adapting
to dwellings which lacked modern conveniences. Thus, it
was Fairbanksans who most often ended up living in saunas,
garages, quonset huts, partially-built or partially-destroy-
ed dwellings, storage sheds, tents or other types of

unconventional housing. Some Outsiders slept in the back
seats of their cars, in tents, or on the river bank; but
the winter cold soon chased them indoors or out of town.

An alternative explanation for the failure of anticipated impacts to materialize is that the expected population influx simply did not occur. The question of population
size in Fairbanks during the pipeline period will forever be
unanswered. No census was taken and no head-counts were made
during this period. All of the population figures cited for
Fairbanks have been projections based on the 1970 Census.
Standard methods for these projections are problematic because of faulty or unfounded assumptions. One projection
made by the U.S. Census Bureau was clearly inaccurate because it used only births and deaths in the formula and did
not account for the massive in-migration. The report actually suggested a net migration out of Fairbanks of 3,800
people from mid-1973 to mid-1974 and a reduction in population of 500 persons, even though pipeline construction
began in 1974.[7]

Other methods of projecting population size which
do not rely totally on vital statistics use other indicators
which may not have behaved properly during the pipeline
period. One such commonly-used factor is school enrollments.
Many people who came to Fairbanks did not bring the "average"
family with them, however, and school enrollments underrepresented the population influx. There is a similar problem
with using new housing construction in conjunction with
household density as a population indicator. Because household density changed dramatically and many people were living
in dwellings which were not new housing, to use 1970 census
data to obtain a household density figure and then multiply
it by new housing would underrepresent population increases.

Recognizing some of these problems, some population
projections were developed using unconventional approaches.

In some cases, population density figures were fabricated
on whim. Other approaches have been more elaborate, such
as developing a mathematical equation based on the assumption
that there is a direct relationship between the distance
from Fairbanks to the construction camp in which a pipeline
worker is located and the amount of additional population
that worker generates in Fairbanks.[8] (While this assumption
is totally unfounded and probably inaccurate, it must be
credited with the sensibility to base the relationship not
on the pipeline worker's fecundity, but rather on economic
multipliers. It is likely, however, that more accurate
figures could have been generated using fecundity as a
basis.)

Unconventional approaches for projecting population
have enabled local governments to generate self-serving
figures. State and federal revenue-sharing and state impact
funds were based on population figures, as were a variety
of other types of grants and budgets. Hence, it was to the
financial benefit of the community to estimate the population
as high as possible. In a door-to-door census commissioned
by the City of Valdez, it was discovered that the actual
population was nearly one-third less than the figures which
had been used by the local government and local businesses.[9]
With due respect for this type of potential upward bias,
population estimates for the Fairbanks North Star Borough
are presented in Table 7.

Another problem with population figures is determining whether transients are included in the tally and how to
define "transient" in the context of the pipeline construction period. While one could conservatively assume that
population was not as high as the estimates in Table 7, indicators suggest that there was indeed an influx of people.
Because Fairbanks is relatively remote, there are only a few
ways people can enter the town. The two most common ways

Table 7

Population Estimates
Fairbanks North Star Borough

Year	Estimated Population	Precent Change Over Previous Year
1970	45,864$^+$	+ 5.8%
1971	44,151*	- 3.8%
1972	45,751*	+ 3.6%
1973	45,571*	- .4%
1974	50,762*	+11.4%
1975	63,350$^\psi$	+24.8%

$^+$ U.S. Census figure

* Figures prepared by Alaska State Department
of Labor; July 1 estimate

$^\psi$ Revenue Sharing Figures used by Alaska State
Department of Community & Regional Affairs;
July 1 estimate

for Outsiders to enter Fairbanks are via the Alaska-Canadian
Highway (ALCAN) and by air. The volume of airline traffic
(Figure 14) and ALCAN border crossings (Figure 15) increased
significantly during the pipeline period. Increased local
traffic volume and demand for housing and public utilities
also suggest a significant population increase.

If one accepts the assumption that the population of
Fairbanks did increase, by whatever percentage, then it is
necessary to explain why the impacts which were expected to
accompany that population increase did not happen. The
hypothesis offered here is that impacts are not simply a
function of population increases, but rather result from the
structure of in-migration and the structure of the community.
An important corollary to this principle of structure provides yet another reason why some impacts did not materialize: a community is not merely a passive recipient of change;
it has the power to affect the shape of change.

The campaign to discourage people seeking pipeline
jobs from coming to Fairbanks unless they had adequate resources to sustain themselves is one example of acting to
affect the shape of change. There are other examples in
which Fairbanks did not remain a passive recipient of anticipated impacts. One of the impacts most feared by people
concerned about the Fairbanks environment was that the increased traffic would raise the carbon monoxide levels in
the downtown area, already plagued by poor air quality. In
spite of the increased traffic due to both more people and
more activities, downtown carbon monoxide levels were less
severe during the pipeline construction period than prior
to that time. The simple reason for reduced carbon monoxide
levels was that the city implemented a traffic plan which
converted several major arteries into one-way streets,
thereby reducing automobiles idling in the downtown area.

Air quality provides another example of anticipated

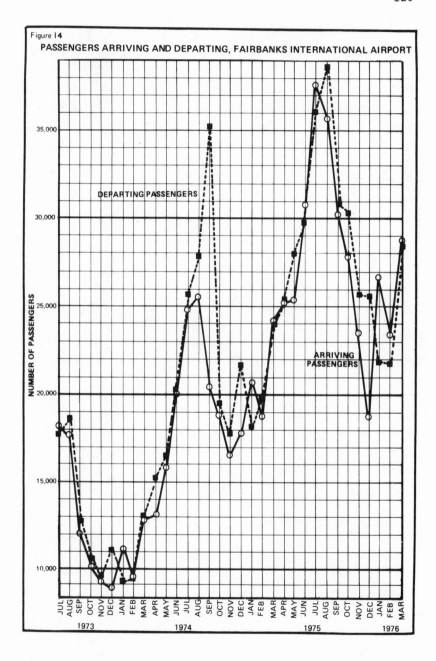

Figure 14

PASSENGERS ARRIVING AND DEPARTING, FAIRBANKS INTERNATIONAL AIRPORT

NUMBER OF PASSENGERS

DEPARTING PASSENGERS

ARRIVING PASSENGERS

35,000

30,000

25,000

20,000

15,000

10,000

JUL AUG SEP OCT NOV DEC JAN FEB MAR APR MAY JUN JUL AUG SEP OCT NOV DEC JAN FEB MAR APR MAY JUN JUL AUG SEP OCT NOV DEC JAN FEB MAR

1973   1974   1975   1976

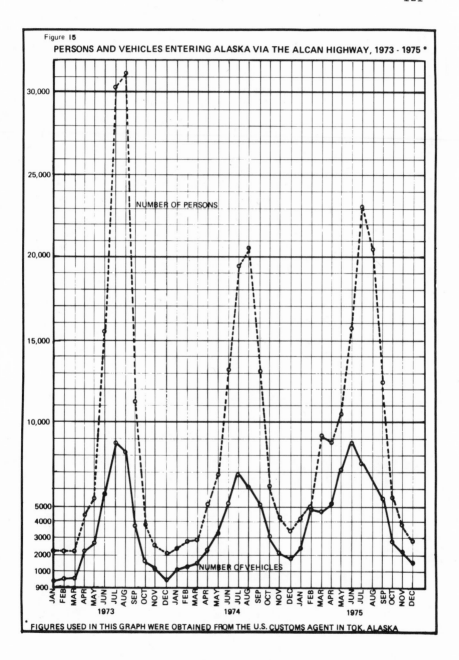

Figure 15

PERSONS AND VEHICLES ENTERING ALASKA VIA THE ALCAN HIGHWAY, 1973 - 1975 *

NUMBER OF PERSONS

NUMBER OF VEHICLES

* FIGURES USED IN THIS GRAPH WERE OBTAINED FROM THE U.S. CUSTOMS AGENT IN TOK, ALASKA

impact which was controlled by the community. It was assumed
that increased population activities would increase both
the intensity and number of days of ice fog in Fairbanks,
and that this in turn would restrict landings at the local
airport due to poor visibility. While this situation did
occur during the winter of 1975-76, it was not inevitable.
In response to the problem, the airport installed a new
instrument landing system enabling planes to land in reduced
visibility, thereby mitigating the effects of increased ice
fog on airport traffic movement.

These examples illustrate that a community can act
to avoid, reduce or control anticipated impacts. However,
Fairbanks did not always exercise its power to affect the
shape of change.

Chapter 7
BOOM/BUST DILEMMA

Just three months after pipeline construction officially began, Fairbanks Municipal Utilities System (FMUS)
announced that it had "run out of telephone numbers" and
that no new customers could be added to the existing system
until new equipment was installed to increase the switching
capacity. The new equipment would take two years to obtain
from the time it was ordered until the time it was installed.
No relief was in sight until 1976.

Under these conditions, the telephone system was overloaded and it often took several tries and several hours to
complete calls. From May 1974 to May 1975, the number
of telephone trouble reports increased by 69 percent, and
the number of people who had made deposits and were waiting
for telephones increased by 125 percent. While FMUS provides telephone service for the entire borough, it is under
the political control of the City of Fairbanks. Residents
of the rapidly growing outlying areas were powerless to influence investment decisions which would have provided more
service to areas outside city limits. At least half of the
1,564 people on the waiting list for telephone service in
May 1975 lived in areas where there simply were no facilities
to provide the service. Even when the new switch was installed the following year, it did not increase telephone service
for outlying suburban areas.

When FMUS and Chamber of Commerce officials met to
examine the causes of the telephone crisis at its breaking
point in July 1974, they found that there was a lack of
ready capital to expand and upgrade the system's facilities.
At that time, the city manager was authorized to issue up to
$5.5 million in bonds for telephone facilities, but the

management of FMUS and community leaders believed that further bonding would be intolerable.[1] They sought to have the $3 million in impact funds for Fairbanks committed to the telephone system, but officials administering the impact funds from Juneau rejected the plan because telephone problems existed prior to the pipeline and the crisis was due to poor planning rather than impact.

The next crisis was a housing shortage. Prior to pipeline construction, there was little increase in rental housing. Postal vacancy surveys conducted in November 1973 indicated that there was a 7.2 percent vacancy rate in apartments; by November 1974 the rate had dropped to 2.2 percent. A postal vacancy rate survey conducted in May 1975, indicated a .5 percent vacancy rate. After pipeline construction began, most of the larger apartment complexes were fully occupied with waiting lists. The amount of rental housing advertised in the local newspaper, mostly reflecting smaller apartment complexes and duplexes, declined gradually during the first summer of pipeline construction and then decreased dramatically during the first few months of 1975, reaching its low point in March (see Figure 16). The decline in availability of rental housing was accompanied by increased rents, some exorbitant:

- A family living in the downtown area for two years was notified that their rent would increase from $290 to $350 on May 5, 1975, and to $400 on July 1, 1975. The landlord cited increased costs of maintenance and electricity as justification for the increases; but, the tenants complained, they paid the electricity and the landlord had not maintained the building.

- A family residing in the downtown area had rented their three-bedroom apartment in 1973 for $475 per month. In 1974, the rent was raised by $50 per month; the tenants were notified of a further $225 increase on May 1, 1975, making the monthly rent $750.

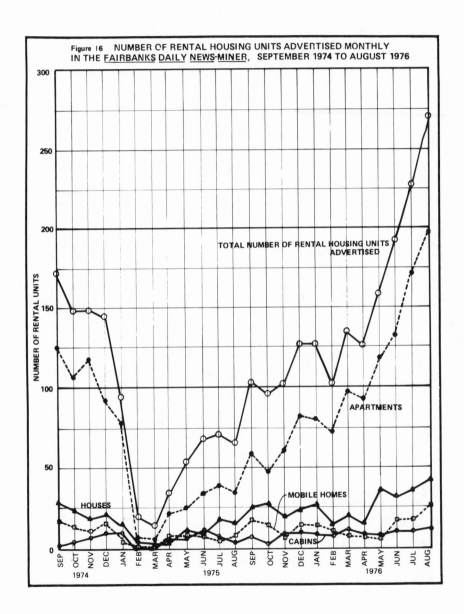

Figure 16   NUMBER OF RENTAL HOUSING UNITS ADVERTISED MONTHLY IN THE FAIRBANKS DAILY NEWS-MINER, SEPTEMBER 1974 TO AUGUST 1976

- In February 1975 tenants were evicted from
an apartment when the landlord told them
that the building was being sold. The
building was not sold and the apartment
which had rented for $240 per month was
rented to persons in pipeline-related
jobs for $375 plus utilities.

Many of the more drastic rent increases occurred in
conjunction with real estate transactions. Landlords who
wanted to sell property raised rents to show high income to
prospective buyers. Rental housing in Fairbanks seemed like
a good investment to buyers in Seattle and other areas, who
immediately raised rents to pay off mortgages during the
pipeline period.

After stories of exorbitant rent increases became
known, the state Commissioner of Commerce conducted public
hearings in Fairbanks and declared a housing emergency in
accordance with the Emergency Residential Rent Regulation
and Control Act (AS 34.06). The Commissioner decided to pro-
mulgate regulations using "the rifle approach" rather than
"the shotgun approach." On May 14, 1975, a Rent Review Office was established in Fairbanks and a three-person Rent
Review Board was appointed to hear cases of alleged rent
gouging. Tenants who believed their rents were raised unfairly could appeal to the Rent Review Board, which examined
their landlords' financial records and only approved rent increases where profit on the property was not more than fifteen percent.

Once established, the Rent Review Board apparently
served as a deterrent against further outrageous rent increases. Actions of the Board were not retroactive, however,
and the price of housing did not decline until after the
Board was established. Moreover, the Board had no control
over prices of new housing in the rental market. The Rent
Review Board might have served to relieve the personal crisis
which occurred when a tenant was the victim of rent gouging

and had no other housing alternatives, but it did not solve the community crisis with regard to the housing shortage.

Several factors contributed to the housing shortage. First, there were few lots with water and sewer connections upon which to develop housing. Second, there was little money available for financing apartment complexes. Since local banks did not offer commercial mortgages, apartment complexes had to be financed by outside investors. The cost of labor and materials during the pipeline period, in conjunction with the cost of borrowing money, meant that even "modest" apartments built would have to rent for $400 to $600 per month. While people with pipeline jobs might have been able to afford such rents, it was uncertain whether the units would be able to sustain themselves after pipeline completion. For this reason, apartments were not attractive investments to most builders and bankers. A study by the Department of Housing and Urban Development (HUD)[2] issued in June 1975 estimated the annual demand for new non-subsidized housing in the Fairbanks area over the following two years to be 665 single-family houses and 1,065 multi-family units. During 1975, the local lending institutions only financed 412 single-family homes and 118 multi-family units.

Third, builders tended to construct speculative housing which was overpriced in comparison to housing needs. By June 1976, 41 percent of the housing advertised for sale was $75,000 or more and only 20 percent was less than $55,000.[3] The HUD study projected a need for 31 percent of new housing under $55,000 and only 26 percent over $75,000. To buy a $75,000 house with a 30-year mortgage required $11,140 in cash and monthly payments of $666 to $708.[4] Many Fairbanksans and their bankers were convinced that even if the prospective buyer could afford the house during the pipeline period, it might be difficult to make such high payments after pipeline construction ceased. Faced with little rental

housing and unaffordable housing for sale, many people living
in Fairbanks opted for less conventional housing, discussed
in the preceding chapter. Some chose to cope with the high
cost of housing by obtaining higher paying jobs, such as
pipeline employment, and/or for spouses who had not previously worked to enter the labor force. Again, these types
of solutions might have helped individuals through their
personal housing crises, but they did not solve the community
housing crisis.

For the community as a whole, the only viable solution to the housing problem appeared to be mobile homes and
modular units which were constructed outside Alaska at a
relatively low price and shipped to Fairbanks. From April
1974, when pipeline construction was just beginning, to
July 1976, the number of mobile homes in the Fairbanks North
Star Borough increased from 2,237 to 3,482. During that
period, mobile homes comprised an estimated 49 percent of
the new housing units in Fairbanks.[5] Instead of realizing
the dream of "broad streets, row upon row of attractive
homes," the pipeline period brought row upon row of mobile
homes crammed close together to minimize the cost of providing utilities to the lots in the mobile home courts.

During the summer of 1975, the housing shortage began
to ease gradually as new houses were brought onto the market
and new mobile homes were brought into the community. By
winter, Fairbanksans were preoccupied with yet another crisis.
This time it was electricity.

Most of the residential and commercial growth in the
Fairbanks community during the pipeline period occurred in
areas which depended upon Golden Valley Electric Association
(GVEA) for its electricity. In 1974 and 1975, GVEA added
approximately 2,800 new service connections, a 36 percent
increase in its services. The peak electric demand grew from
49,700 kilowatts in 1973 to 82,600 kilowatts in 1975,

a 66 percent increase in needed generating capacity. Prior
to this period of intensive growth, GVEA relied on the abun-
dant coal resources in Interior Alaska for most of its power.
During the pipeline period, however, GVEA increased its generating capacity by depending upon more expensive fossil fuels.
While five to six years are required to get a coal-fired
steam plant on-line, it only takes 18 months or less to acquire gas turbines and diesel generators, and the initial
investment is one-third less. According to GVEA management,
the electrical cooperative could not obtain the financing
for the more expensive coal-fired plant. It switched its
reliance to oil at a time in which oil appeared to be an in-
expensive fuel source for Alaskans and would provide energy
for what appeared to be short-term increases in demand without massive investments.

GVEA management found that it was responding to needs,
"not on a five year basis, but almost on a year by year
basis." Because electrical consumption grew faster than
GVEA's generating capacity, every time a large generator
broke down the whole system threatened to break down. During
the winter of 1975-76, GVEA issued "peak load alerts" in
which it implored customers to restrict their useages of
electricity when the generating capacity was reduced due to
equipment malfunctions. During some of these emergencies,
street lights and head-bolt heater parking outlets were
turned off, public offices and schools were closed, and
television stations suspended broadcasting. At one point
GVEA ran out of fuel oil. As GVEA management jumped from
crisis to crisis, so did its consumers. The greater reliance
on oil as a short-term response to needs meant that consumer
prices for electricity escalated by 49 percent during the
pipeline period.[6]

Telephones, housing and electricity are all a part

of what is commonly called the community's "infrastructure."
While it was evident that the infrastructure would have to
be expanded to accommodate increased demands during the pipeline period, there was confusion about how this should be
done, to what extent, in what time period, and with what
funds. Expanding the infrastructure was an expensive pro-
position. Fairbanks is spatially distributed such that expansion of public utilities is especially costly. The types
of capital expenditures needed to expand the infrastructure
required investments of either public funds in the form of
bonds or private funds from lending institutions. Commit-
ments of public or private resources to long-term loans
required assurances that the money could be repaid with interest. This type of assurance had to be based upon a stable
economy or a prospective period of long-term growth.

Historically, Fairbanks has had anything but a stable
economy. From its earliest days as a gold rush town, Fairbanks has followed a classical boom/bust cycle. In 1901,
Captain Barnette docked Lavelle Young on the Chena River
where the town of Fairbanks was to spring up the next year
after Felix Pedro announced a gold strike just north of the
location. The gold rush of 1903 to 1910 brought the first
boom to Fairbanks as the area population grew from 3,000 in
1904 to 11,000 in 1910.[7] During the bust period which followed, from 1910 to 1920, the population declined by 67 percent.[8] After the Alaska Railroad was constructed in 1923.
mining became economically feasible in the Fairbanks area,
and the Fairbanks Exploration Company ("F.E. Company") began
prospecting in 1924. Gold mining became profitable during
the Depression years, and Fairbanks had another boom in the
1930's.

Construction of Ladd Air Force Base, later to become
Ft. Wainwright, touched off the beginning of a military construction boom which peaked in 1951-52 with annual

expenditures of $160 million for construction, $40 million
in payrolls, and $6.2 million in local purchases.[9] The boom
of the 1940's, 1950's and early 1960's was created not only
by construction of Ladd Air Force Base, Eielson Air Force
Base, and Ft. Greely, but also by employment on those bases.
For example, the authorized personnel for Ft. Wainwright
grew from 2,000 in 1961 to 5,443 in 1965.[10] In 1967, a
major flood halted economic activity in Fairbanks. Then
there was a boom from 1968 to 1970 from post-flood rehabilitation programs, university expansion construction, and
federal-state highway construction programs. From 1970 to
1973 there was another bust period as disaster loans expired,
military personnel were withdrawn from the area, and uncertainty clouded the future of Prudhoe Bay oil development.
Thus it was that the trans Alaska oil pipeline era was ushered
into the economic history of Fairbanks with the anticipation
that it would start yet another boom/bust cycle.

During each of the booms Fairbanks has experienced,
the community has been unwilling or unable to make the capital investments necessary to cope with the increased demands
of the times. During the first boom, it is reported, "The
little camp of Fairbanks was ill-prepared for such a rush
and the early stampeders were unable to obtain needed equipment and provisions."[11] Descriptions of subsequent booms
reinforce the belief that history does indeed repeat itself.

> The rapid growth of Fairbanks since 1940,
> due mostly to the impact of military con-
> struction and operation, has brought with it
> a host of problems for the residents and city
> fathers of the municipality. Growth of utili-
> ties and other civic necessities could not
> keep pace with the mushrooming city. As a
> consequence, Fairbanks emerged from World War II
> with a hopelessly inadequate civic plant.
> Schools were placed on dual shifts, the utility
> system was capable of taking care of only a
> fraction of the new population, public buildings
> and equipment were highly antiquated and

outgrown, sanitary conditions needed
attention, streets were in disrepair and
there was a pressing shortage of housing.[12]

Similar to the dilemma faced during the pipeline period, the
community did not know how much to expand during the military
boom because it had no control over the decisions which would
affect its future:

> Future military activity is dependent upon
> the course of world affairs, on new military
> strategy, on the national political and
> economic scene and upon Congress and the
> funds that will be authorized for military
> commands in Alaska.[13]

The same could be said about the current situation if one
were to substitute "energy resource development" for "military" in the foregoing sentence.

Despite this history of economic instability, when
the trans Alaska oil pipeline construction began the pro-
spects of long-term economic growth were quite favorable.
It has been said that there is enough oil and gas at Prudhoe
Bay to build six pipelines. At least one gas pipeline from
Prudhoe Bay has been in the planning stages since before oil
pipeline construction began. Other oil developments north
of Fairbanks are imminent, most notably Outer Continental
Shelf (OCS) development and "Pet 4," the former Naval Petroleum Reserve on the western portion of the North Slope of
the Brooks Range. As the prices of natural resources climb
in the world market, the potential for hard rock mining and
mineral extraction north of Fairbanks escalates. With the
existing transportation systems, Fairbanks would be the
natural supply and administrative center for many of these
developments to the north. Employment from these projects
would continue to stimulate the Fairbanks economy. While
this potential resource development is speculative, there
are other types of economic development which are sure to
affect the Fairbanks economy, such as investments generated

by the Alaska Native Claims Settlement Act through Native
Corporations.

In light of this potentially rosy future, one must
question why the necessary investments to expand the community's infrastructure were not made prior to and during
the pipeline period. To understand the decision-making
processes with regard to expanding the infrastructure, one
must understand the political and economic structure of the
community. Basic to this understanding is the knowledge
that local businessmen controlled local politics and thereby
controlled decision-making relative to public expenditures
for such things as public utilities.

Most local businesses have been family organizations
established in Fairbanks over a period of years. Many of
the business people and community leaders were born and
raised in Fairbanks, and their expectations have been shaped
by their experiences in the community. While Fairbanks pre-
sents opportunities which might attract enterprising young
people, it is so far from major business and communication
centers that it does not attract sophisticated business persons who are competent at making risk-taking decisions.
Furthermore, most Fairbanks business persons were fairly un-
knowledgable and unsophisticated about the world of finance
outside of their community. This meant that they had limited
access to financial resources. Unlike the large national
businesses which moved into Fairbanks relatively recently,
local enterprises could not afford to sustain losses over
long periods or to wait patiently for decisions outside of
their control. For example, if Sears, Roebuck and Company
builds an initially unprofitable store in Fairbanks, it could
absorb the losses in its large operation. But if a local
clothier decides to build a new store which fails to return
a profit for a few years, he could find himself bankrupt and
out of business.

In 1970 it appeared that the pipeline construction
boom was imminent and many forward-thinking business persons
in Fairbanks expanded their inventories and operations to
accommodate the anticipated increased demands. Due to the
delay in pipeline construction, their investments were not
profitable and many sustained heavy losses. The businessmen
felt they had been "burned" by planning ahead. These recent
experiences, coupled with the long boom/bust history of
Fairbanks, led many to believe that it was more realistic
to view the pipeline period as a temporary boom and more
responsible to react accordingly by limiting their investments. They applied the same principles to decision-making
in the public realm and received reinforcement from consultants and state agency personnel. One economist stated in
1970:

> In view of the frequent and marked changes
> of the past five years, it would take a
> presuming (if not foolhardy) economist to
> forecast the rate-of-expansion, or to pro-
> ject the growth magnitudes in each of the
> major fields of economic activity of the
> Fairbanks area. This is not alone due to
> economic ups and downs but to the fact that
> prospective developments are heavily de-
> pendent on factors that are not economic
> but governmental in character--governmental
> decisions that will vitally affect the
> future of Fairbanks.[14]

In 1971 the Alaska State Housing Authority published a report
on projected needs for housing, classrooms, police and fire
protection, public utilities, recreational facilities, and
health and welfare and employment services. It offered the
following advice:

> In planning to meet these needs the state and
> local government should give cognizance to
> the temporary nature of the pipeline con-
> struction and its accompanying increase in
> employment and community population. In this
> situation, communities should look for flexible
> methods of meeting temporary public needs

> to avoid investing in permanent capital
> improvements which will be underused in
> the future. The flexibility afforded by
> accommodations such as temporary class-
> rooms and trailers is appropriate in re-
> sponding to the temporary impact of pipe-
> line construction.[15]

The "flexible" or "temporary" approach meant avoiding the
investments necessary to expand the community's infrastructure.

To business and community leaders, it seemed more
responsible to "only bet on a sure thing." "Because of lack
of committment by the oil industry," the Borough Mayor told
a public gathering in 1975, "it was difficult for people
here to justify spending money, either their own or the
public's, on preparation for the boom, that might never
come."[16] Most gamblers would probably say that betting on
a sure thing is not gambling at all. By the time assurances
are given, it's too late because the lead time needed for
investments is no longer available. This presented a very
tricky timing problem. If houses were built before there
were people to occupy them, then the investment might result
in losses. If houses were built after people had innundated
the community, however, there would be a period of housing
shortage in which returns on investments could have been
forthcoming if the investments had been made sooner. Given
their experiences and the advice of others, the local businessmen and leaders opted for the more conservative wait-and-
see approach.

Another characteristic of most local business persons
was that growth was viewed in terms of profits rather than
assets. This type of short-term thinking meant that local
business persons assumed they could maximize their profits
by minimizing their expenditures for such things as taxes
and capital investments. One example of this type of short-
sighted approach was the attitude of downtown merchants

toward public transportation. Because they wanted to avoid
the taxes necessary to subsidize such a program, downtown
merchants were the most vocal opponents of public transportation. At the same time, with parking shortages and traffic
congestion in the downtown area, downtown merchants would
stand to gain the most from a public transportation system
by not losing their business to retailers springing up in
suburban areas. The emphasis on minimizing taxes meant that
the community could not grow, which turned the boom/bust
cycle into a self-fulfilling prophecy.

Not every Fairbanks business person fit the conservative image described here. A few notable entrepreneurs developed
sources of financing outside the community, made massive investments in times of relative uncertainty and realized substantial profits. While these persons were regarded with
respect, and sometimes with awe, they did not occupy leadership positions in the local community. Some were involved
in the state and national political arenas and stayed aloof
from local politics. Others were viewed with a certain
amount of suspicion by the local power structure. Thus, the
more adventurous and successful business persons did not tend
to significantly influence local decision-making processes.

In addition to the inherent conservatism of the
political-economic structure of the community, many formal
leaders were ideologically conservative. They ascribed to a
body of theory, usually called "free enterprise," which was
interpreted literally to mean that the greatest economic benefits could be derived from a homeostatic regulation of supply
and demand in a market place not influenced or regulated
by government decisions. While this economic theory assumes
that positive adjustments are made in the market place over
the long-term, the kinds of dramatic short-term fluctuations
in supply and demand encountered in the pipeline construction
situation could not be resolved smoothly if left to the open

market, and instead resulted in a series of crises. Leaders who abided by the principles of free enterprise tended to view these crises as temporary.

The free enterprise philosophy conflicts with planning, differing in the agents of decision-making and the timing of decisions. Planning involves a comprehensive approach which can usually only be accomplished by a government entity, while free enterprise opposes government intervention in the market place, seeks to reduce the role of government, and places the responsibility for decision-making on businesses and consumers. According to free enterprise decisions are made in the market place, while planning entails earlier decisions. Thus, the following scenario for dealing with the housing shortage in Fairbanks would have been unacceptable to the leadership:

> Prior to the pipeline people in Fairbanks
> realized that there would be an intensive,
> if brief, demand for housing in Fairbanks.
> They also recognized that Fairbanks was
> plagued by substandard, inadequate, un-
> attractive, and sometimes unsafe housing.
> One of the goals of the community was for
> the pipeline to generate "a beautiful city"
> with "wide streets" and "row upon row of
> attractive housing." To accomplish this
> goal, the community formulated a strategy
> that would maximize housing availability
> during the pipeline period and improve the
> general quality of housing after the pipe-
> line. To do that, new housing would be
> encouraged prior to and during pipeline
> construction. Lenient building codes and
> relaxed zoning regulations would enable
> substandard units to be used during the
> shortage. It was understood, however, that
> after the population began to decline,
> building codes and zoning ordinances would
> be strictly enforced to weed out substandard
> housing and generally improve the quality of
> housing. In this way there would be an in-
> centive for people to build new housing be-
> cause they would know that the market would
> not be flooded after the population began
> to decline.

Because it involved government intervention in the
market place, this scenario was never even contemplated by
the local leadership. However, the Borough Assembly did
debate creating a public campground to accommodate tourists
and job seekers. While it was possible that such a campground would have generated more tourism and, thereby, more
business in Fairbanks, the Borough Assembly decided against
the proposal because government would have been competing
unfairly with private campgrounds in the area. Leaders in
local government who ascribed to conservative ideology felt
that private enterprise could respond to needs in the community and it would be unnecessary for the government to
interfere.

The philosophy of making decisions in the market
place rather than planning influenced decisions which were
clearly in the public realm, such as those relating to public utilities. Decisions about investments in public utilities were made in crisis situations when demand exceeded
supply, similar to the way in which decisions would be made
in the market place, rather than by projecting needs and
planning to meet them. Community leaders did not find it
inappropriate to jump from crisis to crisis. In fact, many
in leadership positions viewed this as a more responsible
approach than planning ahead and making investments which
might be unnecessary.

Inherent conservatism in the economic-political
structure of the community and ideological conservatism of
some leaders help to explain why the community's infrastructure was not expanded before and during the pipeline period
to accommodate the increased demands. However, one might
anticipate that the resultant repeated crises in combination
with the long-term potential for growth might serve to change
the economic and political structure and leadership of the
community.

Chapter 8
THE CHAMBER AND THE CHURCHES

> Not a totem pole could be unearthed by the
> most enthusiastic archeologist, but enough
> telephone, electric light and telegraph
> poles are in evidence to make amends. . . .
> Eskimos are never seen except at the picture
> shows and fewer Indians visit here than is
> the case in almost any of the Western towns
> in the states. In fact, first sight and
> more extended acquaintance compel the im-
> pression that Fairbanks is a busy industrial
> center. . . .[1]

Thus Fairbanks was portrayed in a promotional booklet issued
by local merchants in 1916. The Fairbanks Commercial Club
attempted to dispel frontier stereotypes, deny any distinctly
Alaskan cultural heritage, and characterize Fairbanks as a
modern city. ·

In more recent years, the Chamber of Commerce has
represented the local business community by promoting economic and industrial development in Fairbanks. The announced
discovery of commercial quantities of oil at Prudhoe Bay in
1968 gave focus to the goals of the Chamber of Commerce which
led the campaign for a trans Alaska oil pipeline route, and
later for an all Alaska gas line route. "When oil was discovered 300 miles to the north," according to Mary Clay Berry,
"a sort of mass hysteria swept through the city . . . it was
a wave of irrational fear that the city and its 21,000 people
would somehow be deprived of their slice of the petroleum
pie unless they did something to attract the oil industry to
Fairbanks."[2]

Led by the Chamber of Commerce, Fairbanks set about
to woo the oil industry. In August 1968, businessmen from
Calgary were invited to Fairbanks to offer advice about how
to attract oil development. Three months later, the city and

borough mayors traveled to Houston, Dallas and Los Angeles
to talk to oil company executives. Local business persons
believed that a road from Fairbanks to Prudhoe Bay was essential for Fairbanks not to be by-passed as a supply center.
They lobbied for the winter haul road, later known as the
"Hickel Highway," which became a *cause célèbre* among conservationists. When it appeared that the pipeline would be delayed by Native claims settlement, the businessmen attempted
to influence the Native claimants. On April 11, 1970, 200
businessmen, contractors, and labor leaders met in Fairbanks
to collect money and send a delegation to Stevens Village to
persuade residents to drop their suit which was the basis for
an injunction against pipeline construction.

While the business-dominated leadership of the community seemed to favor development at any cost, not everybody in Fairbanks agreed with those values. Some people came
to Alaska to escape urbanization and wanted to keep the community from growing. Others were concerned about environmental issues related to the pipeline and economic development. "I am a homeowner and a taxpayer, and I'm one of the
species that the politicians and the press of Alaska consider
a rarity if I exist at all," Celia Hunter told a public hearing. "I'm a homegrown 100 per cent Alaskan conservationist."[3]
Although Ms. Hunter perceived herself to be in a minority,
feelings about the need to promote environmental quality were
not as rare as she believed. During the first year of pipeline construction, Jay Hammond was elected governor of Alaska
on a platform which stressed the need to distinguish between
positive and negative development, rather than promoting all
types of development. The majority of Alaska's electorate
agreed with the need to balance development with other values,
such as environmental conservation and social well-being.

After pipeline construction began, some Fairbanksans
were disturbed by alcoholism, child abuse and neglect, racial

and sexual discrimination, the plight of the elderly, and
other problems which they believed were being aggravated by
the rapid development. They wanted local government to give
more attention to these types of social problems, rather than
focusing on minimizing taxes and services in order to maximize the profits to businesses and individuals who were bene-
fiting from the pipeline construction boom. Some felt that
the business-dominated leadership was callous to the social
problems. In regards to the housing crisis, for example, a
banker told the president of the Chamber of Commerce, "We'll
just have to hold our noses and live through it." People
who were suffering from the realities of the housing crisis
recognized most of the business leaders could afford to "hold
their noses and live through it" because they were secure in
owning their homes.

　　　Other Fairbanksans, not necessarily suffering from
social or economic inequities of the pipeline impact situation, simply questioned the values of individualism, the
profit motive, and economic gains that were represented by
the Chamber of Commerce. In a memorable farewell address,
Don Gilmer, who had been borough planning and zoning director
from the time oil had been discovered at Prudhoe Bay until
the end of the second season of pipeline construction, declared, "I am concerned about the greed that this community
is showing and that greed is probably worst in the people who
have been here the longest. . . . It's not the pipeliners,
it's not the newcomers, it's the people who have been here 5,
10, 15, 20 years." "There are prices being charged here now
that have no reason to be charged except for the lack of competition," he said, citing an example in which the business
community had moved to block the entrance of more competitive
businesses into the community.[4]

　　　"Don Gilmer was right." That was the message sent to
the Chamber of Commerce by the Tanana Valley Bar Association

one month after Mr. Gilmer made his farewell speech. The
state bar association had wanted to hold its annual meeting
in Fairbanks, but there were not enough vacant hotel rooms
to house 600 or more lawyers under the same roof for the
convention. When the bar association asked the University
of Alaska Fairbanks Campus for accommodations for their convention, the university followed its policy of not providing
housing for such functions in competition with local hotels
and motels without the approval of the Chamber of Commerce.
The Board of Directors of the Chamber of Commerce deliberated
on the issue and decided that the lawyers should be distributed among vacant hotel rooms in Fairbanks and bussed to a
convention site. If the attorneys did not agree to this
plan, the Chamber of Commerce decided that it would rather
see the state bar association hold its meeting in San Francisco than at the university campus. In response, the lawyers passed their resolution affirming Don Gilmer's statement
about greed and decided to hold their annual meeting in Anchorage.

When conflicts in values between the Chamber of Commerce and other groups in the community became public issues,
the business people asserted that the differences were borne
out of ignorance. People who were not working for private
businesses, they maintained, were not capable of understanding
the issues and comprehending the principles of free enterprise.
More than a third of the workforce in Fairbanks was employed
in government jobs, which the business leaders assumed auto-
matically disqualified them from understanding the perspective
of private business.[5] Furthermore, the population of Fairbanks has been unusually young and well-educated, compared
to the rest of the nation. The business people maintained
that by virtue of age and time spent in school, a large segment of the Fairbanks population has not had the types of
business experience which would enable them to understand the

conservative values of the business community. Although the business community supported the University of Alaska Fairbanks Campus as an institution which spends $23.8 million in Fairbanks each year, for the most part it did not value the university's intellectual, academic and cultural contributions to Fairbanks. The separation between "town" and "gown" kept most of the university people out of local politics.

Among the diverse groups in Fairbanks with different goals and value orientations, the most powerful was the Chamber of Commerce. This may be explained in part by the fact that the Chamber of Commerce was one of the best organized groups with the most stable membership and the greatest funds. Another reason why business interests were allowed to dominate is that labor unions were very strong in Fairbanks. Organized labor was so powerful that business did not prosper at the expense of labor--they prospered together. Since Fairbanks was plagued traditionally by high rates of unemployment, both business and labor had a real desire to develop industry in Fairbanks. People who did not necessarily benefit from such development were people outside of business and organized labor: professionals, government employees, non-union workers, people who were unable to work, retired persons and others on fixed incomes, and some minorities and women who historically have not had access to labor unions or upward mobility in business management. Although these persons comprised a significant portion of the community, they were not well-organized and lacked visible leadership.

As pipeline construction commenced, the need for leadership among those who would feel the adverse affects of the pipeline became more pressing. At the same time, there emerged in the Fairbanks community a group which was seeking a role of social and moral leadership. The group, which became known as the Social Concerns Committee of the Fairbanks Council of Churches, grew out of a statewide ecumenical

movement. At the First Biennial Assembly of the Alaska Christian Conference in 1973, a Legislative and Social Action Task
Group was formed to write resolutions relating to "Christian
concerns in the State of Alaska."[6] To minimize logistical
problems, it was decided that the membership of the Legislative and Social Action Task Group would be drawn from the
Greater Fairbanks Council of Churches. The three-member
Legislative and Social Action Task Group remained inactive
for nearly a year as they tried to decide what kind of role
they ought to play. Late in the Fall of 1973, the Fairbanks
Council of Churches decided that there was a need for a forum
to investigate the potential social impacts of the impending
trans Alaska oil pipeline construction. At that time, the
Legislative and Social Action Task Group of the Alaska
Christian Conference became designated as the Social Concerns
Committee for the Fairbanks Council of Churches.

    To help plan the impact forum, the ministers invited
members of the Fairbanks community to meet with them. Soon
they were asked to expand the forum to include the secular
community. The Pipeline Impact Social Concerns Forum, held
in Fairbanks on February 23, 1973, served to articulate many
of the concerns and needs of the community which had not been
expressed publicly prior to that time. At the forum, a con-
tinuing source of information about the impacts of the pipeline on Fairbanks was proposed. The Social Concerns Committee
led the campaign to establish an impact information center
to meet the need for public monitoring of the social effects
of pipeline construction. The business interests wanted any
such program to be run by the Chamber of Commerce but the
Social Concerns Committee maintained that a disinterested,
independent group ought to be responsible for the project.
The debate was resolved when the Borough Assembly agreed to
establish the Impact Information Center as a Borough function.
    The chairperson of the Social Concerns Committee and

the president of the Chamber of Commerce were among the first
to be appointed to the advisory committee to direct the Impact
Information Center. Later, the chairperson of the Social
Concerns Committee was elected the first chairperson of the
Impact Advisory Committee and became an active spokesperson
for issues related to social impacts of the trans Alaska oil
pipeline.

Based on these experiences, the Social Concerns Committee decided that it could best promote social change by
bringing social issues before the public and community decision-makers. Rather than issuing resolutions and pro-
nouncements, the Social Concerns Committee continued to follow its format of holding public forums.

Disturbed by the growing visibility of prostitution
and gambling in Fairbanks during the first season of pipeline construction, the Social Concerns Committee recognized
increased potential for legalizing prostitution and gambling
as a means of coping with it. Late in 1974, the group in-
vestigated the idea of holding a forum on public morality.
They invited local experts in law enforcement, legislation
and politics, the judicial process, and mental health to meet
with them to discuss the issues in preparation for such a
forum. The meeting was sensationalized on the front page of
a local newspaper in a story which implied that the Fairbanks
ministers supported legalized gambling and prostitution.[7]
Realizing the potential for being misinterpreted on such
volatile subjects, the ministers decided against pursuing the
issues of prostitution and gambling in a public forum. They
did, however, present a series of meetings on the subject in
an ecumenical program held during Lent.

Seeking to explore a less controversial issue with
broader significance, the Social Concerns Committee began to
plan a second forum on pipeline impact and community growth.
In a more grandiose approach, the Social Concerns Committee

organized a Forum Advisory Committee of 17 persons who represented various interest groups in Fairbanks, applied for and
received a $10,000 grant from the Alaska Humanities Forum,
and hired a fulltime coordinator and staff for the event.
What emerged was "Fairbanks and Interior Alaska: A One Day
Community Forum on Growth," attended by 350 or more persons
on a Saturday in April 1975. Organized discussions covered
a variety of topics:

> Hiring for pipeline jobs--are Alaskans getting
>   enough pipeline jobs?
>
> Oldtimers and newcomers--what happens when you
>   don't have a pipeline job?
>
> Youth--what is happening to young people?
>
> Congestion and hassles--is it getting too
>   crowded here?
>
> Housing crises--can anything be done?
>
> Family life under impact
>
> Business and commerce--does the pipeline mean
>   more profits or more overhead?
>
> Land and community--is land use planning
>   possible?
>
> A walk on the wild side--what's happening with
>   organized and unorganized crime that
>   polite people don't talk about?
>
> Oil and gas industry--are we getting our fair
>   share?

A discussion group with a moderator and knowledgeable resource
persons was organized for each topic. In addition to local
people and Alyeska Pipeline Service Company management personnel, the Lieutenant Governor and several state commissioners
participated in the event either as resource persons or just
to listen to what local people had to say.

An officer of the Chamber of Commerce was on the Forum
Advisory Committee, members of the Chamber of Commerce were
asked to be resource persons for the discussion groups, and
the chairperson of the Social Concerns Committee attended a

Chamber of Commerce meeting to issue a special invitation.
Yet the business people felt that they were underrepresented
in the public forum. When the Chamber of Commerce met the
following week, one member lamented, "There were many new
and impressionable state commissioners who got a concensus
of the community that was drastically opposed to your views."[8]
Another businessman who had attended the forum reported, "I
went to three of the meetings and was attacked in two out of
three."[9] One of the Chamber board members dismissed the
subject by saying, "If we are going to be effective we need
a different type of forum--maybe of forum of the citizens
who are paying the bills and not one of the people on state
payrolls, federal payrolls and different types of government
grants."[10] Underlying the criticism by the Chamber of Commerce was the recognition that the Social Concerns Committee
had organized an effective demonstration of public concern.
So the event would not be easily forgotten, the Social Concerns Committee published and distributed a summary of the
One Day Community Forum on Growth.[11]

The next community-wide event sponsored by the Social
Concerns Committee was intended to educate people about con-
sumerism and the consumer movement. The director of the
Alaska Public Interest Research Group (AkPIRG), a Ralph-Nader-
type of organization located in Anchorage, was invited to
Fairbanks to meet with various groups to discuss consumer
issues and explain how to organize such a group. Many Fairbanksans came to hear the talks and expressed an interest in
having a consumer group in Fairbanks. The Fairbanks Consumer
Group was formed in early 1976, but it suffered from lack of
attendance, focus and organization. Unlike the Anchorage
group, Fairbanks did not have a leader willing or able to
work fulltime for the consumer group.

Emergence of the Social Concerns Committee in a role
of political leadership ought not be interpreted as a case of

the churches versus the Chamber of Commerce. Many business
people were active in their churches and supported the efforts
of the Social Concerns Committee. Rather, it was a case of
the churches becoming a more powerful force in community
secular life. In addition to their burgeoning role of political leadership, some of the churches in Fairbanks addressed
social needs by directly providing commodities and social
services. During the pipeline period, a new type of needy
family emerged in Fairbanks. These were families which had
never received public assistance or other state social services. While their income levels were too high to qualify
for public assistance and they were too proud to seek such
services, they were suffering from accelerated inflation
which created financial hardships. Many of these families
also were suffering from the housing shortage, double-shifting
in the schools, a shortage of child care, or other pipeline-
related problems. Even those who did qualify for public
assistance and sought that type of financial aid found it to
be inadequate. For example, the maximum housing supplement
provided by the state was $180 per month, well below the
amount needed to rent an apartment. Existing agencies were
unable to assist this group and no formal institutions were
developed by state or local government to meet their needs.
To fill this community void, the churches and their ministers
became sources of emotional and physical support for these
newly-needy persons, as well as others in the community.

The role of the Rescue Mission and the Salvation Army
in providing food and shelter for people caught in the jaws
of the housing crunch has already been discussed. Various
churches also permitted people who were stranded to sleep in
their buildings and use their shower facilities. Some churches
collected food, clothing and money which they gave to individuals and groups in need, not necessarily their own church
members. Many churches opened their doors to community

groups and provided them meeting places in a town where space
was a rare commodity. Churches also became the primary
source of space for pre-schools, nurseries, and other types
of child care. In addition, churches provided such needed
social services in Fairbanks as a receiving home for children
who were abandoned or otherwise in need of care and a placement facility for teenage girls. And, ministers served on
various advisory groups related to social services in the
Fairbanks area.

Not every church in Fairbanks was involved in the
secular life of the community. In 1975, there were about 65
churches in the Fairbanks area, mostly Christian, with congregations ranging from 16 to 900 members.
Significant theological differences permit the churches to be
classified into fundamentalist, conservative and liberal
groupings. While there are fewer churches in the liberal
category in Fairbanks, they have the largest congregations,
with a mode of 250 members. By comparison, the fundamentalist
churches have a modal membership of 50.[12]

Interviews with local ministers indicated that the
churches which were more involved in secular life were those
which espoused a more liberal theology.[13] "I do not see the
common division between sacred and secular. God made the
whole world, He made it good, and so everything must be at
once both sacred and secular," said the minister of a liberal
denomination. "Social action is the visible expression of
the Gospel," said another. In discussing theology, the pastors of congregations with more liberal theologies were likely
to cite portions of the scriptures in which "Jesus teaches
that those who will enter into the Kingdom prepared are those
who fed the hungry, gave water to the thirsty, invited strang-
ers into their homes, clothed the naked, and visited the sick
and the prisoners, all in Jesus' name." In contrast, pastors
of congregations with more fundamental theologies cited

portions of the scriptures which suggest that suffering is just punishment for sin, such as, "He who does not work shall not eat." "If the church concentrates on the spiritual man," said one minister of a fundamentalist church, "the transformed life will make social concerns vanish."

At the same time, the structure of the churches affected their theology. The churches which became involved in secular affairs in Fairbanks were those which belong to denominations with large national or international organizations, as opposed to those having small local congregations without outside affiliations. This may be explained by the economic and political structure of the churches. Ministers of small churches without denominational affiliations were dependent upon their local congregations for their survival. Persons in those congregations were generally quite conservative and the minister avoided controversial social issues to which they might be opposed. The approach with the least political controversy was to restrict activities to a fundamental interpretation of the Bible.

Ministers of larger congregations which were parts of larger national and international religious organizations had to respond to the church hierarchy as well as the local congregation. In general, these churches were wealthier and thus were able to engage in missionary activities which led to the establishment of diverse congregations. Social needs of the poor or oppressed filtered upward through the church hierarchy to create an emphasis on social responsibility which then filtered down to ministers of individual churches. In addition to hierarchical support for social activism, ministers of this type of church might be moved from congregation to congregation and were, therefore, not solely dependent upon the local congregation for their survival. For example, churches which historically have conducted missionary activities in remote areas of Alaska were more likely to be active in secular affairs in Fairbanks in order to address the needs of their Native members. Thus, the secular roles of churches functioned to develop and maintain the theological interpretations relating to social responsibility.

The interdependence of theology and internal political and economic structure of churches helps to explain why the churches which were most socially active in Fairbanks were characterized by liberal theologies and were part of larger national and international religious organizations; whereas, the churches which were least active socially were characterized by small congregations restricted to the local area and fundamentalist theology. Since more socially active churches were few in number, only a handful of Fairbanks ministers accepted responsibility for social and moral leadership in the community and were active in the Social Concerns Committee.

While trying to meet community needs, ministers also faced increased demands from their own congregations. In a survey of 19 churches, 42 percent of the ministers indicated that they had experienced changes in counseling needs because of problems which were directly related to pipeline impact, including financial stress, marital conflicts due to prolonged absence of spouses working on the pipeline, housing problems, and family disruption. [14] Ministers were not immune from the problems which their parishioners faced. Escalating prices made it difficult for ministers to support their families; increased demands forced them to spend less time at home; and impact situations, such as double-shifting in the schools, created additional pressures on their own families. At the same time, church internal affairs demanded ministers' time and attention. Community population growth led several churches to expand, build new buildings, and start new congregations. While two-thirds of the ministers surveyed reported that financial contributions to the church had increased during the pipeline period, in many cases the additional income was offset by higher costs.[15] "Maintenance of buildings, especially, has tremendously increased--particularly fuel costs," reported one minister, "so increased contributions have barely kept ahead of inflation."[16]

After two years of trying to meet the special needs of the community with regard to pipeline impact as well as the intensified needs of his own congregation and family, one of the most socially active ministers in Fairbanks described himself as being in a state of "compassion fatigue." Another minister who was a leader in ecumenical and community affairs described the effects of the pipeline impact on his congregation:

> The pipeline has been a relentless, all-consuming activity, which has left people worn out and troubled and isolated from one another. The church has been one of those places of gathering, where the old-timers and new-comers, where the "haves" and "have-nots," have been able to come together in a unity of feeling and purpose. At the same time people have very little energy left to commit themselves to other activities besides their jobs. There is a yearning to participate but a fatigue level that frustrates.

Either from exhaustion, or a need to re-evaluate the potential for achieving their goals, or for preservation of self, the socially active ministers gradually began to withdraw from community leadership positions by either taking advantage of the structure of their churches' hierarchies to move to another position or activity, or by redirecting their attentions from the whole community to the church communities of their particular congregations.

Chapter 9
UNEXPECTED IMPACTS

During the pipeline period other forces were at work
to change the community power structure. The influx of investment capital resulted in a gradual decentralization of
business activities from the urban center to new suburban
shopping and industrial areas. With this type of change in
land use came alterations in cash flow and eventually in the
power structure. At the same time other factors affecting
the community power structure were evolving as a result of
population in-migration which brought new businesses and professional people to Fairbanks. One of the more visible examples was a change in the power structure of the health care
industry in Fairbanks.

In the decade before pipeline construction, most of
the private physicians in Fairbanks were organized into two
competing clinics. Doctors working for the two clinics received both salaries and a portion of the profits from their
clinic. Since there was a strong financial incentive to keep
business away from the competing clinic, it was not uncommon
for doctors to refer their patients to specialists in Seattle
rather than across the street. Because of the divisiveness
of the system and the relatively small population in Fairbanks,
the community boasted very few medical specialists prior to
pipeline construction.

When oil was discovered at Prudhoe Bay in 1968, there
were 27 private physicians in Fairbanks, representing eight
specialities.[1] In anticipation of population increases due
to the pipeline, by 1973 the clinics had increased their
staffs to a total of 40 private physicians representing ten
specialities.[2] Several physicians who felt a need for
an alternative structure of health care delivery in Fairbanks

broke away from the clinics in 1973 and began construction of a building to house independent practitioners. The
building was ready for occupancy in 1974, as pipeline construction began. The number of private physicians in Fairbanks continued to grow in anticipation of needs generated
directly and indirectly by pipeline construction. By 1976,
there were 57 private physicians in Fairbanks, representing
12 specialities.[3] Over a third of the doctors were practic-
ing independently of what were formerly the two major clinics.
The net result was a significant change in the power structure
of the medical community. The traditional style of competition was altered as large contracts rather than individual
patients became the prize.

When pipeline construction began, the smaller of the
two clinics received the contract to provide medical services
under the Teamsters Union pre-paid medical plan, which accounted for about 15 percent of the clinic's patient volume.[4]
At first many of the local doctors were involved in providing
pre-employment physicals for pipeline workers, at a cost of
$78 to $125 per examination. Later Alyeska Pipeline Service
Company decided that the physicals were too costly and contracted with the larger of the two clinics to provide approximately 120 pre-employment examinations each day at an average
cost of $67.[5] Rather than hiring additional doctors, the
physicians in the larger clinic decided to work in shifts and
do the physicals on an "overtime" basis. At the same time,
the larger clinic experienced a 30 percent increase in patient
load, exclusive of the pipeline employment physicals.[6] Large
contracts and increased patient loads enabled the clinics to
expand and build new facilities. Physicians who were not
affiliated with the two clinics concentrated their efforts on
serving the local population, also experienced expanded patient
loads and planned to build yet another professional office
building. A reduction in medical needs after pipeline

completion may lead to competition for rental of office space,
rather than competition for individual patients.

Because the structure of the medical profession
changed, the population expanded, and the number of medical
specialists increased in Fairbanks, the local hospital was
utilized in a different way. More types of surgery were performed in Fairbanks instead of being referred to Seattle. In
addition, persons injured while working on the pipeline north
of Fairbanks and south to Isabel Camp were evacuated to Fairbanks Memorial Hospital. From May 1, 1975, to April 30, 1976,
a total of 1,283 medical emergencies were sent to Fairbanks
hospital from pipeline camps, an average of 3.5 medical evacuations per day.[7]

Fairbanks Memorial Hospital was a relatively new
facility owned by the non-profit Fairbanks Community Hospital
Foundation. The community raised $2.6 million which was
matched by $6 million in state and federal funds, so that the
hospital was debt-free when it opened in April 1972. In 1974,
the hospital added 28 orthopedic beds on its third floor.
That year the 116-bed hospital experienced a 67.7 percent
occupancy rate. It was anticipated that the hospital would
be able to accommodate the Fairbanks community for several
years, with expansion being unnecessary before 1978. By
February 1975, however, the hospital was experiencing an 80
percent average occupancy and on some days every bed was
filled. Most hospitals find 80 percent occupancy the maximum
limit for effective functioning, since greater levels of
utilization create problems of patient mix. While it was
possible to add 12 beds by converting two day rooms, a fathers'
waiting room, and a doctors' dressing room, it was not possible to expand the facilities to keep up with immediate
demands.

To cope with the demands for inpatient health care,
doctors moved patients out of the hospital a little faster

than before, used the extended care facilities of a local
private convalescent home, and delayed elective surgery. In
accommodating the overflow from the hospital, the 88-bed private extended care facility found itself with a 90 percent
occupancy rate, and a need to expand.

In addition to the increased demand for inpatient
services, the hospital was overwhelmed by emergency room
activities. Prior to the pipeline, the two clinics in town
effectively opposed any emergency room services provided by
the hospital. Hence, the emergency room was not staffed and
patients were required to call their doctors, or a doctor
from the same clinic, to meet them at the hospital emergency
room. Each of the two clinics had a doctor on call for emergencies. Unknowingly, many newcomers assumed that Fairbanks
had the emergency room services of a general hospital. Both
because they did not have family doctors in Fairbanks and
because many types of health insurance cover hospital visits,
but not office calls, many of the people new to Fairbanks
sought routine medical care from the hospital emergency room.
The emergency room also was flooded by persons in need of
alcohol detoxification. About the time that pipeline construction began, the community eliminated its drunk laws and
the local alcoholism program eliminated its detoxification
services. As a result, people who were seriously inebriated
were taken to the hospital emergency room. The emergency
room was also the recipient of more medical emergencies during
the pipeline period, as there were more traffic accidents,
fires, industrial accidents, and psychiatric traumas.

One of the potentially most significant results of
pipeline construction on the Fairbanks medical industry was
an increase in the number of persons covered by union and
industrial health insurance programs. The most visible short-
term effect of this was the pipeline pre-employment physical
exams, which pumped more than $1.2 million into the medical

industry in Fairbanks each year of pipeline construction.[8]
More long-term consequences are expected from union health
insurance programs. As the union memberships increased from
pipeline employment, more people were eligible for comprehensive medical insurance programs and union trust funds for
these purposes grew significantly. The largest union with
the most comprehensive health care benefits was the Teamsters
Union Local 959. The growth in union membership and trust
funds has made it more economically feasible for the Teamsters
to provide health care services directly to their membership
rather than contracting the services. In Anchorage, the
union built a $36 million hospital and a $5 million professional clinic to house the approximately 30 physicians who
provide a health maintenance organization for Teamsters. To
provide the same kind and quality of service to its Fairbanks
members, in 1975 the Teamsters Union considered building a
hospital in Fairbanks.

Directors of the Fairbanks Memorial Hospital were
concerned about a second hospital in the same community.
They felt that two hospitals would drive up the cost of inpatient care, particularly for Fairbanks Memorial Hospital
which must accept Medicare and Medicaid patients. Since
Teamsters hospital would be a private institution, it would
siphon patients whose bills fully cover expenses and not incur
the financial loss from Medicare and Medicaid patients. In
addition, the Teamsters hospital would reduce the number of
patients at the Fairbanks Memorial Hospital and possibly
cause under-utilization of specialized facilities. Since
there was a definite need for more hospital beds in Fairbanks
and Fairbanks Memorial Hospital was in the process of making
expansion plans, they invited the Teamsters to participate
in the expansion of the existing hospital. Before accepting
the plan, Teamsters insisted that they have adequate representation on the Board of Directors of Fairbanks Memorial

Hospital. This offended most board members who regarded the hospital as a community effort which ought not to be controlled by any special interest. After initial negotiations failed, the Teamsters continued plans to build their own hospital in Fairbanks. More than any other event during the pipeline period, this could have changed the structure of health care delivery and the power structure of the medical community in Fairbanks.

More subtle potential long-term effects of the increased number and percentage of people in Fairbanks who were eligible for industrial and union health care insurance was the shift in emphasis from acute care to preventive medicine, greater access to and utilization of health care institutions, an expansion of the medical industry in Fairbanks, and, possibly, better health for Fairbanksans.

Unexpected impacts of pipeline construction on the health care industry illustrated, once again, the importance of structural analysis in predicting impacts. By postulating a direct relationship between population size and the need for hospital beds and health care professionals, the health care industry in Fairbanks was deemed adequate and no impacts were anticipated, aside from the increased demands on the state laboratory. The state laboratory was the one case in which numerical formulas were relatively accurate--the number of syphillis serologies performed by the state lab jumped from 4,745 for the six-month period from April through September in 1973 to 12,892 for the same period in 1974,[9] in direct relationship to the number of pipeline physical exams performed. Contrary to the other predictions, however, changes in the structure of the health care delivery system and other aspects of the community caused the hospital and long-term care facility to be inadequate and changed the demands for health care manpower.

This type of structural analysis is also helpful in

explaining another set of unexpected impacts. It was anticipated that, although employment opportunities would increase
during the pipeline construction period, the influx of pipeline job seekers would perpetuate high levels of unemployment
and there would be no problems filling local jobs. Contrary
to these predictions, structural factors intervened to make
local employment one of the most annoying and pervasive
problems related to pipeline impact.

Local employment problems may be attributed to several
factors: (1) as the community expanded, more local jobs were
created; (2) more local people sought pipeline jobs than had
been anticipated; (3) people who came to Fairbanks did not
fill the local employment needs. The third factor was the
most unexpected. It has been explained in part by the circumstances affecting the in-migration of pipeline job seekers,
who were mostly people fairly determined to obtain pipeline
jobs. Other factors also affected their failure to fill the
local employment needs. Some Outsiders seeking pipeline jobs
had unemployment insurance as a source of income while waiting for a pipeline opening; they did not have to work at
local jobs. The cost of living in Fairbanks was so high that
many in-migrants could not afford to work at the lower-paying
local jobs, and chose instead to leave Fairbanks temporarily
or permanently. Those who took local jobs did so on a temporary basis, which created exceptionally high turnover rates.

Nearly all businesses and agencies in Fairbanks experienced high employee turnover rates during the pipeline period.
For example, the Post Office hired 150 employees for its 210
jobs in 1975, a turnover rate of 65 percent.[10] While there
were only 30 mail carrier jobs with the Post Office, an average of 10 new mail carriers were hired each month.[11] Another
major employer in Fairbanks, the University of Alaska, experienced high turnover rates in its non-professional staff--in
the first six months of 1975, 79 employees terminated from

the university's maintenance services department in which
there were 77 jobs. By April 8, 1976, a 15-person mortgage
and loan department in a local bank had only three employees
with more than one year's tenure.[12] Problems of employee
turnover were even more monumental in local jobs with union
affiliation, because people could work at them just long
enough to become eligible for pipeline jobs. Employees of
the Municipal Utilities System power plant were members of
Operating Engineers Local 302. For 34 employment positions
at the power plant, there were 48 terminations and new hires
in 1975. By March 1976, less than 10 employees at the power
plant had more than one year's experience.

High turnover rates were costly in terms of both recruitment and training, and caused a multitude of other problems. Inexperienced people are more likely to make mistakes
and function inefficiently. Inexperienced auto parts employees tended to order the wrong parts, delaying automobile repairs. Inexperienced clerks at the hardware stores often
could not find items, which meant longer lines at counters
and frustration from doing without needed materials. And,
inexperienced mail carriers seemed to put mail in the wrong
boxes. When people are employed only for a short time, there
is less accountability and nobody takes responsibility for
workmanship. A common complaint of Fairbanksans during the
pipeline period was that they could not get their automobiles
repaired properly, and "the mechanic who worked on the car
last week has left town." The power plant supervisor at the
Municipal Utilities System complained that people working at
the power plant were just "putting in time" and did not understand the importance of their jobs. Hiring untrained and inexperienced people to work on complex and expensive power plant
equipment resulted in more "down time" and excessive maintenance. In some cases, people working at jobs without proper
training might have created hazardous situations, such as in

furnace repair.

In the absence of skilled or knowledgeable personnel, some services simply could not be provided. One of the three laundries in Fairbanks closed its doors during the pipeline period because it could not find skilled personnel to do the work. A local bank decided not to finance new housing construction in 1976 because the executive familiar with the local housing market had resigned.[13] In many cases, unfilled positions created more work, greater pressure, and longer hours for employees who remained. Because of the greater demands on them, it was not uncommon for long-tenured employees to take early retirement options. This, in turn, contributed to the lack of experience and knowledge among employees of local businesses and agencies.

Employers developed several strategies for coping with the high turnover rates in Fairbanks: (1) reduce services (a laundromat, for example, decided to close on Sundays); (2) raise wages and benefits to make jobs more attractive (this was the basic strategy of the State of Alaska, which became one of the highest paying employers); (3) develop more intensive training programs to reduce the mistakes and inefficiency of new employees (this strategy was used by the University of Alaska, banks, and the Post Office, among others); (4) recruit employees from Outside (a local cab company hired a Cuban manager who brought with him a cadre of Cuban cab drivers from Florida and, in a short time, Fairbanks had developed a community of 40-50 Cuban immigrants[14]). In addition to these strategies, many employers simply refused to hire persons whom they thought were waiting for pipeline jobs, which in general meant people who were new to the community.

In the context of high turnover rates during the pipeline construction period, local people who normally had difficulty finding jobs became more desirable as employees. Particularly for the lowest paying, or entry level, positions,

more physically and mentally handicapped persons were able
to find jobs in Fairbanks. Vocational rehabilitation counselors found that marginally handicapped persons were more
likely to find jobs on their own, and that more attention
could be given to the severely handicapped who were previously considered unemployable. Perhaps as a result of greater
job opportunities, public assistance to the disabled declined
by 30 percent from 1972 to 1975 (see Figure 11). At least
one vocational rehabilitation counselor observed that the
pipeline period gave disabled people a chance to prove themselves on the job and that their jobs would not be threatened
by the changed employment situation after pipeline construction was completed.

High turnover rates also created greater employment
opportunities for persons who were socially handicapped by
poor work records or English as a second language, for women
who only wanted to work part-time, and for teenagers.

Chapter 10
TEENAGERS TAKE OVER IN FAIRBANKS

Fresh face. Eager smile. Hair pulled back with a bright silk scarf. You couldn't help but notice the youthfulness of the person handing back your change at the cosmetic counter of the drugstore, the sportswear section of the department store, the check-out line at the grocery store, or the teller's window at the bank. She couldn't be more than 19, you think. She was probably closer to 16.

While high school students in the "Lower 48" states were babysitting, mowing lawns and finding other odd jobs to earn their weekly spending money, the teenagers of Fairbanks were accumulating substantial savings accounts as they kept the town going by taking jobs vacated by persons working on the pipeline. Young people could be seen holding responsible jobs in nearly every local establishment. They worked as bookkeepers, stock persons, secretaries and clerks. They pumped gas, repaired vehicles, cooked and waited tables. And, they did a variety of more menial jobs--boxboy, dishwasher, maid.

Fairbanks Memorial Hospital is located just behind the high school, an easy commute for the 30 to 40 high school students who worked part-time jobs that had been filled full-time by adults. The teenagers earned $4.10 per hour working in housekeeping, the kitchen, and the office of the hospital. Three high school students had enviable positions working in surgery.

High school students in Fairbanks received a mixed blessing with the pipeline. Their lives were disrupted considerably when the school board decided that the only way to prepare for the anticipated population influx was to use the high school facility in two shifts. Two separate high schools

were created, each with its own administration, faculty,
staff, and student body. [But, they used the same building.
One school met from 7:00 a.m. to 12:03 p.m.; the other school
held classes from 1:00 p.m. until 6:00 p.m. Many of the
traditional after school activities had to be curtailed.
The unconventional school hours often created logistical
problems for families. Many of the young people objected
to a schedule in which they turned off the alarm clock at
5:00 a.m., could barely keep their eyes open during their
first period class, and ate lunch early in the morning]

Not unlike other small towns, Fairbanks teenagers had
always complained that "there's nothing to do." There weren't
many organized activities for teenagers in Fairbanks; furthermore, teenagers didn't seem to like organized activities.
Traditional teenage gathering places--MacDonalds, the Dairy
Queen, the drive-in root beer stand--got boring after a while.
During the pipeline period the boredom and frustration of being
a teenager in a small town seemed to disappear. By going to
school only half-day, teenagers found that they could take
many of the jobs vacated for pipeline work. Unlike adults
who could not afford to live in Fairbanks on the wages of the
low-paying local jobs, teenagers who were already supported
by their parents found those jobs attractive. The jobs provided a challenge, a learning experience, a source of income,
and an adult role in the community.

In a joint effort between a high school economics
class and the Impact Information Center, nearly half of the
high school students in Fairbanks were surveyed in December
1974 to determine the characteristics of their participation
in the local labor force. The distribution of the sample by
school and grade are given in Table 8. At the time of the
survey, 50 percent of the students in the sample reported
that they were employed. As indicated in Table 9, older
students had slightly higher employment rates than younger

Table 8

Description of Sample of High School Students
Surveyed by School and Grade

	Morning High School			Afternoon High School			Total		
	Total Number Students	Number in Sample	Percent in Sample	Total Number Students	Number in Sample	Percent in Sample	Total Number Students	Number in Sample	Percent in Sample
Freshmen	391	102	26.0	315	163	51.7	706	265	37.5
Sophomores	360	133	36.9	325	124	38.1	685	257	37.5
Juniors	330	159	48.1	257	115	44.7	587	274	46.7
Seniors	298	144	48.3	120	78	65.0	418	222	53.1
TOTAL	1379	538	39.0	1017	480	47.2	2396	1018	42.5

165

Table 9

Teenage Employment Rates by Grade and School

	Morning School		Afternoon School		Total	
	Number Employed	Percent Employed	Number Employed	Percent Employed	Number Employed	Percent Employed
Freshmen	39	38.2	73	44.8	112	42.3
Sophomores	60	45.1	40	32.2	100	38.9
Juniors	94	59.1	52	45.2	146	53.3
Seniors	105	72.9	41	52.5	146	65.7
TOTAL	298	55.4	206	42.9	504	49.5

students, and those attending school in the morning were more likely to be employed than those attending afternoon classes. Table 10 gives an inventory of the jobs most commonly cited by the employed teenagers in the sample.

Most of the employed teenagers found their jobs through an informal network of communications. Nearly 40 percent said that they first heard about their jobs from friends and another 20 percent said that they learned about job openings from their parents. For the most part, the teenagers surveyed did not use formal job placement services. Less than 5 percent located their jobs from newspaper advertisements, and only 3 percent used the state employment office.

"See all the shiny new cars in the parking lot?" asked a high school principal as he pointed out the window of his office. "That is the student parking lot. Now, if you go out the back door when you leave, you will see a parking lot full of old Volkswagens. That is the teachers' parking lot."

Most of the employed students surveyed were earning more than the $2.60 minimum hourly wage, as indicated in

Table 10

Jobs Held by High School Students Surveyed

Job	Number in Sample	Percent Employed Teenagers in Sample	Percent of all Teenagers in Sample
Salesperson	51	10.1	5.01
Stock-person	34	6.7	3.33
Secretary-Clerical	34	6.7	3.33
Cook-Waitress	30	6.0	2.95
Janitor	25	5.0	2.46
Vehicle Repair	17	3.3	1.67
Boxboy	17	3.3	1.67
Dishwasher	13	2.6	1.28
Gas Station Attendant	9	1.8	.88
Maid	9	1.8	.88
Bookkeeper	9	1.8	.88
Other	177	35.1	17.38
No Answer	79	15.7	7.76
TOTAL	504		

Table 11. Approximately 45 percent of the employed students surveyed said that they were earning $3.00 per hour or less, and 42 percent said they were earning more than $3.00 per hour. A total of 18 students in the sample reported that they were earning more than $6.00 per hour. Several local tax accountants said that they had prepared income tax returns for teenagers who had earned more than $30,000 in 1974.

Not all working teenagers owned automobiles. When asked what type of transportation was used to and from work, 31 percent reported that they used their parents' automobiles, 29 percent walked, and 19 percent drove their own cars. The others either rode with friends (14 percent), hitchhiked

Table 11

Hourly Wages for High School Students
Surveyed in December 1974

Hourly Wages	Number in Sample	Percent of Employed Teenagers in Sample	Percent of All Teenagers in Sample
Less than $2.60	79	15.7	7.76
$2.60 - 3.00	149	29.6	14.63
$3.01 - 3.50	74	14.7	7.26
$3.51 - 4.00	66	13.1	6.48
$4.01 - 6.00	53	10.5	5.21
More than $6.00	18	3.6	1.77
No answer	65	12.9	6.39
TOTAL	504		

(4 percent), or found another means of transportation (5 percent).

Contrary to myths about teenagers and cars, automobiles did not have the highest priority in most of the working teenagers' plans for spending their earnings. Only 12 percent said that they had purchased or planned to purchase an automobile, while 13 percent planned to travel, 15 percent were saving for college, and 17 percent were using their wages to purchase necessities, which could mean anything from supplementing the family budget to buying clothes or records. The largest group of working teenagers, 30 percent, were saving their money without any specific goals for spending. This suggests that the work experience was more important than the economic incentives to work.

Fairbanks employers seemed pleased with their teenage employees, and most teenagers were proud of the responsibilities of their adult roles in the community. Yet young people seemed to be trading one set of frustrations for another. Before it was difficult to be a teenager in an adult world; now it was difficult to be an adult in a teenage world. Young persons working at adult jobs in the morning went to school in the afternoon and were told that they had to get a pass to go to the toilet. One young person said that she dropped out of school because she resented being locked in the lunch room. She wrote a petition to have that policy changed and gathered signatures from her fellow students. When she presented the petition to a school administrator, he tore it up in front of her. It became difficult to respect the institution of school, when the school didn't seem to have much respect for the student.

Teenagers began to place greater emphasis on their working roles than on their student roles. Nearly half the employed teenagers reported working more than 20 hours each week and a quarter worked 31 to 40 hours (see Table 12).

Table 12

Reported Number of Hours Worked Each Week
by High School Students Surveyed

Hours Worked Per Week	Number in Sample	Percent of Employed Teenagers in Survey	Percent of all Teenagers in Sample
Less than 10	47	9.3	4.62
10 - 20	127	25.2	12.48
21 - 30	118	23.4	11.59
31 - 40	68	13.5	6.68
More than 40	38	7.5	3.73
It Varies	25	5.0	2.45
No Answer	81	16.1	7.96
TOTAL	504		

Teachers observed that more students were falling asleep in class and being generally unresponsive. Increasing numbers of students tended to either graduate early in their senior year or to drop out of school. During the 1974-75 school year, high school enrollment declined by 331 students, or 20 percent. Some of the students left school to take pipeline jobs.

High school counselors reported that fewer graduating seniors were applying for college. Some parents were concerned about changing educational values. "What is going to happen to these kids after they get used to earning pipeline wages?" asked one parent. Other parents believed that it was good for their children to work and take advantage of pipeline employment opportunities before deciding whether or not to pursue higher education. During the pipeline period, there was a general awareness in the community that skilled trades, or even unskilled labor, had greater earning power than a college diploma.

According to the 1974 survey, about half the teenagers in Fairbanks probably led lifestyles similar to their counterparts in other small towns in the United States. Some experienced new wealth as a by-product of their parents' new wealth. When a group of high school students went on a school-sponsored weekend trip to Whitehorse, they were told to take no more than $25 on the excursion. According to the adult chaperones, most of the teenagers exceeded the $25 limit and several had more than $100 with them. "They had more money than we did," said one chaperone. A school principal reported that one of his students was given a $40-a-week allowance "for taking out the garbage." As some parents acquired new wealth from the pipeline boom, their children acquired new automobiles, snowmobiles, stereo record players, and other symbols of affluence.

Some teenagers, however, experienced greater neglect as a by-product of their parents longer working hours and work in remote areas during the pipeline boom. In some cases, teenagers were left alone while their parents went to work in a pipeline camp. A parent who did not have a pipeline job found his own work so demanding of his time and energies that he gave less time to his children. Expressing a common concern, he said, "The less time I spend with my teenager, the less she will be influenced by my values and the more she will be subject to the values and pressures of her peers." Perhaps because of parental neglect or increased wealth, or other factors--higher rates of divorce, greater availability of drugs, a "rip-off" mentality, ineffective law enforcement, the influence of television, or national trends, there was an inordinate increase in runaways and criminal activity among Fairbanks teenagers.

From 1972 to 1975, the number of runaways brought to the attention of authorities nearly doubled, from 122 to 243.[1] The increase was greatest among girls, from 65 in 1972 to 165 in 1975.[2] Many runaways were never reported to the police or the Division of Family and Children Services. Often teen-age boys were "kicked out of the house," and therefore not reported as runaways. "The parents we have run into don't care," said one social service worker. "They either encourage kids to run away or kick them out of the house."

The director of a group foster care facility for teen-age girls in Fairbanks was involved with many cases of teen-age runaways. During the pipeline period, he observed a different pattern of runaways emerging: a core of at least 20 to 30 teenagers provided a network for runaways. Parents of some of these young people were working at pipeline jobs either locally or in more remote construction camps, leaving their children unsupervised and their houses unattended. Groups of teenagers floated from house to house where adults were absent, obtaining food and shelter without having to return home. In some cases, older men provided shelter for

the runaway teenagers. In the fall of 1974 the Fairbanks
police arrested runaways living in three houses--15 teenagers
between the ages of 14 and 17.

With drugs or sex young people could "buy into" the
network in which teenagers provided for each other during
runaway episodes. A drug abuse counselor reported, "We are
seeing a lot of runaways about 15 years old and every one is
involved in drugs, including amphetamines and LSD." According
to persons working in drug abuse programs, the pipeline construction period attracted more LSD, speed, and cocaine into
the Fairbanks community. Cocaine, which is often called a
"champagne drug" because it is so expensive, became especially popular, possibly because of the increased wealth. Teenage drug and narcotic violations brought to the attention of
law enforcement agencies in Fairbanks more than tripled from
1972 to 1975, from 50 to 215.[3] A 17-year-old Fairbanks boy
who disappeared July 5, 1975, was reportedly murdered because
of his involvement in drug dealings.

Drugs seemed to be associated with other serious crimes
involving Fairbanks teenagers during the pipeline period. A
young man arrested for armed robbery told his attorney that
he was "so high he didn't know what he was doing." In the
first two months of 1976, there were 25 armed robberies in
Fairbanks, 14 of them occurring in the first 16 days of February. Many of the robberies were conducted by teenagers,
and had a certain juvenile naiveté about them. A 17-year-old
accomplice sat in the "get away vehicle" with his infant
nephew while his two 16-year-old companions sprayed a pizza
parlor full of bullets and took $100 from the cash register.
In his court trial, he testified that he used his portion of
the "take" to buy gasoline for his truck and candy for his
nephew.[4] In another armed robbery, two teenagers wearing ski
masks held up a gas station attendant for $90, at the same
time that he was filling up a taxi cab with gasoline. The

taxi driver alerted the police on his radio and proceeded
to follow the two young robbers.[5]

Some of the robberies attributed to Fairbanks teenagers were more sophisticated. In broad daylight, three
armed teenagers robbed a Fairbanks bank of $16,000. A 16-
year-old Fairbanks youth who planned and committed three
armed robberies had his juvenile status waived and received
an adult trial because the judge believed his alleged crimes
showed a "certain amount of guts," degree of sophistication
and planning that "exceeds normal 'juvenile offense.'"[6] Perhaps the judge was also responding to community pressures to
stem the tide of teenage armed robberies by making an example
out of the offender. The Juvenile Intake Officer said that
he did not want students to see armed robbers "walking around
school like nothing had happened to them."[7]

The number of auto thefts reported to the police increased from 235 in 1973 to 771 in 1975.[8] During the same
period, the number of juveniles apprehended for joy riding or
auto theft increased from 26 to 100.[9] Near the end of 1975,
Fairbanks police arrested a "ring" of nine teenagers for
stealing cars.[10] About 20 cars were recovered in various
locations where they had been used for playing "Chicken" and
"demolition derby." Some of the cars were full of bullet
holes. Two months later, two other youths were arrested for
stealing five vehicles which they had used for similar purposes.[11] Reasons for the auto thefts among teenagers could
not have been monetary, since the autos were neither sold
nor used as transportation. It was more of a game, something
to do, a response to peer group pressure, a way to rebel and
possibly to attract the attention of parents, an expression
of disregard for property, and a lack of reality orientation
possibly due to drugs. At least one of the teenagers arrested
for joyriding was found guilty of heroin use.[12]

During the pipeline period, there was also a rise in

174

shoplifting among teenagers. A total of 73 teenagers were
apprehended for shoplifting in Fairbanks in 1973, compared to
188 in 1974.[13] Teenagers were not "stealing to survive,"
said one local authority, who attributed the increase to a
lack of regard for personal property. Shoplifting is a way
of acting out anger, frustration, and rejection, said another
adult who works with juveniles.

Increases in runaways, armed robberies, auto theft
and shoplifting among teenagers might have been coincidental
with pipeline construction. While the increase in juvenile
crime was disproportionately greater than the increase in
juvenile population in Fairbanks, it is possible that some of
the criminal activity could be attributed to influences such
as television or other factors which have given rise to teenage crime as a national trend. Nevertheless, the pipeline
construction created several conditions which may have affected teenage crime activities.

A "rip-off" mentality became prevalent in Fairbanks
during the pipeline period. It was an accepted fact that
many of the people employed on the pipeline were earning exceptionally high wages without doing very much work. Large
sums of money became so commonplace that people began to lose
a perspective on money. It was not unusual for people in
Fairbanks to pay for a $5 lunch with a hundred dollar bill.
When a security guard asked a pipeline worker to remove his
change before passing through a metal detector on his way to
an airplane, the man put his hand in his pocket, pulled out
a wad of bills so thick he could barely hold it in his fist,
and laid the money on a tray in front of the security guard.
As though she had been through the same scene a hundred times
before, the guard responded with total boredom, "That won't
make the buzzer ring."

As people lost perspective on the value of money,

respect for personal property diminished. Alyeska Pipeline
Service Company became "Uncle Al" to people who saw it as a
provider of all kinds of goods. Even though pipeline employees were well paid, many had the feeling that the pipeline company had a surplus of supplies and that a few items
wouldn't be missed. When they went home at night, local
persons working as craftsmen on the pipeline project at
Ft. Wainwright lined their pockets, or their trucks, with
copper fittings or tools or other commodities with which they
had been working. A worker leaving a construction camp with
nine weeks paychecks in his pocket also took with him a pil-
lowcase full of grapefruit from the camp's kitchens. Even
management personnel seemed to be "on the take."

The list of articles stolen or missing from the pipeline included tools, building materials, clothing, radios,
calculators, tires, bedding and linen, and petty items:
stamps ($65), wall clock ($18), coffee pot ($30), fire ex-
tinguishers ($30), 40 pounds of laundry detergent ($30), a
case of prime rib ($120).[14] In the Fairbanks area alone,
during 1975 a total of $78,755 worth of pipeline property was
reported as lost or stolen, not including 34 vehicles valued
at $285,000.[15]

Young people in the community could not avoid seeing
the distinctively marked stolen property in their own homes
or in the homes of friends and neighbors. In many cases,
there was no attempt to hide or disguise the stolen articles
and "ripping off Uncle Al" was often talked about as one of
the fringe benefits of the job. Given the environment in
which a "rip-off" mentality became prevalent, it was not
likely that crimes against personal property would be taken
seriously by teenage members of society. This may have been
one factor affecting such criminal activities as shoplifting,
auto theft and armed robbery.

Another factor, already mentioned, is longer working

hours which inevitably led to a certain amount of parental
neglect and a greater need for young people to turn to their
peers for reinforcement. In a revealing letter to the editor
of the local newspaper,[16] one Fairbanks parent wrote:

> Dear Editor,
>
> Recently I received a call from the Police
> Department in Fairbanks shortly after 5 p.m.
> It seems that one of my boys who goes to the
> Junior High at Main was picked up for shop-
> lifting. Believe me I was depressed, to say
> the least, after a somewhat harder than usual
> day on the job of having to drive all the way
> to town and back in the ice fog was no fun.

The parent went on to say:

> I presumed he was picked up by himself but when
> I walked in the police station, he was among a
> half dozen other kids. . . .I knew at a glance
> had my boy been with himself he would not be
> sitting in the police station. . . .I asked him
> why he did this. His answer was the same ex-
> perienced in our younger days ourselves: "They
> dared me to, and when I didn't, called me chicken."

Before signing the letter as "A Concerned Parent," the writer
concluded:

> We parents may not always show it but we love each
> and every one of our kids. So kids, please try
> to stay out of trouble and give your parents a
> break they fully deserve.

The Juvenile Intake Officer who handled most cases of
teenage crime and saw both the teenage offenders and their
families, held parents responsible for their children's behavior. "The buck is so important to them that they overlook
problems with their children," he said. One way for children
to get the attention from their parents was to misbehave. A
mental health counselor cited a case in which a teenage boy became involved in drugs after his father's business became so
busy from pipeline activities that the father no longer had
time for his son.

Yet another factor in teenage crime may have been the

emergence, or propulsion, of teenagers into adult roles in the community. Among teenagers, as among adults, some assume traditionally responsible roles and others do not.

Chapter 11
A NEW SPECTATOR SPORT

"Go slow, Harold," a middle-aged woman commanded her husband as he drove their sedan the two blocks between stop lights on Second Avenue, "I want to get a good look."

Two secretaries on their lunch hour crossed the street to deliberately walk on the south side of Second Avenue. Their conversation dwindled as their eyes remained fixed on the other side of the street.

Four o'clock in the afternoon. A businessman entered his attorney's office and found the lawyer gazing out his second story window onto Second Avenue. The attorney looked up at his client, nodded his head toward the window, and said, "Look at this one."

Starting in the summer of 1974, Fairbanksans developed a keen interest in what was to become the town's newest spectator sport--watching prostitutes solicit on Second Avenue. The first challenge for the spectators was identifying the players. Most prostitutes working Second Avenue made themselves relatively easily identifiable to potential customers and spectators alike by their costumes which usually included platform shoes and large handbags. There was something a little more subtle which set them apart from most women in Fairbanks, something which one observer called "big city slick." The carriage and clothes of a model, coiffured hair, and carefully applied make-up seemed to distinguish the women of the streets from the harried housewife or the frontierswoman. Even so, the uninitiated weren't sure whether they had identified "a real prostitute" or an especially attractive career girl.

Keen observers were not satisfied with only identifying the players; they wanted to know who was on what team. Some

178

of the women worked together and some worked with pimps.
Pimps who fit the stereotype--Black, lean, dressed in fancy
clothes, driving flashy Cadillacs--were easiest to spot.
With time and patientce, however, spectators could identify
pimp and prostitute teams by watching the non-verbal communications between a woman on the north side of Second Avenue
and a man standing on the south side of the street or sitting
in a car nearby.

Fairbanksans who worked in offices or stores on Second
Avenue or frequented the area for other reasons, soon began
to keep score cards. They could tell which prostitutes were
new to the area and how successful they were at attracting
customers. Observers tried to identify solicitation strategies. "A Second Avenue observer says he has noticed a new
strategy among some of the prostitutes," the Fairbanks Daily
News-Miner reported. "It seems that one woman at a time will
occupy the southeast corner of the intersection of Second and
Cushman and wait for a customer to show up in a car. When she
leaves another one takes her place. In a way, it's like base-
ball workup, he notes."[1]

At parties and other gatherings it was not uncommon
to hear Fairbanksans discussing the number of times they had
been propositioned on Second Avenue, and what the going rates
seemed to be. One hundred dollars a trick or $300 for the
night was the reported cost for services of the Second Avenue
prostitutes.

Prostitution took many forms in Fairbanks during the
pipeline period--call girls, dating services, brothels, those
who solicited in the bars, and those who worked the streets.
Women who worked the streets received the most attention from
the general public and the police, possibly because these were
the prostitutes who were most visible, most easily observed
by persons who did not want to become involved directly, and
the source of contact between most Fairbanksans and the whole

institution of prostitution. In the first 11 months of 1975,
21 of the 58 arrests for prostitution were made on Second
Avenue and an additional 26 arrests were made in the two
Second Avenue bars at whose doors most of the street-workers
loitered in an attempt to attract customers.[2]

The two-block area of Second Avenue came to symbolize
prostitution and the other vices associated with a boomtown.
During the pipeline period, journalists and newcomers dubbed
the stretch of pavement "Two Street." This was a part of
the boomtown that everybody expected, that attracted reporters
seeking sensationalism and tourists wanting "an experience."
Pipeline workers, businessmen and visitors had to spend at
least one night "doing the bars," so that they could tell
their friends back home about the wild and woolly North.

Prostitution had deep roots in the history of Fairbanks, from its beginnings as a mining town. According to
local folklore, the first women in Fairbanks were prostitutes
who, because of their trade, accumulated massive amounts of
cash and thereby became powerful forces in banking and real
estate. When epidemics swept through the tiny gold mining
town, according to legend, the ladies of the night became
sisters of mercy, nursing the sick back to health. In the
early days, prostitution was considered more of an institution
than a problem. Women who worked as prostitutes lived on
Fourth Avenue in little log cabins which were called "the
cribs," and checked in regularly with the police. It was not
until the 1950's, when the military pressured the local
government into taking action, that prostitution became illegal
in Fairbanks.

Perhaps because Fairbanksans viewed the old Fourth
Avenue "line" with nostalgia, or because there was a genuine
tolerance of diverse lifestyles, or because a frontier environment did not breed a puritanical ethic, most Fairbanksans did
not view the concept of prostitution as inherently evil.

Rather, they tended to approach the subject with humor.
"Prostitution is a 'whore-ible' problem," joked one minister.
In a spoof in the Fairbanks Daily News-Miner, a local writer
recounted his meeting with an old girl friend:

> You can imagine how surprised I was to
> see her on Second Avenue in a long black coat,
> long boots, with heavy green and purple make-
> up on her eyelids. . . .
>
> (She explains:) "It's not what you think
> at all. I am simply a graduate student in
> anthropology come up to Alaska to do field
> work. . . .Now I'm working on my doctoral
> thesis entitled 'Adaptation of the Eastern U.S.
> White Anglo-Saxon Protestant Prostitute to
> the Alaska Environment and Her Attitudes
> Toward Ecology'."

As she hurried down the street after a "tall, bearded guy
in cowboy hat and high-heeled mukluks. . .in a green Alyeska parka that matched the color of the hundred dollar bills
bulging out of his pockets," the writer concludes: "Don't
be too quick to judge a girl on Second Avenue just because
she is dressed in a certain way. She might be an anthropology student or even an old friend from your past."[3]

Fairbanksans were not alone in viewing prostitution
in a comic light. Nationally-syndicated cartoonist Milton
Caniff featured an encyclopedia-selling "Pipeline Polly" in
his comic strip, "Steve Canyon."

Even those in the trade seemed to have a sense of
humor about their business. As flights originating in the
pipeline camps landed at Fairbanks International Airport near
the end of 1975, the passengers were met by a man who handed
them a leaflet advertising "Paradise Dating Service," "Operated BY Pipeliners FOR Pipeliners." "No Duds--No Dogs--No
Rip-offs," the advertisement stated. "Paradise girls are
carefully screened for honesty, beauty, hygiene, and pleasant
personality." According to one knowledgeable source, the man
who handed out the leaflets and ran Paradise Dating Service

had only one employee, his wife, who had three wigs: blonde, brunette, and red.

⌐ [While the attitude of most Fairbanksans toward the concept of prostitution was a mixture of curiousity, acceptance and humor, there was some concern about the by-products of prostitution.] As trans Alaska oil pipeline construction brought Fairbanks into the national spotlight, journalists tended to focus on the Second Avenue prostitutes. Many community leaders feared that this would give the town a bad reputation and adversely affect potential investors, tourists, and other sources of economic growth. They were also afraid that this type of publicity would make Fairbanks more attractive to vice peddlers who would migrate to the community and aggravate the problems.

Streetwalking was not a traditional form of prostitution in Fairbanks. The theory held by law enforcement officials was that the massive influx of prostitutes into the community during the pipeline construction period led to a situation in which supply exceeded demand and caused them to be more aggressive. They emerged from the bars to solicit in the streets. As more women worked the streets, the more aggressive they became. At first it was not uncommon for a man walking down Second Avenue to be asked, "Do you wanna party?" Later the come-ons got stronger: "Mmmm, I like your body." And by the summer of 1976 men driving down Second Avenue were accosted by women who hopped into their cars at the stop signs. Some men found it flattering, others found it annoying. There was no real drive to crack down on prostitution, but there was pressure to clean up Second Avenue. In March 1976, the Fairbanks City Council passed an ordinance requiring a mandatory jail sentence of 60 days and raising the maximum fine to $1,000 and imprisonment to one year for persons convicted of prostitution. Previously the maximum penalty

was a 60-day jail sentence and a $600 fine, with most jail
sentences averaging 10 days. In July of that year the City
Council passed an ordinance forbidding "loitering for the
purposes of prostitution."

Not only were Fairbanksans concerned about the community's image as a result of open prostitution, but also
some were genuinely concerned about public safety. Law enforcement officials and others believed that drugs and violence follow prostitution. In Fairbanks, there was some evidence to support that stereotype. A call girl who had worked
in Fairbanks told a reporter, "The pimps control the streets."
Drugs were a big part of the streetwalkers' life, she said.
"You gotta get high to stand hanging around on a street-
corner."[4] The body of a murdered woman who was reported to
be a prostitute heavily involved in drug traffic was found
in Fairbanks in September 1975.

The violence which was most often associated with
prostitution was "rollings." Sometimes women worked in pairs
or in groups of three. When a customer accompanied a prostitute to a motel room, he was met by another woman or two who
took his wallet, assaulted him if he resisted, and fled. Some
prostitutes were more discreet, providing sexual services
first and then lifting their customers' wallets without them
knowing until the following morning. Teamwork not only faci-
litated taking advantage of the unwary customer, but also
served to protect the prostitutes who were themselves victims
of violence. Cases in which the customer assaulted the prostitute were less likely to come to the attention of the police
because the prostitute would have been subject to prosecution
rather than being treated as a victim. In one reported case,[5]
a 19-year-old woman solicited a customer on Second Avenue,
accompanied him to a hotel room, and provided her services as
a prostitute. After the sex act was completed, the customer
struck her on the back of the head with a broken bottle, beat

her, tried to strangle her, and forced her into sexual inter-
course. Partially for protection against these kinds of incidents, most of the prostitutes who worked the streets of
Fairbanks carried knives in their purses.

While the safety of the customer and his wallet were
somewhat endangered as a by-product of prostitution, Fairbanksans were more concerned about public safety in a more
general sense. There was a general feeling that "night life"
in Fairbanks had become less safe. Traditionally, bars had
been social centers and gathering places for many Fairbanksans. Most bars had regular clientele who seemed to know
each other. They were more like clubs--complete with activities
such as dart boards, pool tables, and electronic games--than
impersonal places to order drinks. Each of the many bars
seemed to have its own personality and its own "type" of customer. Local people classified the establishments as "military bars," "Native bars," "bars for university-types," "work-
ingman's bar" and so forth. Groups such as softball teams,
drama organizations or labor groups met regularly in certain
bars. During the pipeline period, however, the character of
many bars seemed to change. New faces appeared making the
old familiar places seem less comfortable to the regulars.
People's sense of trust seemed to erode and the bars felt
less safe.

In some cases, conflicts in territoriality led to
overt hostility. Late in the summer of 1975, hostilities escalated to open violence in the streets. At that time street
brawling became the newest spectator sport. In the early
hours of the morning, people congregated on the streets and
parking lots in the downtown area to watch fights which often
started in bars. When the police arrived on the scene, spectators inhibited their efforts to quell the action. The number of assults on police officers jumped from 15 in 1973 before pipeline construction began to 57 in 1974 and 55 in 1975.

Some of the street violence also included vandalism, as bot-
tles and other objects were thrown through storefront windows.

Reasons for the street brawling were complex and not
well understood. It appears that the conflicts had racial
dimensions, as most of those involved were Natives and Blacks,
who have had tense racial relations for a long time. According to observers, the traditional racial hostilities were
fueled by several factors indirectly associated with the pipeline construction period. With more money as a result of
pipeline employment, there were more Natives and more Blacks
frequenting bars on Second Avenue. Many of the Second Avenue
prostitutes were Black women armed with knives, and many of
the pimps were also Black. Traditionally, Natives had used
Second Avenue as a popular meeting place where one could find
friends and relatives from the villages. It was possible that
their use of the territory was threatened by the growing visibility of Blacks. As the prostitutes working Second Avenue
found that many of their potential customers were seeking
instead Native women in the bars, they might have felt threatened by this additional competition. Much of the brawling
reportedly started as name-calling among people who were usually drunk and led to various forms of assult, of which fist-
fighting and knifing seemed to be the most common.

After weekend fights involving 70 persons on Saturday
night and as many as 100 on the following Sunday night in mid-
August of 1975, the Fairbanks Native Association asked the
city to close the bars earlier than their 5 a.m. legal closing
time. Bar owners insisted that the solution to the problem
was better law enforcement, rather than earlier closings which
would have hurt their businesses. The bars remained open and
the street activities gradually cooled off as winter weather
approached. However, sporadic fights in bars, assaults on
police officers, stabbings, vandalism, and other forms of
violence were reported from time to time. While some people

viewed rioting in the streets as a kind of boomtown recreation, for others the disturbances threatened their sense of personal security.

In addition to the new faces in the bars, new prostitutes on the streets, and new forms of street hostilities, many Fairbanksans perceived that night life in Fairbanks had taken on a seamier quality. Perhaps nobody was more aware of the seamy side of Fairbanks night life than the local cab drivers. Because there was a high turnover rate among cab drivers and working at night enabled people to attend daytime calls at the union hall, many of the unemployed persons seeking pipeline jobs did stints as nighttime cab drivers. The naive were soon to learn that being a cab driver involved more knowledge than memorizing the city map and a broader function than chauffering people. Far from the stereotype of a cab driver as an Everyman philosopher and observer of life, cab drivers in Fairbanks played a central role in the matrix of illicit activities. They became pimps when their fares asked them to find prostitutes; they transported prostitutes and their customers to motels; they assisted persons who were picking up and delivering heroin and other drugs. Because of their access to information about illicit activities and their participation, cab drivers were very vulnerable. At times they were offered bribes in the form of large tips, or they were threatened not to reveal information. After becoming accessories to criminal activities, it became relatively easy for cab drivers to become more involved and to reap more of the financial rewards. Those who decided to play it straight often feared for their own safety. In addition to the dangers of being accomplices in crimes, many of the cab drivers were themselves victims of armed robberies and assault.

After a cab driver was killed in January 1976, several of the remaining cabbies resigned and others began to carry guns. Although carrying a concealed weapon was illegal in

Fairbanks, the cab drivers felt it was necessary for self-
protection. Just five months later, another cab driver was
murdered. The slain cab drivers had several characteristics
in common: each had left his family Outside and had come to
Fairbanks to seek a pipeline job and each was murdered for
motives apparently unrelated to robbery, since cash was found
on each of the victims. It appears that drugs may have been
involved as a motive in at least one of the cases. As a tri-
bute to the victims, Fairbanks cab drivers formed caravans
to escort the coffins of their slain comrades to the airport
where the bodies were shipped to hometowns in the Lower 48
states for burial.

While it is not uncommon for cab drivers to be murdered in larger cities in the United States, these were the
first such incidents in Fairbanks in over a decade.[6] One cab
driver told a reporter, "I think they need to clean up the
whole town. I've never seen a place where the whores, pimps,
and gambling is so open." He felt that the armed robberies
and murder were part of the general crime picture of the city.
"Evidentally, it's the way the people want it or it wouldn't
be that way," he said. "A town is no better than the people
who live in it."[7]

In a small town, isolated incidents tend to outweigh
statistics in the minds and perceptions of residents. The
actual figures on crimes reported to the Fairbanks police in
1973, 1974, and 1975 are given in Table 13, with the percentages of change each year. Percentages are highly misleading
in light of the small numbers, however. For instance, an increase from two murders in 1973 to three in 1974 can be represented as a 50 percent increase even though it means only one
additional case. A favorite trick which journalists played
on local and national audiences was to cite the percentages
of increase in various categories of crime without giving the
actual numbers. In spite of the distortions created by well-

Table 13

Fairbanks Police Department Activity Report

Category of Crime	1973	1974	1975	% Change 1973-1974	% Change 1974-1975
Murder, Non-negligent Manslaughter	2	3	2	+50.0%	-33.3%
Forcible Rape	10	14	11	+40.0%	-21.4%
Kidnapping	2	2	3	0	+50.0%
Robbery	21	47	62	+123.8%	+31.9%
Burglary (Breaking & Entering)	258	281	351	+8.9%	+24.9%
Larceny Theft (Except Auto Theft)	1,056	1,248	1,859	+18.2%	+49.0%
Auto Theft	231	345	771	+49.4%	+123.5%
Aggravated Assault	60	98	115	+63.3%	+17.3%
Other Assaults	235	263	317	+11.9%	+20.5%
Assault on a Police Officer	15	57	55	+280.0%	-3.6%
Interfering with a Police Officer	8	6	33	-25.0%	+450.0%
Arson	20	17	19	-15.0%	+11.8%
Forgery and Counterfeiting	29	16	33	-44.8%	+106.3%
Fraud	46	62	83	+34.7%	+33.9%
Embezzlement	17	21	15	+23.5%	-28.6%
Buying, Receiving or Possessing Stolen Property	2	2	8	0	+300.0%
Defrauding Innkeeper	0	16	31	-	+93.8%
Prostitution & Commercialized Vice	2	16	68	+700.0%	+325.0%
Sex Offenses (except Rape & Prostitution)	30	57	50	+90.0%	-12.3%
Narcotic Drug Law Violations	182	276	221	+51.6%	-20.0%
Gambling	13	3	2	-77.0%	-33.3%
Vandalism	215	251	368	+16.7%	+46.6%
Carrying, Possessing Weapons	34	67	142	+97.1%	+111.9%
Bomb Threats	8	5	10	-37.5%	+100.0%
Driving under the Influence	159	197	261	+23.9%	+32.5%
Liquor Laws	108	186	123	+72.2%	-33.9%
Drunkenness	230	540	173	+134.8%	-68.0%
Disorderly Conduct	123	244	354	+98.4%	+45.1%
Offenses against Family & Children	36	28	22	-23.3%	-21.4%
Runaway	99	173	234	+74.7%	+35.3%
TOTAL COMPLAINTS*	5,072	6,851	9,788	+35.1%	+42.9%

*
Note: Totals include complaints not listed in the table.

188

publicized isolated incidents and the use of percentages
which contributed to a feeling that crime was rampant in Fairbanks, the figures do suggest that there were significant increases in nearly every category of crime during the pipeline
construction period.
High visibility of prostitution combined with overall
increases in crime led some to speculate that organized crime
was entering Fairbanks. Local law enforcement officials felt
that some of the prostitutes who worked in Fairbanks were
part of a ring which traveled in circuits from Seattle to
Anchorage to Fairbanks to Valdez and back to Seattle, or some
similar schedule. The Chief of Criminal Investigations for
the Alaska Department of Public Safety maintained that some
of the cash passing hands in the three known illegal gambling
establishments in Fairbanks was backed by Las Vegas sources.[8]
During the pipeline construction period, each week an estimated
$80,000 to $100,000 exchanged hands in illegal gambling in
Fairbanks. Investigative reporters from the Los Angeles
Times[10] and the Anchorage Daily News[11] revealed that the Alyeska warehouse in Fairbanks was staffed by Teamsters with
criminal records, seeming to support alleged connections between organized labor and organized crime. After a three-day
visit to Alaska, a federal Law Enforcement Assistance Administration official declared, "It would appear that just about
every conceivable manifestation of organized crime and/or
organized criminal activity is present in Alaska."[12] In a
memo recommending federal support for an investigation of organized crime in Alaska, the official said, "Despite the lack
of 'hard' data, it is obvious that the state of Alaska is falling heir to an increasing level of organized criminal activity."[13] Contrary to these allegations, the governor of Alaska maintained that the greatest problem was "disorganized"
crime attributable to general population increases and alcohol-related incidents.

One type of "disorganized crime" requiring considerable organizational ability is fraud, which seemed to increase
during the pipeline period. The most common type of fraud
was writing phony checks. In addition to the numerous bad
checks written by persons who later left town, there were
organized check forgery operations in Alaska. The local
banks printed a large advertisement in the Fairbanks Daily
News-Miner warning the business community that

> Within the last six months, a professional
> ring of forgers has been operating in the metro-
> politan areas of Alaska, primarily the Fair-
> banks-Anchorage area. Several of our well-known
> businessmen and all of our banks have been
> victims of this forgery ring. THEY ARE STILL
> AT LARGE AND OPERATING IN ALASKA.[14]

The advertisement described the ring's methods of operation:
(1) a member of the forgery ring (usually female) sought employment with a large local company; (2) forgery ring members
gained access to offices, check supply, and check protecto-
graph and stole company checks, usually from the back of the
check supply; (3) this professional group of forgers had
Alaska identification and cashed the forged checks after holi-
days, on Mondays and Fridays.

Problems with check forgery and bad checks plagued
local businesses and created additional hassles for legiti-
mate Fairbanks consumers. Many businesses which had previously cashed checks for their customers discontinued that service.
Persons wishing to make purchases with checks were required to
show two or more pieces of identification, and at least one
establishment required customers who wrote checks to endorse
them with fingerprints. A new business called "Check-Rite"
opened in Fairbanks to serve as both a collection agency for
bad checks and a credit-rating service which gave local businesses lists of persons who had written bad checks. Normally
responsible persons who bounced checks when their accounts

became inadvertently overdrawn found themselves in the em-
barassing position of having credit denied and being treated
like criminals. Some Fairbanksans found this situation annoying, and many felt that the general attitude toward check
cashing was indicative of the changes which made Fairbanks
more impersonal and less trusting.

In addition to bad checks, there were several con
games ranging from fake gold sales to the mailing of bogus
Telex invoices to local businesses for advertising which they
had not purchased. Another type of fraud which occurred was
the emergence of agencies claiming to provide pipeline employment. The housing shortage in Fairbanks also created a
climate conducive to fraud. In one case, a group called
Fairwood Associates advertised "Fairwood Apartments" for rent
and charged prospective tenants $500 deposits. Approximately
26 persons paid deposits for the apartments which they were
told were prefabricated and in transit to Fairbanks where
they would be placed on property on the south side of town.
Fairwood Associates left town with the deposits, the housing
never materialized, and a subsequent investigation revealed
that the group did not even own the property which they identified as the housing site to prospective renters.

"Disorganized crime" was only half the problem. The
other half was "disorganized" law enforcement. Two law enforcement agencies were responsible for public safety in the
Fairbanks area. The Fairbanks Police Department served the
City of Fairbanks and the State Troopers, Detachment I of the
Alaska State Department of Public Safety, served the area outside the city limits. Detachment I included most of the northern region of the state, from Tok to Barrow, and most of the
pipeline corridor. Because the State Troopers did not keep
statistics on their activities in the Fairbanks North Star
Borough distinct from their other activities in Detachment I,
most of the figures cited are from the Fairbanks Police

Department and reflect only the crimes committed within city limits. Both of the law enforcement agencies experienced increased demands for their services and both suffered from manpower shortages.

City police in Fairbanks were the highest paid in the country, and an inexperienced state trooper starting to work in Fairbanks in October 1975 could earn $1,578 per month.[15] Pipeline security guards, however, earned $1,400 per week.[16] Many of the local law enforcement officers could not resist the temptation, including the Chief of the Fairbanks Police Deaprtment, who opted to work on the pipeline after 21 years of service to the city. It was difficult to fill the vacancies created when police left for pipeline jobs, because the housing shortage in Fairbanks limited recruitment potential. As a result, both the state troopers and the city police experienced manpower shortages. In March 1975, the Fairbanks Police Department was budgeted for 50 employees, but there were only 36.[17] Eleven of the 13 who resigned from the Fairbanks Police Department in the first quarter of 1975 were destined for pipeline jobs. At the same time, the Alaska Department of Public Safety had authorized 17 troopers to cover the 215,000 square mile area of Detachment I, but only 12 positions were filled.[18] From January to August 1975, 18 troopers in Detachment I resigned and only nine were hired as replacements.[20]

As a result of the manpower shortage, fewer police were patrolling the streets and highways, and those who did patrol worked longer hours. By October 1975, the Department of Public Safety's civil section in Fairbanks was behind in serving 600 to 700 warrants.[21] Both the troopers and the city police failed to investigate minor accidents and ignored many complaints of larceny and burglary. When investigations did occur, they were often delayed and inadequate. A small store in an outlying area of the Fairbanks North Star Borough was burglarized four times in 1975. After the second break-in, the store owner gave the troopers serial numbers of the stolen rifles, but the troopers didn't have time to give the numbers to local pawn shops, the procedure which is usually followed to help recover stolen articles and track down thieves. Three weeks later, the store was broken into for a third time and it took State Troopers two hours to arrive on the scene. That day one of the three troopers assigned to patrol the Fairbanks area had been sent to Tok to pick up a prisoner and another trooper was talking to school children. That left only one trooper to patrol the entire 7,361 square mile area. On his way to investigate the break-in, he was diverted to check on a driver who had passed out behind the wheel of his car. Two months later the store was burglarized for the fourth time and the owner, discouraged and angered, announced that he wanted to sell his establishment.

In addition to the manpower shortage, other factors made it difficult for state and local police to enforce vice laws. Small police departments in small towns cannot maintain undercover forces to infiltrate gambling houses and catch prostitutes soliciting. The police departments found it impossible to keep strange faces on the streets. After a night or two of work, the "undercover" agents were easily recognized by people involved in illicit activities. Some of the prostitutes who were arrested charged that there was discrimination in the laws and their enforcement. Since most of the women arrested for prostitution were Black, they alleged that there was racial discrimination on the part of the police department. Others challenged the law which arrested women for prostitution but did not penalize the male partner in the act. These charges of discrimination put the police in the uneasy position of pursuing cases which might not lead to convictions and demoralized their efforts to "clean up Second Avenue." Police were further demoralized by the rising incidents of assaults on officers.

Law enforcement activities might also have suffered
from misplaced priorities. During the pipeline construction
period, one of the highest priorities of law enforcement was
the control of narcotics. The Area-wide Metropolitan Narcotics Team, called "Metro Team," was formed in a joint effort
between state troopers, city police and agents of the Federal
Drug Enforcement Administration. After months of investigation using former drug addicts as informants, the Metro Team
made 24 arrests for hard drug charges in December 1975. The
24 arrested ranged in age from 16 to 61 and included 14 whites,
nine Blacks, and one Indian.[22] Among law enforcement officials and many community leaders, this was touted as one of
the greatest successes in local law enforcement. Among people involved in drug rehabilitation programs, the busts were
considered disastrous.

According to street people and drug rehabilitation
program personnel, there was an informal network in Fairbanks
through which people who used drugs sold to their friends.
Those arrested by the Metro Team were not "big-time" dealers,
but local people who sold mostly to their friends. The Metro
Team acknowledged that most of the people arrested were friends
or acquaintances of the two informants.[23] A leader of the
Metro Team declared, "I thought the Metro Team, in this instance, got about as far into local heroin traffic as they'll
ever be able to go."[24] He explained that the larger heroin
dealers would be hesitant to make a sale to anyone but a
junkie, for fear that the purchaser would go to the police.
By destroying the informal network of drug sales without going
to the source of drugs for the community, the police created
a climate in which the more sophisticated drug dealers could
move into the community. Because local persons were too para-
noid to share their drug supplies with friends, addicts were
forced to go directly to more organized dealers who charged

about twice as much. According to some knowledgeable sources, this pressure was responsible for many of the armed robberies which occurred in the following months.

Thus, while the police cleaned up one type of illegal activity, they may have opened the door to more serious problems.

Chapter 12
MENTAL HEALTH

Community mental health is a relatively elusive and ill-defined concept. Nevertheless, mental health practitioners and researchers recognize that individuals respond to changes in their environment in a variety of ways, some involving changes in mental or emotional well-bring. The concept of stress plays an important role in models which relate events in the community or family to an individual's mental health. In developing a model for measuring and monitoring stress in communities, Francis T. Miller and his associates at the University of North Carolina School of Medicine conceive of "individuals existing in a matrix of events, some satisfying and rewarding, some tension-producing and stressful, and some neutral or of little import."[1] If the balance between stresses and satisfactions is greatly altered, the individual's capacity to cope may prove inadequate, and he may need mental health or other helping services. Events or changes in the community, the family, or the individual are viewed as potential precipitators of emotional distress.

Certainly, construction of the trans Alaska oil pipeline was a significant event producing changes in the community, in families, and in the roles of individuals. Changes in the community which could have intensified stress on the individual included rapidly rising rates of inflation, everyday annoyances from increased traffic to longer lines, and a diminished sense of security resulting from unfamiliar faces in the community, rapid change toward an uncertain future, and increased crime.

Changes in the family related to pipeline construction also could have created stress on the individual. The most obvious of these changes was the absence of a spouse, parent,

196

child, or other family member working in a remote pipeline camp. Even the families which were not disrupted by the absence of a member might have found that longer working hours and double-shifting in the schools created conditions in which the family spent less time together. Another pipe-line-related condition was the housing shortage which caused crowding and forced some families to change residences be-cause of rent increases or evictions. Buying or building a home can further stress marriages and family relationships.

The pipeline also changed the structure of the com-munity in ways which created new roles for individuals or accelerated the pace at which they adopted new roles. The combination of expanded employment opportunities and high turnover rates often meant promotions resulting in pressures from more responsibility and greater demands. Women entering the workforce for the first time, or re-entering the work-force after a period of domestic activity, or entering levels of employment never before open to them, developed new iden-tities as a result of new roles at work, as well as at home. Similarly, teenagers finding employment during the pipeline period adopted new roles in the community, at school, and in their families. Many Fairbanksans who had never worked on construction projects before elected to seek pipeline employ-ment, leading to new roles in relation to unions, employers and co-workers. In addition, pipeline workers experienced relative deprivation from long working hours and the isolation of pipeline construction camps.

At community, family and individual levels, the pipe-line project may be viewed as an event potentially increasing stress. These developments, however, must be considered in the context of community mental health prior to the pipeline. Like other areas in the arctic and subarctic, Fairbanks has been characterized by a high incidence of alcoholism and poor mental health, apparently related to the extreme climate and

social environment. Folks who live in Fairbanks usually
attribute mental health problems to the long, cold, dark
winters which isolate people by limiting their mobility, reduce sensory stimulation, and induce feelings of depression.
Another folk explanation for poor mental health in Fairbanks
is the lack of recreational opportunities forcing people to
congregate in bars where they develop tendencies toward alcoholism.

Contrary to these folk beliefs, mental health workers
consider other factors more significant. They point out that
psychological casualties are more likely to occur during good
weather, rather than in the winter. One explanation for this
is that people use the winter weather as an excuse for their
problems. When spring comes, people are forced into the
realization that their problems are due to other causes and
then seek help for depression, troubled marriages, and other
problems, or give in to their problems through suicide attempts, divorce, or other means. The folk belief that a
harsh climate is responsible for poor mental health in the
North probably serves as a mechanism for helping people cope
through the winter, but it does not adequately explain the
relatively higher incidence of alcoholism and poor mental
health.

According to mental health professionals, the Northern
environment plays a different kind of role in determining the
rate of psychological problems. To many people, Alaska is
still considered a frontier. Because of its remoteness and
frontier quality, Fairbanks attracts people who are trying to
escape from their former lives and "start all over again." In
a recent survey, more than 50 percent said that "a chance to
be independent to start something new" was an extremely or
very important reason for coming to Fairbanks.[2] According
to the survey, this was by far the most significant factor
affecting in-migration. While some find satisfaction in their

move, others find that they cannot escape from their problems.
Alcoholism may be a manifestation of this need to escape.

In addition to being "the end of the road" for many
people, Fairbanks is so remote that people who move to this
isolated community find themselves removed from their traditional support structures. When a new baby comes along,
Momma and Grandma aren't there to give advice or take charge
when a screaming child makes his mother feel like she is
losing control. A long distance call is too expensive when
a person feels like discussing a problem with an older brother
or life-long friend. In the absence of extended families,
Fairbanksans tend to develop family-like relationships with
people to whom they are unrelated by marriage or kinship.
These relationships take a long time to develop, however, and
most people avoid making that emotional investment in a newcomer whom they fear may be transient.

Another factor which may contribute to the general
status of mental health in Fairbanks is the significant portion of the population who are military personnel. Persons
in the military are often subject to an unusual degree of
stress, as are their families. This often creates mental
health problems, for example, greater incidence of child
abuse and child neglect.[3]

To assess changes in community mental health, Miller
and his colleagues suggest a variety of indicators, including
births, deaths, marriages, divorces, suicides, hospital admissions, ambulance and rescue calls, utilization of social
services and mental health facilities, alcohol consumption,
and crime. Recognizing that it often takes as long as three
years for a stressful event to precipitate a crisis which is
then manifest in community mental health records, some of the
indicators reviewed here are in the short-term context of the
pipeline construction period.

Births and deaths in the Fairbanks Election District,

an area larger than the Fairbanks North Star Borough, are
given in Figure 17. The birth figures reveal a declining
number of births in the years preceding pipeline construction, consistent with national trends. In 1975, however,
there was a 10 percent increase in births. This may be attributed to several factors: increased population, greater
affluence, more marriages, a reactionary movement against
abortion, and higher costs of abortion. The 10 percent increase in births is less than the estimated 25 percent increase in population from 1974 to 1975. This may be explained
by the fact that many of the people migrating to Fairbanks
were unmarried or did not bring spouses with them. In addition, the figures reflect only births to Fairbanks residents and many of the in-migrants may not have considered
themselves as such.

Unlike births, the total number of deaths of Fairbanks
residents remained fairly constant in spite of population
growth (see Figure 17). When deaths are considered by age
group (Figure 18), some patterns begin to emerge in the pipeline construction period. Deaths for persons under the age
of 34 remained fairly constant during the six years from 1970
to 1975. However, for the age group over 65, there was an
abrupt increase in deaths in 1974, followed by a decline in
1975. The increased number of deaths of older persons in
1974 may have been associated with the commencement of pipeline construction; for example, housing pressures may have
forced elderly people into institutions or other housing
situations which they found so depressing that they gave up
the will to live. Conversely, increased mortality in the
over-65 age group may have been due to extraneous factors:
(1) because of Fairbanks' demographic history, an increasing
number of people were attaining the age of 65; (2) because of
the Longevity Bonus, or other factors, fewer Fairbanksans
were leaving the state after they retired; (3) because of a

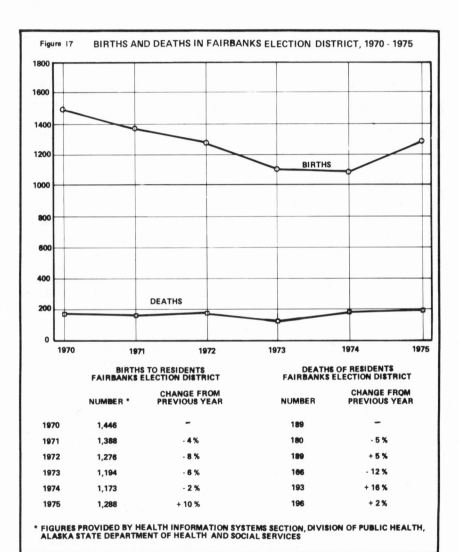

Figure 17   BIRTHS AND DEATHS IN FAIRBANKS ELECTION DISTRICT, 1970 - 1975

	BIRTHS TO RESIDENTS FAIRBANKS ELECTION DISTRICT		DEATHS OF RESIDENTS FAIRBANKS ELECTION DISTRICT	
	NUMBER *	CHANGE FROM PREVIOUS YEAR	NUMBER	CHANGE FROM PREVIOUS YEAR
1970	1,446	—	189	—
1971	1,388	- 4 %	180	- 5 %
1972	1,276	- 8 %	189	+ 5 %
1973	1,194	- 6 %	166	- 12 %
1974	1,173	- 2 %	193	+ 16 %
1975	1,288	+ 10 %	196	+ 2 %

* FIGURES PROVIDED BY HEALTH INFORMATION SYSTEMS SECTION, DIVISION OF PUBLIC HEALTH, ALASKA STATE DEPARTMENT OF HEALTH AND SOCIAL SERVICES

202

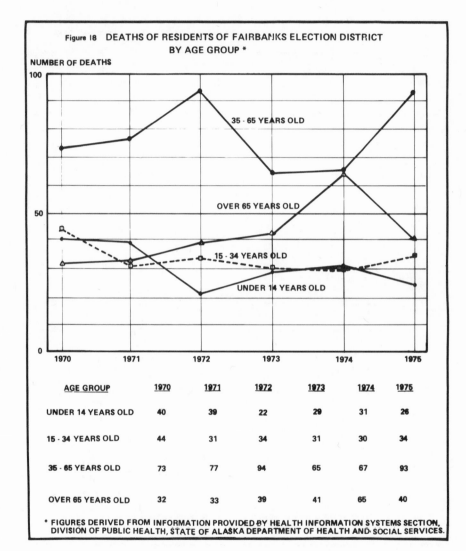

Figure 18 DEATHS OF RESIDENTS OF FAIRBANKS ELECTION DISTRICT BY AGE GROUP *

AGE GROUP	1970	1971	1972	1973	1974	1975
UNDER 14 YEARS OLD	40	39	22	29	31	26
15 - 34 YEARS OLD	44	31	34	31	30	34
35 - 65 YEARS OLD	73	77	94	65	67	93
OVER 65 YEARS OLD	32	33	39	41	65	40

* FIGURES DERIVED FROM INFORMATION PROVIDED BY HEALTH INFORMATION SYSTEMS SECTION, DIVISION OF PUBLIC HEALTH, STATE OF ALASKA DEPARTMENT OF HEALTH AND SOCIAL SERVICES.

greater scope of medical care, more ill people were staying
in the state rather than seeking health care Outside. Of
course, these hypotheses do not explain the decline in deaths
among the elderly in 1975. One possible explanation is out-
migration to places of less costly and less-stressful living
conditions. Another explanation is that 1974 was an excep-
tional year and that during 1975 there was a return to the
norm. None of these hypotheses has been tested.

Among those between the ages of 35 and 65 there was
a significant increase in deaths in 1975. Again, this could
be explained as a variation from or return to a pattern,
given the comparable number of deaths in the non-pipeline
year of 1972. Those seeking a pipeline-related explanation
could postulate greater risks of fatalities from transportation and construction accidents. To test that hypothesis
would require data correlating age with cause of death, data
not readily available.

Marriages and divorces are presented in Table 14. Divorce complaints filed in the Fairbanks Superior Court may
be a more useful mental health indicator than actual divorces
decreed, since a lengthy period of litigation often ensues.
Divorce complaints reflect problems with marriages rather
than the ultimate dissolution. Information presented in
Table 14 suggests that divorces were increasing at a more
rapid rate than marriages, with a significant rise in the
number of divorce complaints filed occurring in 1974 and 1975.
In 1975, however, there was a marked increase in marriages,
possibly associated with greater affluence, population growth,
or a greater number of single or divorced persons available
as marriage partners.

Statistics related to suicide are often misleading.
Because life insurance often does not apply to suicide cases,
and for religious and social reasons, there is a strong moti-
vation to classify suicides as accidental deaths. Furthermore,

Table 14

Marriages, Divorces, and Divorce Complaints, 1967-1975

	Marriages, Fairbanks Election District[φ]		Divorces to Residents of Fairbanks Election District		Divorce Complaints Filed in Fairbanks Superior Court [*]	
	Number[φ]	Percent Change	Number[φ]	Percent Change	Number	Percent Change
1967	424	+10%	--	--	235	--
1968	502	+18%	--	--	262	+11%
1969	527	+ 5%	--	--	300	+15%
1970	545	+ 3%	108	--	351	+17%
1971	522	- 4%	48	-56%	389	+11%
1972	586	+12%	207	+331%	440	+13%
1973	577	- 2%	200	+ 3%	468	+ 6%
1974	618	+ 7%	340	+70%	586	+25%
1975	832	+35%	453	+33%	783	+34%

[*]Marriages and divorce figures were provided by Health Information Systems Section, Division of Public Health, Alaska State Department of Health and Social Services. These numbers represent marriages which occurred in the Fairbanks Election District, but not marriages of residents who were married outside the district. Divorce figures are for residents of Fairbanks Election District.

[φ]Figures derived from dockets of Fairbanks Superior Court; not all complaints filed resulted in divorce, and some divorces were decreed in years following the year in which the complaint was filed.

it is difficult to distinguish suicides from accidents, particularly when there are no witnesses to the event. Rather
than relying on suicude figures *per se*, Robert Kraus and
Patricia Buffler have developed a category of death called
"mortality due to violence," which includes suicides, homicides, accidents, and deaths due to alcohol.[4] In Alaska,
where violence is the leading cause of death, alcohol is a
significant component of most suicides, homicides and accidents. Figure 19 shows deaths in the Fairbanks Census District according to selective causes. Deaths due to violence
may be compared to deaths due to chronic disease. There are
no clear trends, possibly because the numbers are relatively
small. Deaths due to violence increased during the first two
pipeline construction years, but still remained below the
number of such incidents during the more economically depressed years of 1970 and 1971.

After a period of relatively gradual growth from 1970
to 1973, hospital admissions increased by 35 percent in 1974
and another 19 percent in 1975, as indicated in Figure 20.
For the most part, this rise in hospital admissions during
the pipeline period may be attributed to the changes in the
structure of the health care industry in Fairbanks discussed
in Chapter 9. Emergency evacuations from the pipeline construction camps also contributed to a rising hospital census.
Hence, it may be inappropriate to use hospital admissions as
an indicator of changes in community mental health.

Similarly, it is difficult to use ambulance runs as
a mental health indicator for this period. Equipped with
three emergency vehicles, the City of Fairbanks Fire Department provided ambulance service to persons residing within
city limits. While there was a steady growth in the number
of ambulance runs during the pipeline period, much of the
increase might be attributed to the transportation of injured
or ill pipeline workers from the Fairbanks airport to the

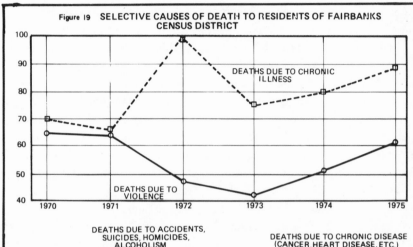

Figure 19   **SELECTIVE CAUSES OF DEATH TO RESIDENTS OF FAIRBANKS CENSUS DISTRICT**

	DEATHS DUE TO ACCIDENTS, SUICIDES, HOMICIDES, ALCOHOLISM		DEATHS DUE TO CHRONIC DISEASE (CANCER, HEART DISEASE, ETC.)	
	NUMBER *	CHANGE	NUMBER *	CHANGE
1970	65	–	70	–
1971	65	0	66	- 6 %
1972	47	- 28 %	98	+ 48 %
1973	42	-11%	76	- 22 %
1974	52	+ 24 %	80	+ 5 %
1975	61	+ 17 %	89	+ 11 %

* FIGURES DERIVED FROM INFORMATION PROVIDED BY HEALTH INFORMATION SYSTEMS SECTION, DIVISION OF PUBLIC HEALTH, ALASKA STATE DEPARTMENT OF HEALTH AND SOCIAL SERVICES

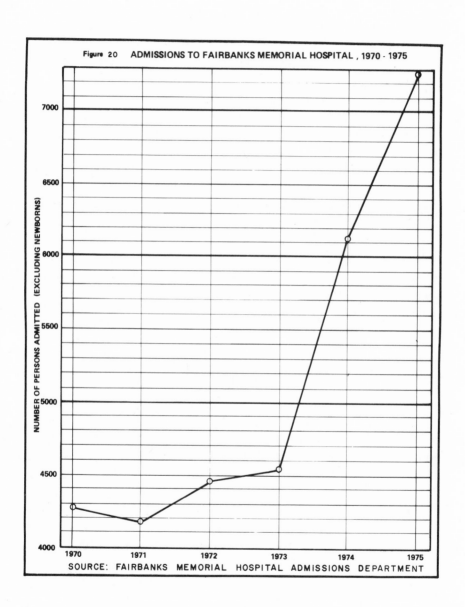

Figure 20   ADMISSIONS TO FAIRBANKS MEMORIAL HOSPITAL , 1970 - 1975

SOURCE: FAIRBANKS MEMORIAL HOSPITAL ADMISSIONS DEPARTMENT

hospital. In the four months from March to June 1975, for
example, 178 of the 908 ambulance runs, or 20 percent, were
for the purposes of transporting pipeline employees. Figure 21 shows the increase in total number of ambulance runs,
ambulance runs for emergencies, and those for life and death
situations. Frequency of overdoses, gunshot wounds, and mental
disturbances are also displayed in the graph. These types of
emergencies related to mental health did not have the marked
growth of the total ambulance service.

Utilization of social services and mental health
facilities has also been suggested as an indicator of changes
in community mental health. As discussed in Chapter 6, there
was a dramatic reduction in the utilization of categorical
assistance and food stamps. The number of public assistance
cases declined by 36 percent from 1972 to 1975 (see Figure 11)
and the number of food stamp cases declined by 90 percent
between 1973 to 1976 (see Figure 10). Distribution according
to race of heads of households remained relatively constant.[5]
The distribution of food stamp recipients by age group indicates a declining percentage of recipients under 25 years old
(33 percent in 1973, 16 percent in 1976) and an increasing
percentage over 60 years old (12 percent in 1973, 25 percent
in 1976).[6] Table 15 gives other indicators of change in food
stamp distribution. In addition to the overall decline in
food stamp recipients, the most significant change since pipeline construction began was a relative increase in new cases
as a percentage of the total number of cases. These figures
suggest that not only were fewer people receiving food stamps,
but there was a greater turnover in food stamp recipients
and they were receiving food stamps for shorter periods of
time. Both the total number of cases and the number of new
cases declined, particularly among young people, suggesting
greater economic well-being and independence.

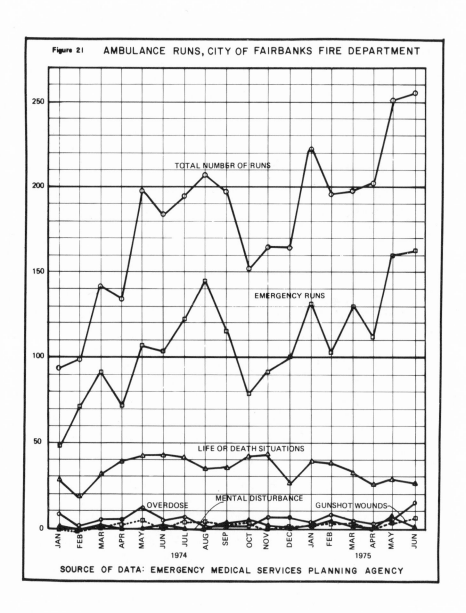

Figure 21   AMBULANCE RUNS, CITY OF FAIRBANKS FIRE DEPARTMENT

TOTAL NUMBER OF RUNS

EMERGENCY RUNS

LIFE OR DEATH SITUATIONS

OVERDOSE   MENTAL DISTURBANCE   GUNSHOT WOUNDS

1974   1975

SOURCE OF DATA: EMERGENCY MEDICAL SERVICES PLANNING AGENCY

Table 15

Indicators of Change in Food Stamp Distribution
in Fairbanks, 1973-75

	1973	1974	1975	Percent Change 1973-1975
Average Number Families Receiving Food Stamps Each Month	792	497	223	-72%
Average Number of New Cases Each Month	70	46	41	-41%
Number of New Food Stamp Cases	845	551	494	-42%
Average Monthly New Cases as a Percent of Total	10%	10%	19%	+90%
Average Monthly Percentage of Continuing Cases	90%	90%	81%	-10%
Average Monthly Government Transfer Payments for Food Stamps	$76,716	$57,320	$28,612	-63%

Source of data: Alaska Department of Health and
Social Services

210

In addition to categorical assistance cases, which
are partially funded by the federal government, the state
provided some types of general assistance. From September 11,
1974, to May 16, 1975, the state spent $12,791.70 in general
assistance funds to send people who were unable to cope with
pipeline impact from Fairbanks to places outside Alaska.[7]
The 62 people who were sent out of state included six mental
patients, one of whom was running from the devil; 20 destitute
men who left their families in another state and came to Fairbanks where they were unsuccessful at finding jobs; several
families with from one to seven children who could not find
or afford housing in Fairbanks; several single people who
did not have adequate skills for coping with the Fairbanks
situation; and two or three people whose lives had been
threatened. According to the social worker who handled general
assistance cases in Fairbanks, "Most of these people have
always had a hard time making a living and coping regardless
of where they were. It will be the same for them in the future,
but to expect them to make it in Boomtown Fairbanks is utterly
unrealistic."[8] Helping these people leave the state seemed
in their best interest, as well as alleviating the need for
the state to continue to provide economic assistance.

Although there may have been a reduced need for economic assistance, it appears that there was an increased need
for counseling services. The Alaska State Mental Health
Clinic located in Fairbanks admitted 40 to 50 percent more
new clients during the pipeline period than before pipeline
construction began (see Figure 22). According to the clinic
staff, the caseload did not represent newcomers to the community. The increased caseload might be attributed to Fairbanksans experiencing stress from changes in the community,
challenged with changing values, or confronting different decisions than they had made before. Stress in the community

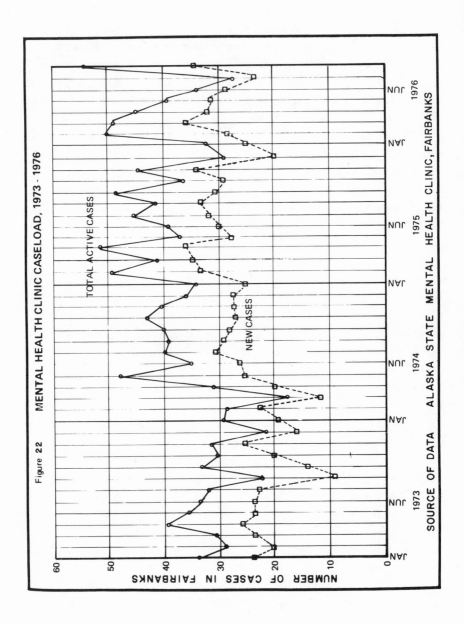

Figure 22   MENTAL HEALTH CLINIC CASELOAD, 1973 - 1976

SOURCE OF DATA   ALASKA STATE MENTAL HEALTH CLINIC, FAIRBANKS

did not manifest itself with any specific symptoms. According
to the clinic director, "We are seeing more of everything
which we saw before."

Fairbanks Crisis Line is an anonymous telephone crisis
intervention, information, and referral service. Crisis calls
increased from 29 percent of all calls in the spring of 1973
to 49 percent of all calls in the spring of 1975. More than
five times as many people called Crisis Line in suicide-
related contacts in spring of 1975 than during the same period
of 1973. During the year from May 1974 to April 1975, 396
of the more than 6,000 calls received by Crisis Line were
related to problems directly caused by pipeline impact, such
as housing, or spouses or parents absent due to pipeline employment. While the changing use of Fairbanks Crisis Line
might have reflected changing mental health needs in Fairbanks,
the increased number of calls might also have been related to
the increased awareness and acceptance of this mental health
facility. The declining percentage of calls from people who
were lonely and wanted to talk with somebody may have resulted
from people being busier and having less time to be lonely.
The director of another counseling center observed that people
had less time to focus on themselves and dwell on their own
problems. At the same time, he noted, people had less time
to spend with each other to "negotiate" relationships.

In addition to providing public assistance, the Alaska
Department of Health and Social Services also provides counseling and other types of social work. At the same time that
pipeline construction commenced, there was an increased awareness of child abuse and child neglect in the Fairbanks community. This resulted in substantially more inquiries about
potential child abuse and neglect cases which required investigation by the Division of Family and Children Services. However, according to the district administrator, there was no
actual increase in numbers of cases. Despite substantial

population increases, child welfare cases remained fairly constant at approximately 140 cases at any given time and child protection cases remained at approximately 40 cases at any given time. Many cases of child abuse or child neglect are never detected or reported to the Division of Family and Children Services, and therefore an increase in this type of problem may not be revealed in caseload figures. Most reported cases involved families previously residing in Alaska, rather than those new to the community. While the numbers of cases remained relatively constant, according to social workers, the types of cases changed somewhat, becoming more severe and complicated. One of the complicating factors was a reduced number of foster homes and other facilities in which to place children in need of protective custody.

Alcohol abuse appears to be a major mental health problem in Fairbanks and an underlying factor in most criminal behavior and family disruption, but there are no available quantitative measurements to monitor it. During the pipeline period Fairbanks did not have a detoxification center and state-funded alcohol rehabilitation programs only served a small portion of the community. Alcoholics Anonymous, the major treatment and maintenance program for alcoholics in Fairbanks, kept no records of its membership or other activities. Before decriminalization of public drunkenness, arrests for drunkenness in Fairbanks were more than seven times the national average for cities of comparable size. During the pipeline construction period it was not a crime to be drunk in public, so changing incidence of public drunkenness is not retrievable from police records. Because medical insurance often does not cover alcohol-related problems, intoxication was rarely recorded in ambulance logs or hospital admission records.

Although it is difficult to assess changes in alcohol abuse, state excise tax records on the wholesale sales of alcoholic beverages do give an indication of changes in amounts and patterns of consumption. Table 16 shows the numbers of gallons of alcoholic beverages sold in the Fourth Juducial District, an area larger than the Fairbanks North Star Borough. The figures suggest that the more economically depressed period of fiscal year 1971-1972 was a peak year in total numbers of gallons of alcoholic beverages sold, rather than during more recent pipeline construction. During fiscal year 1971-1972, beer accounted for the greatest increase in sales of alcoholic beverages. This may have been due to lowering of the drinking age and/or an influx of young people seeking summer employment in Fairbanks. [After pipeline construction commenced, the sales of liquor increased 51 percent. Both liquor and wine sales were greater in fiscal year 1974-1975 than during each of the previous four years.] This may be attributed to greater affluence, an influx of newcomers with different tastes and consumption patterns, or the fact that it was easier and more efficient to "smuggle" liquor than beer into pipeline construction camps which prohibited alcoholic beverages initially. Although Table 16 indicates that there was a definite increase in consumption of alcoholic beverages during the pipeline construction period, it is impossible to determine to what extent this may have been due to population increase, changes in affluence and drinking patterns, or mental health problems.

Criminal activities in Fairbanks were discussed in Chapters 10 and 11. [The rise in crime, particularly among juveniles, may be interpreted as an indicator of changes in community mental health.] However, crime may be both a cause and a symptom of changing community mental health. In a 1975 survey of Fairbanks residents, 47 percent of the households said that they were the victims of some type of crime in the preceding year. [9]

It is difficult to interpret these indicators of

Table 16

Gallons of Alcoholic Beverages Sold in Fairbanks[*]

	FY/1970-71	FY/1971-72	FY/1972-73	FY/1973-74	FY/1974-75
Liquor	166,919	170,391	166,752	154,740	234,272
Wine	103,393	114,127	124,333	117,956	134,777
Beer	1,001,101	2,329,601	1,197,998	1,169,281	1,695,966
TOTAL	1,271,413	2,614,119	1,489,083	1,441,977	2,065,015

[*]Figures, provided by the Alaska Department of Revenue, are for the Fourth Judicial District, an area larger than the Fairbanks North Star Borough.

community mental health both individually and collectively.
There are no reliable population figures with which to compare their fluctuations. We are forced to consider raw data
rather than rates--number of cases per 1,000 population, for
example--and some of the data lack time depth. The unknown
direct effect of population change on mental health indicators
is further complicated by the fact that some fluctuations
may be attributed to changes in the structure of the community, rather than changes in mental health. Moreover, changes
in some of the indicators may be a reflection of national
trends rather than particular to local events. When considering the indicators collectively, one is faced with the problem
of weighting. How does one balance the increase in crime
against the decline in public assistance?

A general review of the various mental health indicators does not suggest a sweeping picture of emotional de-
vastation. Enduring the vicissitudes of pipeline impact was
probably not as traumatic as some of the crises which humans
have survived. Wars, famines, concentration camps, disasters
caused by earthquakes and tidal waves, all suggest levels of
human suffering much greater than that of pipeline impact.
The question here is not how much stress humans are capable
of enduring. Rather, we are faced with the problems of considering how the construction of the trans Alaska oil pipeline affected the quality of life and emotional well-being
of the residents of Fairbanks, and how Fairbanks residents
coped with changes in the community resulting from the construction project.

Construction of the trans Alaska oil pipeline had some
characteristics which may have served as inherent mechanisms
for coping with stress from community change. Because the
project was scheduled for completion in three to four years,
the duration of pipeline impact was well-defined for Fairbanks

residents. They knew that the inconveniences caused by the pipeline were temporary and could feel more hopeful about the future. Furthermore, the pipeline offered a reference point from which one could develop a greater sense of identity. This may have come from new associations, such as being part of the pipeline project or becoming a member of a labor union, or from identifying with one party of a perceived dichotomy-- good guys versus bad guys, residents versus Outsiders.

Characteristics of the community of Fairbanks suggest other types of built-in coping mechanisms. Even before pipeline construction began, a majority of the Fairbanks population was relatively transient. Many people came to Fairbanks from more urbanized areas and may have possessed mechanisms for coping with the conditions which emerged from pipeline impact. While many Fairbanksans may have been displeased about the increased traffic, for example, they might have acquired skills for driving under those or worse conditions Outside before moving to Fairbanks.

Another characteristic of Fairbanks is that the town historically experienced periods of boom and bust. Impacts of massive population in-migration and major construction projects were not new phenomena to Fairbanksans. Most people considered the gold rush a positive era in Fairbanks history and many analogies were made with it during the pipeline period. This helped people view the pipeline project with a sense of history and excitement. A local bank developed an advertising campaign drawing upon this sense of history with the phrase, "Alaska's spirit is high."

Fairbanksans who can't remember or appreciate the gold rush can remember Fairbanks directly before pipeline construction began. And unless they are engaged in reinterpreting history, their memories will recall that prior to the pipeline Fairbanks was plagued with a high cost of living, inadequate telephone service, and electric outages. Because these problems were not entirely new to the pipeline period, people had developed some mechanisms for coping with them. Thus, many changes in the community from pipeline construction were changes of degree rather than kind of problem. The major kinds of new problems facing Fairbanksans were changes in roles and values.

The concept of environment as a determinant of mental health employs not only the factor of stress, but the "balance between stresses and satisfactions."[10] One hypothesis that explains the relative neutrality of mental health indicators despite rapid community change during pipeline construction is that at the same time Fairbanksans experienced stress and displeasure with changes in the community, they also experienced personal satisfaction as a result of better jobs and/ or higher incomes. This satisfaction could be directly related to a feeling of success from rapid career advancement, a sense of pride in assuming greater responsibilities, a greater feeling of self worth from attaining economic independence, or feelings of accomplishment or greater security from having the financial resources to achieve such goals as buying land, building a house, traveling, or paying off debts. While feeling pessimistic about the future of Fairbanks, people could feel optimistic about their personal futures.

To help test this hypothesis, several questions were included in a survey of 408 families in Fairbanks conducted in the spring of 1975 by John A. Kruse of the University of Alaska's Institute of Social and Economic Research. When asked for a general impression of how Fairbanks had changed over the past three years, only 14 percent said the community had changed for the better and 56 percent said it had changed for the worse. People who lived in Fairbanks the longest and people who were not working on the pipeline were more likely to view the community changes as negative.

While Kruse's preliminary results showed a general

dissatisfaction with changes in the community, they also indicated a significant increase in family income. In 1973, 35 percent of the families surveyed were earning less than $12,000 per year, while in 1976 only 9 percent were earning less than $12,000. Families with incomes greater than $40,000 increased from 6 percent of the Fairbanks population in 1973 to 39 percent in 1976. Changes in personal income distribution (Figure 23) suggest dramatic gains during the pipeline period.

One of the survey questions asked for agreement or disagreement with the statement, "The growth of Fairbanks today makes me more optimistic about my personal future, but less optimistic about the community's future." In response, 45 percent agreed, 26 percent disagreed, and 29 percent were neutral. Greater agreement was voiced by blue collar workers and those living in Fairbanks more than 10 years.

In general, preliminary results of the Fairbanks Community Survey seem to support the hypothesis that many Fairbanksans experienced personal satisfactions during the pipeline period at the same time that they experienced disappointment with changes in the community. The survey also explores the extent to which Fairbanksans believed that they had to sacrifice some of their values during the pipeline period. Among the respondents, 52 percent of the pipeline workers and 43 percent of the non-pipeline workers said that they had sacrificed some of their values.

Effects of pipeline construction on community mental health will probably be different in the long run than in the short term. Nevertheless, the immediate situation suggests three types of changes in community mental health:

1. Many people experienced increased personal satisfaction, particularly in relation to better jobs
   and higher income, which may have offset their

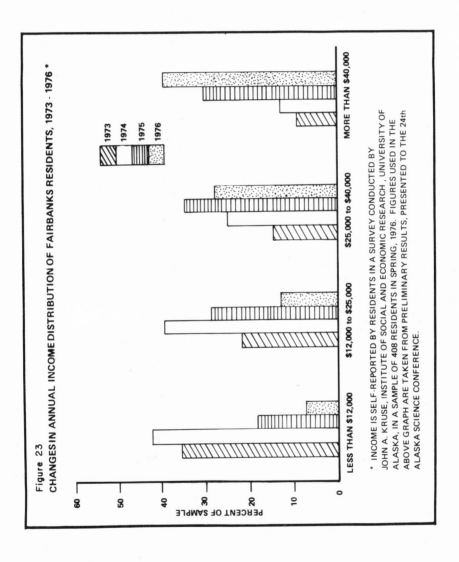

Figure 23
CHANGES IN ANNUAL INCOME DISTRIBUTION OF FAIRBANKS RESIDENTS, 1973 - 1976 *

1973
1974
1975
1976

PERCENT OF SAMPLE

60   50   40   30   20   10   0

LESS THAN $12,000 $12,000 to $25,000 $25,000 to $40,000   MORE THAN $40,000

* INCOME IS SELF-REPORTED BY RESIDENTS IN A SURVEY CONDUCTED BY
JOHN A. KRUSE, INSTITUTE OF SOCIAL AND ECONOMIC RESEARCH, UNIVERSITY OF
ALASKA, IN A SAMPLE OF 408 RESIDENTS IN SPRING, 1976. FIGURES USED IN THE
ABOVE GRAPH ARE TAKEN FROM PRELIMINARY RESULTS, PRESENTED TO THE 24th
ALASKA SCIENCE CONFERENCE.

222

disappointments in perceived negative changes in
the community. This affluence and personal opti-
mism may be reflected by lower rates of public
assistance, more marriages, more births, and relatively fewer deaths due to violence in relation
to population increases.

2. As a result of greater employment opportunities
for women and teenagers, as well as new jobs and
career advancement for men, people established
new roles and new identities in the community and
in their families. At the same time, people were
forced to consider conflicting values between jobs
and families, affluence and change in lifestyle.
The new roles and value conflicts may have contributed to stress within individuals and families.
These types of stress may be reflected by greater
utilization of counseling services, more marital
problems and divorces, and increases in runaways
and juvenile crime.

3. Although most people were able to cope with the
higher cost of living and physical changes in the
community, there were some who were "pushed over
the brink" by those changes. Most of these were
people who had chronic problems of emotional instability. The intensification of their problems
as a result of stress in the community may be reflected by increased number of suicide calls to
Crisis Line, more severe and complex problems
relating to child welfare, and the general relief
caseload increase.

This typology seems to account for the differential trends in
mental health indicators and reflects the perceptions of mental health professionals in Fairbanks.

Mental health is a complex subject. There were some

people who experienced stress during the pipeline period who did not get married or divorced, did not give birth to a child, ride in an ambulance, commit a crime, or visit a social service or mental health agency. Some of these people had real problems, yet were never counted in the statistics. Some were able to cope with their problems, even though they did not receive any satisfactions from the pipeline construction period. These were the people with the most to lose and the least to gain.

Chapter 13
PEOPLE WITH THE MOST TO LOSE
AND THE LEAST TO GAIN

Rapid upward mobility as a result of pipeline construction did not affect people whose employment was not influenced by expansion or high turnover rates or increased income. One such group was the professional staff at the University of Alaska in Fairbanks, whose only pay raises during
the pipeline period were cost of living adjustments. Their
relative incomes declined in relation to people employed in
other types of jobs and other educational institutions, such
as community college and secondary education, in which teachers
were unionized and thus able to negotiate higher wages during
the pipeline period. Despite the relative loss of income
from university employment, many professors had consulting
jobs and more funds for research to study various aspects of
resource development.

People employed in other spheres which were relatively
unaffected by pipeline construction activities had the option
to change employment, an option which many exercised. Sometimes this involved sacrificing values, particularly those
values associated with family, work and leisure time. Those
who were committed to their careers or lifestyles, and did
not want to sacrifice their values, often found themselves
bearing the costs of pipeline impact without receiving the
benefits. This net loss included both relative income and
aspects of lifestyle which were important to them.

The Fairbanks Community Survey conducted by the Institute of Social and Economic Research in the Spring of 1976
asked residents whether they felt they had received the benefits or borne the costs of pipeline construction. Among sample
respondents who had worked on the pipeline, 57 percent said
they had received the benefits, while only 10 percent said

they had borne the costs. The opposite was true of people
who had not worked on the pipeline, of whom 15 percent said
they had received the benefits and 59 percent said they had
borne the costs. Newcomers to Fairbanks were more likely to
have worked on the pipeline, and therefore were more likely
to have received benefits rather than bearing the costs. This
is reflected in the survey finding that 39 percent of the
people who had lived in Fairbanks less than two and a half
years perceived themselves as receiving the benefits of pipeline construction and 35 percent perceived they had borne the
costs. By comparison, 17 percent of the people surveyed who
had lived in Fairbanks more than 10 years said they had received the benefits, and 56 percent said they had borne the
costs.

Most people in Fairbanks had the option to make certain kinds of trade-offs between jobs, income, lifestyle,
amount of time spent with family, and other values. While
every group probably experienced some gains and some losses,
it appears that those with the most to lose and the least to
gain were the very young and the very old. Both were outside
the labor force, and therefore not direct beneficiaries of
changes in the employment situation. Options of the very old
were trade-offs between undesirable alternatives: whether to
pay high rents or move into a home for the aged, whether to
save taxi money by walking or save money on food by eating
starches, and so forth. They also faced the ultimate decision
of whether to stay in Fairbanks and endure a lower quality of
life resulting from higher cost of living and changes in the
community, or to leave what may have been home for the past
quarter of a century. In either case, the trade-offs seemed
to involve primarily losses. The question of trade-offs is a
moot point among the very young, who have no control over decisions which affect their lives.

The Very Young

Most children have very little power in the decision-
making processes which affect their lifestyles and environments. Furthermore, they are rarely polled to find out how
they feel about changes in the family. Thus it is difficult
to reflect a child's point of view of how pipeline construction affected his or her lifestyle. Two conditions which may
have affected the very young were families spending less time
together and more mothers working at gainful employment. [Ac-
cording to the Fairbanks Community Survey, 55 percent of the
families surveyed said that they spent less time together
during the pipeline period, and mothers were working in 52
percent of the families with children under five years old.]

Under these conditions, child care became a major
component in the lifestyle of the very young. In October 1974
there were five licensed day care centers in Fairbanks with a
total capacity to care for 130 children. A sixth licensed
child care center, with a capacity for 34, opened in March 1975.
A year later one of the child care centers serving 48 children
closed, citing as reasons "the salaries we are able to pay our
staff are not competitive in the labor market" and "as we lose
employees we are unable to replace them with the same high
caliber persons that we require."

In addition to licensed child care centers, approximately 30 licensed child care homes, serving approximately
200 children, were operated in Fairbanks during the pipeline
period. An estimated 250 persons provided child care in their
homes without licenses, and a religious school offered a
structured religious education program during the day to between 90 and 130 youngsters.

[Both the quantity and quality of child care during the
pipeline period became problematic in Fairbanks. Women traditionally have been providers of child care. Increased employment opportunities for women during the pipeline period

coupled with a higher cost of living made it economically un-
attractive for women to enter the child care business, particularly when rates charged by babysitters were $1 per child
per hour or less.⌋ Child care professionals in Fairbanks recognized that the demand for services far exceeded the supply.
The combination of child care licensing requirements and a
shortage of low cost rental space in Fairbanks during the pipeline period made it nearly impossible to acquire physical
facilities for additional child care centers. For this reason,
churches became the primary locus of child care centers.
Some churches, however, found that increased costs of maintenance coupled with the increased need for maintenance from
children using their buildings, created real financial problems.

        Not only was there greater need for child care during
the pipeline period, but there was also need for different
types of child care. Local pipeline employees usually worked
10 hours a day, six days a week. None of the licensed child
care centers operated during hours which would enable a parent
working at a local pipeline job to place his or her children
there, and only three licensed child care homes accommodated
children during those hours. Unless a parent desiring pipeline-related work could prevail upon relatives or friends to
care for the children, it was not likely that he or she would
be able to find adequate child care during the long working
hours. Some parents with small children sought child care
provisions which would enable them to work at more remote
pipeline jobs. This situation was typified by the following
advertisement in the Daily Job Demand List issued by the Alaska
State Employment Center, October 3, 1974:

          Live-in Babysitter--care for two children,
          2 and 5 yrs. old, cook, do laundry, take
          over household. Mother is on N. Slope.
          Must be responsible. $300 per month +
          R. & B.

It was probably unreasonable to expect any adult to assume
the responsibilities of caring for two small children and
housekeeping for $300 per month, while their mother was earning
more than 10 times that in pipeline wages.

To determine how persons employed at local pipeline
jobs coped with the child care shortage in Fairbanks, the Impact Information Center surveyed 246 pipeline-related employees
in October 1974.[1] The respondents included 156 men and 92
women, all of whom worked at least 60 hours per week. The
questionnaire elicited information about the care of a total
of 185 children. Very different patterns emerged between
male and female respondents with regard to children and child
care. Most of the men (76 percent) did not have children residing in Alaska, while most of the women (70 percent) did.
Although a greater percentage of female than male employees
had children, the men who did have children had proportion-
ately larger families. Female employees had a greater percentage of pre-school age children than did male employees. In
general, the pipeline-related employees in the sample who had
children had young children. More than 70 percent of the
children of those sampled were less than 10 years old. Although men had larger families, they spent significantly less
money on child care than did women. Whereas a majority of men
had wives as a source of cost-free child care, women had to
depend on more costly methods of child care. For male employees with children, the median amount spent for child care
was less than $9 per week, while the median for female employees
ranged between $40 and $49.

The types of child care utilized by pipeline employees
are shown in Table 17. Because of the long working hours,
many pipeline employees had to place their children in more
than one type of child care setting. More than 39 percent of
the female employees with children reported using a combination
of two or more types of child care. A man with two children,

Table 17

Types of Child Care Utilized by Pipeline Employees in Fairbanks

Type Child Care Utilized	Female Respondents		Male Respondents		Total	
	Number	Percent	Number	Percent	Number	Percent
Spouse	13	20.3%	33	89.2%	46	45.5%
Relative	11	17.2%	0	0 %	11	10.9%
Friend	8	12.5%	0	0 %	8	7.9%
Day Care Center	0	0 %	1	2.7%	1	1.0%
Nursery School	8	12.5%	4	10.8%	12	11.9%
Sitter in Her Home	33	51.6%	6	16.2%	39	38.6%
Sitter in Your Home	8	12.5%	1	2.7%	9	8.9%
Care for Selves	15	23.4%	2	5.4%	17	16.8%
Other	2	3.1%	0	0 %	2	2.0%
Combination	25	39.1%	4	10.8%	29	28.7%

Note: Every type of care mentioned was tabulated. Percentages are based upon number of respondents with children (64 females and 37 males). Percentages do not total 100% because some of the respondents used combinations of two or more types of child care.

ages 4 and 6, described some of the problems with using more
than one type of child care:

> We presently make up to four special trips per
> day to transport children to and from school.
> Children attend two schools at two different
> times--no bus transportation.

And a woman with two children expressed displeasure with her
child care arrangements:

> I have two babysitters which is very incon-
> venient. My 6-year-old has to stay with the
> landlord so he can ride the bus to school.
> Then my 6-month-old stays with my friend,
> but she watches too many other children.

A number of pipeline employees did not hire people to
care for their children. A total of 42 children were left at
home to care for themselves (see Table 18). In many cases,
an older child in the family took care of the younger children.
But the sample included three children between the ages of 6
and 10, and 16 children between the ages of 11 and 15, who
were unsupervised during non-school hours while their parents
were working. One parent expressed concern about her 12-year-
old daughter who was left at home alone, particularly since

Table 18

Ages of Children Who Care for Themselves,
According to Sample of Fairbanks Pipeline Employees

Age	Number of Children	Cases with Older Children in Family	Number of Unsupervised Children
0-5 years old	1	1	0
6-10 years old	8	5	3
11-15 years old	24	8	16
16-20 years old	9	-	-
TOTAL	42	14	19

she was unable to obtain a telephone and therefore could not check on her daughter or have her daughter call when problems arose.

Some parents expressed concern that their children were being cared for in situations which did not give them adequate personal attention and deprived them of associations with other children their age or the opportunity for educational growth.

A woman who paid a babysitter $43 per week to care for her 4-year-old child in the babysitter's home complained:

> Prior to moving to Alaska, our son attended pre-school. I felt he had an opportunity to advance and learn much more with planned programs and schedules. Upon inquiring into the nursery or day care facilities in Fairbanks, I found that they are only open five days per week, and usually only 7:00 a.m. until 6:00 p.m., not allowing any time for leaving the children before working hours, or even enough time to allow for driving time to work. Thus, we had to settle for a private babysitter, which, although she takes good care of him, does not provide the educational background that a good day care center or nursery school can provide.

A woman with a 6-year-old child who must walk six blocks to school wrote:

> I am very displeased at having to trust someone else to get my first-grade son to school in the mornings and back in the afternoons. He sometimes is not properly dressed, misplaces his money and is late for school.

Other parents working at local pipeline jobs said they were worried that their children were not being fed well enough.

Working parents who placed their children in child care settings which they considered to be inadequate or unsatisfactory usually experienced some type of internal value conflict. Sometimes they justified their decisions on the grounds that they tried unsuccessfully to find alternative

child care arrangements. In a sense, this places the blame
on the community for not providing viable alternatives. Other
parents were convinced that their 11- or 12-year-old was exceptionally mature, and therefore capable of taking care of
himself. While they may have felt that the child care arrangements were not ideal, most parents did not believe that they
were really neglecting their children.

　　　Although parents were able to rationalize their decisions about child care, it remains to be seen how children
coped. When a parent had to take a child to several babysitters each day and sometimes change babysitters every month,
what effect did this succession of people and environments
have on the child? When a child was placed in an unlicensed
home in which a babysitter was trying to care for too many
children and they had to compete for her attention, what effect did this have on a child? When a parent was working 60
hours a week and came home exhausted and preoccupied, what
effect did this have on a child? There are no data with which
to answer these questions, but the questions themselves suggest the potential for the very young to bear many of the costs
and few of the benefits of the pipeline construction period.

The Very Old

　　　Fairbanks is a city of young people--the average age
of residents of the Fairbanks North Star Borough in 1970 was
22 years, according to the U.S. Census. Fairbanks is also the
home of many older persons, however. The 1970 Census showed
886 persons over the age of 62 living in the Fairbanks North
Star Borough, 544 of them in the City of Fairbanks. Fairbanks
was the home of many of these older citizens for a quarter of
a century or more.

　　　For the most part, age means experience, and with it
comes perspective:

　　　　　　I do not feel that problems in the
　　　　　Fairbanks area are basically related to

the pipeline impact, but have existed previously to a substantial degree. Ice fog
in the winter, dust pollution in the summer
have been increasing for some years as
vehicular traffic and population expansion
accelerated in this area. Telephone service
has always been erratic and lagging behind
subscriber demand for installation. Narrow
streets in the core area have been with us
since the town was founded, and traffic
congestion has occurred periodically during
the times of transient influx a number of
times--such as during the construction of
Ladd (Wainwright) Field and Eielson, during
World War II, and the Russian plane ferrying
program, etc. Between these periods, there
was the seasonal impact of workers for the
F.E. gold dredges with resultant dislocations
of rents, services and transportation facilities.

Food prices have been high, but the wage
scale locally has taken that into account in
the main. Comparison shopping in the Seattle
area (itself a high cost area) usually shows
that except for fresh fruits and vegetables,
prices in Fairbanks compare favorably if
transportation charges are included. Variety
of selection is more limited here, but that
gap is closing from year to year as more chain
stores, markets, and specialty shops open up.
Rental housing has been the most expensive
item comparatively speaking, due part ' to the
climatic demands, and partly to the boom-and-
bust nature of the Fairbanks economy. The
high price of gas and oil is a national and
international problem, so Fairbanks is not
unique in that. High land prices are not
unique to here either and in any event, should
lead to increased borough revenue in the future,
as property tax assessments rise.[2]

Perspective does not always cast the current situation into a
positive light:

Being an old-timer from Territorial days,
I resent the influx of rabble looking for the
"easy buck" and caring little for our traditions.
Increase with that type is not progress. The
pipeline construction brings decay not only to
our "way of life" but also to the ecology of

234

the land. The men coming for gold after '98
were a different type. They came for adventure,
and "to seek a newer world" and build a "brotherhood of man." Now, most of the newcomers seek
money and will leave after making it.[3]

In addition to perspectives from experience, age sometimes brings a sense of powerlessness resulting from poor
health, or an inability to accomplish objectives with the ease
of youth, or from the way a nation or culture regards its
elderly. It was difficult to distinguish the problems of
aging from problems due to changes in the community in response to the pipeline.

These things did not happen as a result of
changes in the community. It is because I am
a semi-invalid and 66 years old and cannot
earn a living on my own power.[4]

Powerlessness sometimes induces a person to accept blame for
problems which were perhaps unavoidable. One elderly man attributed his problems to inflation, rather than impact, without seeing the relationship between the two. Many elderly
suffered the effects of pipeline construction without recognizing that as cause for their problems. Still others acknowledged changes in the community which affected their lifestyles
and attributed those changes to pipeline construction.

We own our trailer, have flowers and a
little garden now. Our trailer is a 12 x 45 and
all larger trailers are to be moved to make room
for the new Pipeline people to put in their
travelling trailers. It is very hard on us
older people to have to move for non-Alaska
people. Their big wages and money always help
to get what they want. I do not think the
pipeline people should be allowed to take over
here from us poorer people.[5]

A number of Senior Citizens had a long list of grievances related to pipeline impact:

It is getting increasingly dangerous for

older people on the city streets at night.
Medical expenses have increased, also lab
fees and medical clinic service charges.
I get medicine out of town; it's too expensive here. Long lines at banks and much more
open drunks in the Northward Building which
can't be locked. The security problem is
bad. Police department ought to be enlarged
and more street patrols on foot. Traffic is
much worse. We need buses for around town
and nearby area. If it wasn't for the Senior
Citizen transportation I couldn't do my
shopping, can't afford taxis. . . .Food
prices are terrible.[6]

Problems created by pipeline construction which most affected
the elderly were inflation, housing, transportation, medical
care, safety and security. While these types of problems affected most Fairbanksans, the elderly were less able to cope
with them for a number of reasons.

As a group, the elderly had incomes substantially less
than the Fairbanks population as a whole. Their primary source
of income was Social Security, a federal program which makes
no adjustments for regional differences in cost of living.
Social Security payments in 1975 ranged from $93 to $340 per
month. The maximum payment of $340 per month applied to per-
sons who earned more than $14,000 per year during the time
that they were making contributions to Social Security. Persons who received Social Security benefits were not permitted
to increase their incomes substantially through employment.
If a person's total yearly earnings exceeded $2,520, the Social
Security Administration held back $1 in Social Security for
every $2 earned for each month in which the recipient earned
more than $210.

Older persons could supplement their Social Security
income through another federal program known as Supplemental
Security Income (SSI). To qualify for this program, a person
had to have less than $1,500 in total resources. The maximum
SSI payments in 1975 were $146 per month, but any amount of

unearned income above $60 per month and half of earned income above $60 per month was deducted from SSI payments. The State of Alaska also provided some public assistance to the aged, but it only supplemented incomes to a level of $250 per month for persons renting or owning their own housing, or $185 per month for persons living with other persons, such as their children.

Unless older retired persons had substantial investments or pension benefits, they probably had monthly incomes less then $300. A survey of Senior Citizens conducted in Fairbanks in March 1975[7] indicated that 31 percent of the respondents had monthly incomes less than $300 (see Table 19). In 1973, every person over age 65 who had been a resident of Alaska for 25 years became eligible for Longevity Bonus, a program to encourage older people to remain in the state. A total of 468 persons residing in the Fairbanks area received $100 per month Longevity Bonus in 1975, an increment which, in some cases, made the difference between "surviving and living," as one administrator stated. Starting December 18, 1971, some Alaskans became eligible for Alaska Native Claims payments. For Fairbanksans, this meant $500 per year for persons who were enrolled in Doyon, Ltd., the Native regional corporation, but not village corporations; and $100 per year for persons who were enrolled in both Doyon and village corporations. Neither Longevity Bonus nor Alaska Native Claims payments were taxable nor deducted from Social Security, SSI, or state public assistance payments. These two programs probably helped push many of the Fairbanks elderly into the monthly income category of $301 to $500. According to the survey of Senior Citizens in 1975, 22 percent had monthly incomes of $301 to $500. The distribution of sources of income by respondents' income levels is shown in Table 20.

While the pipeline employers did not discriminate on the basis of age and some people over 64 years old worked at

Table 19

Distribution of Income of Fairbanks Senior Citizens
Surveyed by the Impact Information Center in 1975

Monthly Income	Yearly Income	Number Respondents	Percentage Respondents	Cumulative Percentage of Respondents
Under $300	Under $3,600	54	31.0%	31.0%
$301 - 500	$3,612-6,000	39	22.4%	53.4%
$501 - 700	$6,012-8,400	22	12.6%	66.0%
$701 - 900	$8,412-10,800	11	6.3%	72.3%
$901 -1100	$10,812-13,200	15	8.6%	80.9%
More than $1100	More than $13,200	8	4.6%	85.5%
No information	No information	25	14.4%	99.9%
		174	99.9%	

Table 20

Distribution of Monthly Income by Source for Fairbanks Senior Citizens
Surveyed by the Impact Information Center in 1975

Source of Income	Total Sample*		Total Monthly Income										
			Under $300		$300-500		$500-700		$700-900		$900-1100		More
Social Security	141	81%	51	94%	36	92%	14	64%	9	82%	7	47%	5	63%
Longevity Bonus	81	47%	18	33%	24	62%	10	45%	7	64%	6	40%	0	25%
Pension	66	38%	3	6%	19	49%	12	55%	9	82%	8	53%	6	75%
Welfare Assistance	33	19%	22	41%	7	18%	1	5%	0	–	0	–	0	–
Private Savings & Investments	32	18%	3	6%	6	15%	9	41%	2	18%	3	20%	1	13%
Employment	29	17%	4	7%	5	13%	4	18%	3	27%	8	53%	2	25%
Land Claims Payments	17	10%	8	15%	7	18%	0	–	0	–	0	–	0	–
Food Stamps	10	6%	9	17%	1	3%	0	–	0	–	0	–	0	–
Money from Children	4	2%	0	–	2	5%	0	–	1	9%	0	–	0	–
Insurance	3	2%	0	–	2	5%	0	–	1	9%	0	–	0	–

*Total includes 25 respondents for whom the amount of income was not reported.

pipeline jobs, most older people could not take advantage of this type of employment for health or other reasons. Cost of living adjustments in other sources of income were based upon national rates of inflation and did not keep pace with the cost of living in Fairbanks or the upward shift in income for most Fairbanks residents. While the Fairbanks Community Survey revealed that 14 percent of the population earned less than $12,000 and 85 percent earned more in 1975, the survey of Senior Citizens showed 72 percent receiving annual incomes under $10,800 and only 13 percent above.

Both as a result of lower than average incomes and incomes fixed in relation to pipeline inflation, many elderly people experienced changes in their lifestyles during this period. Table 21 lists some of the lifestyle changes reported by Senior Citizens surveyed in 1975, the two most frequent being staying home more and spending less on recreation. These may have had ramifications for mental health.

> It is quite difficult to sit home all the time, so I take my car, all of which is paid for, and go visit other friends of which I have known and worked with in all the years I have lived up here. And that takes some of my pension checks for gas, oil and upkeep. In this way I try to control my illness and visits to doctors which are exceedingly high (expensive). . . . [9]

Other lifestyle changes common to Senior Citizens were buying less clothing and walking rather than taking taxis. Nearly 30 percent said that they were buying less food and different types of food than they did before pipeline construction began. Particularly for older persons, this may have affected nutrition and health.

Besides making changes in their lifestyles, older people developed other strategies for coping with the higher cost of living during pipeline construction. Some persons delayed retirement.

Table 21

Changes in Lifestyle Reported by Senior Citizens
Surveyed by Impact Information Center in 1975

Lifestyle Changes in Last Year	Total Sample*		Reported Monthly Income							
			Under $300		$300-700		$700-1100		Over $1100	
Change in Lifestyle	65	37.3%	19	35.2%	22	36.0%	12	46.2%	3	37.5%
No Change in Lifestyle	73	41.9%	20	37.0%	25	41.0%	13	50.0%	5	62.5%
No Answer	36	20.7%	15	27.8%	14	23.0%	1	3.8%	0	–
Total	174		54		61		26		8	
Type Changes										
Staying Home More	65	37.4%	20	37.0%	27	44.3%	5	83.3%	2	25.0%
Spending Less on Recreation	62	35.6%	19	35.2%	27	44.3%	8	30.8%	2	25.0%
Buying Less Clothes	54	31.0%	22	40.7%	20	32.8%	6	23.1%	2	25.0%
Buying Less Food	52	29.9%	16	29.6%	23	37.7%	6	23.1%	2	25.0%
Buying Different Kinds of Food	51	29.3%	16	29.6%	22	36.0%	7	26.9%	1	12.5%
Walking Rather than Cab	34	19.5%	10	24.6%	15	24.6%	5	83.3%	2	25.0%
Making Fewer Visits to Doctor	28	16.1%	9	16.7%	13	21.3%	2	7.7%	0	–
Senior Citizens Lunch Program	25	14.4%	9	16.7%	10	16.3%	1	3.8%	2	25.0%
Senior Citizen Transportation	24	13.8%	11	20.4%	7	11.5%	0	–	2	25.0%
Moves to Less Expensive Housing	10	5.7%	5	9.3%	4	6.6%	0	–	0	–
Sold Home	6	3.4%	0	–	3	4.9%	1	3.8%	0	–
More People Living in Household	6	3.4%	3	5.6%	1	1.6%	2	7.7%	0	–
Total (used in figuring percentages)	174		54		61		26		8	

*Total includes 25 respondents for whom no income information was provided.

I am still working, but I hope to
retire in June 1975, but I do know high cost
of living hurts very much. Very much.[10]

One man stated that he simply couldn't afford to retire, and
others were forced out of retirement.

Came here with retired husband to live
out our lives. Both have been forced to
return to work as his pension will not even
pay rent.[11]

The pipeline not only created a higher cost of living, but it
also created jobs for the elderly.

I went back to work as a full charge
bookkeeper so we could still get by on our
own. Thanks to my working for a sub-con-
tractor on pipeline camp jobs, we are doing
okay at present. Before that we were not
able to get by on Social Security and Alaska
bonus as our only income.[12]

By going to work, however, Senior Citizens who earned more
than $2,520 in a year lost their Social Security payments for
that year.

Another strategy employed by the elderly was to sell
their possessions to make ends meet. "Sold my jewelry," reported one older woman.[13] Another stated that she had sold
nearly everything of value which she owned:

Have had to sell many household items,
antiques, misc. Desparately hunting for
heated one bedroom house or apartment un-
furnished. Sold my home.[14]

Others reported trying to cope with inflation by reducing fuel
bills or in other ways managing their affairs more efficiently.

Problems with housing were closely related to problems
with inflation. Survey results indicated that half of the
Senior Citizens in Fairbanks owned their own homes (see
Table 22). While this helped them avoid the rental housing
crisis, home ownership was not without expenses.

Table 22

Place and Type of Residence Reported by Senior Citizens
Surveyed by Impact Information Center in 1975

Location of Residence	Total Sample*		Reported Monthly Income							
			Under $300		$300-700		$700-1100		Over $1100	
City of Fairbanks	140	80.5%	47	27.0%	41	67.2%	23	88.5%	7	88.0%
Fairbanks North Star Borough	31	17.8%	7	13.0%	17	27.9%	3	11.5%	1	12.0%
Outside Borough	2	1.1%	0	–	2	3.3%	0	–	0	–
Total φ(used in figuring percentages)	174		54		61		26		8	
Type Residence										
Home-Owned	88	50.6%	20	37.0%	32	52.0%	19	73.0%	4	50.0%
Private Rental Unit	40	23.0%	12	22.0%	14	23.0%	5	19.0%	4	50.0%
Government Subsidized Rental Unit	22	12.0%	12	22.0%	6	10.0%	1	4.0%	0	–
Health Facility	8	5.0%	6	11.0%	1	1.6%	0	–	0	–
Live with Children	7	4.0%	4	7.0%	2	3.0%	0	–	0	–
Other	12	7.0%	2	4.0%	6	10.0%	3	12.0%	0	–
Total λ(used in figuring percentages)	174		54		61		26		8	

*Total sample includes 25 respondents for whom income information was not given.

φTotals of locations of residence may be less than sample size used in percentages because one respondent did not provide information on place of residence.

λTotals for type of residence may exceed sample size because some respondents indicated two responses, eg. live with children in a private rental unit.

242

> I paid $113.93 for repair on furnace;
> $37.00 for repair on water heater. My home
> needs repairs--new roof--chimney repair--
> roof leaks and siding is old and water runs
> down the walls--how can I get help to do
> this repair?[15]

Home ownership also required activities, such as shovelling
snow from the roof and drive, which some of the elderly persons were unable to do. Because of changes in the employment
situation and values in the community during the pipeline construction period, it was difficult for older persons to find
youngsters or others to help with these tasks.

Anticipating rapid increases in property tax assessments in the pipeline construction period, in 1973 the legislature initiated a program exempting persons over 65 from
paying local property tax and reimbursing municipalities for
lost revenues.[16] While this relieved financial pressures on
many elderly persons, retired persons under 65 were still con-
fronted with escalating taxes.

> My greatest concern at the moment is
> receiving my tax assessment notice and finding
> the valuation of my property and home has gone
> up $41,000 in one year's time. I realize I am
> living in a business zone but have been for a
> good many years, and to have that tax at the
> mill rate which I am sure will not be less
> than last year is hard to face in lieu of the
> fact that I am living on a fixed income.[17]

Older residents' homes were more likely to be near the center
of town, where land use and property values changed most
rapidly during pipeline construction.

There were two types of rental situations for Senior
Citizens who did not own their homes: private rental units
and government subsidized rental units. The latter have fed-
erally regulated rent structures and income requirements
which tend to select for low income persons. Although many
elderly Fairbanksans qualified for subsidized housing, only

26 such units were designated for persons or families in which the heads of households were older than 65 or disabled. The turnover rate in these units was extremely low; vacancies rarely occurred unless someone died. While there was a high demand for subsidized housing units among the elderly, persons occupying them were not always entirely pleased with their housing arrangements because of rules, regulations, and neighbors.

Subsidized housing presented a trade-off of freedom for security. Persons who rented private housing often found themselves having to contend with rent increases they could not afford. According to the 1975 survey, 25 of the 40 Senior Citizens renting private housing experienced rent increases ranging from $2 to $460 during the pipeline period, with a modal increase of $25. Like others in Fairbanks, the choice of rental housing was limited for Senior Citizens. Unlike other residents, most of the elderly did not have many options for raising their incomes when their rents were raised.

To stay within their budgets, older persons often rented substandard housing. This not only presented potential safety hazards, such as fires, but also made them more vulnerable to the housing shortage and land use and zoning changes accompanying increased demands for space in the city. After a residential hotel burned in 1972, several of the rooming houses in which oldtimers lived were condemned. Some had lived in these at reduced rates for 15 years or more. At that time a campaign was begun to build additional Senior Citizen housing in Fairbanks. A group of energetic Senior Citizens envisioned a 96-unit high-rise apartment, which they called "Golden Towers," and campaigned for financial assistance from state and federal housing programs. They hoped that the housing would be ready before pipeline construction to alleviate housing pressures on the elderly. For the next four years, a series of bureaucratic delays caused the estimated cost of the proposed housing to escalate. As cost estimates increased, the scope of the project diminished until it no longer resembled the originators' vision. Not until 1976, the third year of pipeline construction, was construction of the Senior Citizen housing begun using modular, prefabricated units which initially left many of the Senior Citizens cold and disillusioned.

Transportation was another problem facing Senior Citizens during this period. Driving became more costly, not only for fuel, maintenance, insurance and repairs, but also for associated costs such as parking. Taxis became more difficult to obtain, as well as more costly. Both driving and walking became more hazardous as the traffic volume increased. A special transportation program for Senior Citizens in Fairbanks was established by the North Star Council on Aging. This helped to meet many of the older persons' needs, but it was not a total solution to their problems. The service operated on a restricted schedule with no regular service on weekends or in the evenings. At noontime the system transported persons to the Senior Citizens' lunch program and was therefore not available for other purposes. The transportation program was a "dial-a-ride" type, making it less accessible to persons without telephones.

Aging brings health problems. While pipeline construction cannot be held directly responsible for increasing the health care needs of older persons, it did impinge upon solutions to those needs. Public and private insurance programs fell behind rising health care costs. Like others in Fairbanks, older people had to wait longer to see dentists and sometimes doctors.

Senior Citizens also expressed concern about their safety and security during the pipeline period. Many of the older people lived near the downtown area where criminal activity was most apparent. "Pipeline impact on Fairbanks," said one, "makes the people here less trusting."[18] Another stated

simply, "I feel less safe living alone."[19] The rapidly
changing nature of the community and the new faces also disturbed older persons' sense of security. As one oldtimer
put it, "You can't drive your dogsled to the Post Office any-
more."

Like any other gorup in the community, Senior Citizens
were diverse persons with varying lifestyles, personalities,
and political affinities. Special impact problems for Senior
Citizens were often not distinguishable from problems of the
community as a whole or from general problems of aging. Construction of the trans Alaska oil pipeline created problems
for Fairbanksans which were often felt most severely by the
elderly simply because their alternatives for problem-solving
were most limited by age, health and income. Older persons
with incomes less than $300 per month were unable to compete
for limited local resources with persons earning three or
four times as much on pipeline jobs.

Many older persons in Fairbanks had been citizens of
the community for a long time. Fairbanks is where they built
their homes, raised their children, made their lifelong friends.
Fairbanks was more than a place to earn an income, particularly
since most of the elderly were no longer earning incomes. The
ties that bind people to a community are the sum of experiences
and memories, joys and sorrows, struggles and rewards. Fairbanks is a difficult place to live in many ways, and those who
have lived here the longest have experienced most fully those
difficulties. Because they made these types of emotional investments, they had the most to lose. And as the community
changed, as the relative standard of living for the elderly declined, as others reaped the benefits of employment while the
elderly were no longer in their working prime, these were the
people with the least to gain from construction of the trans
Alaska oil pipeline.

> We will probably sell out in a year or two
> and move back South, but we prefer Alaska. After
> quarter of a century, this is "home" to us.[20]

Photo by Paul Helmar

Figure 24. BOOM/BUST CYCLE REPEATING ITSELF? The trans Alaska pipeline
winds through a valley of mining tailings left by the historic gold
dredge in the foreground. The pipeline descends Fox hill north of
Fairbanks, then emerges from the ground to carry the oil east atop
vertical support members.

Photo by Paul Helmar

Figure 25. OIL COMES THROUGH FAIRBANKS. The trans Alaska oil pipeline
snakes through the woods of the Fairbanks North Star Borough.

Photo by Paul Helmar

Figure 26. ALYESKA PIPELINE SERVICE COMPANY HEADQUARTERS ON FORT WAINWRIGHT. Existing buildings on the army base in Fairbanks were utilized for administrative offices, as an orientation and transfer center for workers en route to construction camps, and as lodging for some of the pipeline workers assigned to the Fairbanks area.

Photo from *Pipeline Impact Collection, Alaska Historical Library*

Figure 27.   DAILY UNION CALL.   Job seekers at the Laborer's Hall wait for their numbers to be called.

251

Photo by Paul Helmar

Figure 28. OUTSIDERS. A group of newly-arrived members of a Boston local of the International Brotherhood of Electrical Workers pose on the steps of the union hall in Fairbanks.

Figure 29. UNCONVENTIONAL HOUSING. Three examples of unconventional housing utilized in Fairbanks during the pipeline construction period: a rooming house in which a job seeker from Phoenix and six others each pay $40 per week to share this basement (upper left); a house in the city which does not meet building codes (upper right); a mobile home park in Fairbanks where by 1976 nearly a quarter of the housing consisted of mobile homes (lower photo).

Photo by Paul Helmar

Figure 30. TEENAGERS AT WORK. A seventeen-year-old teaches a fourteen-year-old how to operate machinery at a commercial printing company in Fairbanks.

Figure 31. FLAUNTING IT!

Figure 32. SECOND AVENUE. The two-block stretch of Second Avenue pictured here became a symbol of prostitution, vice, street crime, and racial conflict associated with the pipeline boom.

Photo by Paul Helmar

Figure 33. OLD GIVES WAY TO NEW. Growth during the period of pipeline construction brought about changes in land use, including an expansion of the commercial areas of downtown Fairbanks at the expense of older residential areas.

Photo by Paul Helmar

Figure 34. FAIRBANKS SKYLINE. Just before an August rain in 1976, this photograph was taken from the top of the Chena View Hotel looking east at downtown Fairbanks with the Cushman Street bridge crossing the Chena River at First Avenue.

Chapter 14
REVIEWING ASSUMPTIONS:
A MODEL FOR PLANNERS

Making assumptions is a tricky business, a little
like fortune-telling. Many people are unwilling to risk their
reputations on their abilities to foretell the future and so
they hire others to be their soothsayers. Decision-makers
can ask for advice and then use the advisor as a scapegoat if
the wrong decision is made. Perhaps this is why consultants
and planners are able to stay in business. Success in the
business of foretelling the future is not dependent upon
having a good track record, for nobody seems to keep score.
It is more a matter of supply and demand. Particularly with
the advent and refinement of the National Environmental Policy
Act of 1969 (NEPA), there has been a growing demand for "experts" to provide decision-makers with visions of the future.
This exercise, usually called "impact assessment," has generated a multitude of voluminous environmental impact statements and planning documents. After the future becomes the
past, few of the documents are examined to evaluate the accu-
racy of the predictions they contain and the processes by
which those predictions were made.

Before construction of the trans Alaska oil pipeline
began, there were some attempts to anticipate the social and
economic impacts of the project on Fairbanks and Alaska. In
compliance with NEPA, the Department of the Interior prepared
an environmental impact statement (EIS) which briefly considered impacts of the proposed pipeline on the economy, population, and Native groups of Fairbanks and the State of Alaska.
To aid the Department of the Interior in preparing its EIS,
the oil companies applying for the right-of-way permit were
required to submit as part of their application information
projecting the socioeconomic impacts of the proposed pipeline.

In turn, Alyeska Pipeline Service Company hired a private
consulting firm to study the problem and make the necessary
projections. Acknowledging that "Even at their best, economic models of sparsely populated regions are not very precise
tools; and sociological models are almost nonexistent," the
consulting firm had to develop its predictions based upon a
variety of assumptions. [1]

Predictions and projections about pipeline impact were
made by others, not so much to comply with laws and regulations as to plan for the future. The state legislature and
administration needed to develop fiscal policy and programs
based upon resources and needs created by pipeline development. Local governments were faced with immediate planning
problems, fiscal policy decisions, development of programs,
and application for impact funds, all of which required predicting impacts of pipeline construction on the local community.
Even private citizens living in Fairbanks had to predict impacts of the pipeline as a prelude to their decision-making
with regard to conducting business, making investments,
changing jobs, and otherwise anticipating needs. At all levels, the process of predicting the impact of pipeline construction required making assumptions or hiring somebody else
to make them.

A review of the documents generated with regard to
predicting the socioeconomic impacts of the trans Alaska oil
pipeline suggests that five basic approaches were used to make
assumptions. The most common approach was to use assumptions
which had already been developed by someone else, particularly
if they were published and/or subjected to review processes
of any kind. This approach has three merits: (1) responsibility for the assumption rests with another party, the orig-
inator of the assumption and/or the reviewing body; (2) it is
quick; and (3) it is cheap. The major problem with this approach, as everybody who regularly reviews published

literature will attest, is that while publication may legiti-
mize a point of view, it does not necessarily validate it.

Using assumptions developed by others usually means
relying on information generated by the industry causing the
anticipated impacts. In the case of the trans Alaska oil
pipeline, federal,[2] state,[3] and local governments[4] all assumed that figures generated by the oil companies were correct.
In the government planning process, critical assumptions were
made using the workforce, timing and cost estimates prepared
by Alyeska Pipeline Service Company. In retrospect, it is
obvious that the industry grossly underestimated all three
critical factors in this case.

The second most common approach to making assumptions
was to draw upon history. In predicting social and economic
impacts of the trans Alaska oil pipeline on Fairbanks, assumptions were based upon three types of historical examples.
Most frequently, the history of the local situation was used,
including both the boom/bust cycle which has characterized
Fairbanks since gold rush days and more recent history. The
use of recent history was explained by one consulting firm
in the introduction to its study ". . . .both in the economic
and social projections, the critical assumption was made that
the underlying determinants of people's behavior will continue
to be what they were in the past."[5]

In addition to utilizing local history, analogies
were often made to the history of other areas in which similar
developments occurred. At the time that the trans Alaska oil
pipeline proposal was being considered, the only other significant oil development which had taken place in Alaska was
that on the Kenai Peninsula. Experiences of oil impact on
the Kenai Peninsula became the basis for some assumptions
about potential impact on Fairbanks. The following example
was first used by a consulting firm hired by Alyeska, and

referenced in nearly every succeeding impact assessment:

> A factor which is likely to be signifi-
> cant will be an increase in the so-called
> victimless crimes, i.e., crimes in which the
> victim is seeking the demise to which he comes.
> Examples are prostitution, gambling, confidence
> games, and other schemes whereby the victim
> loses his property and sometimes his life.
> In both the Kenai oil development and other
> earlier "boom" experiences in Alaska, these
> kinds of crimes increased locally. In the
> Kenai case, however, the increase was predomi-
> nantly in Anchorage, the nearest community to
> which oil workers could go for rest and
> relaxation. It may be presumed that a similar
> series of events will take place during the
> employment boom of the construction period.
> Logical targets for this type of activity in-
> clude the corridor between Fairbanks and Valdez.[6]

Another use of history in the development of impact assumptions was drawing upon personal experience. This approach is rarely acknowledged by consultants and planners because it somehow seems unprofessional, but personal experience is bound to influence judgments about which types of assumptions to rely upon. Individuals who were making assumptions for their own use were more likely to draw upon personal experience. Examples listed below are assumptions based upon personal experience developed by members of the Fairbanks North Star Borough's Impact Advisory Committee at the beginning of the pipeline construction:

- With a winter of normal cold temperatures, Fairbanks will have worse ice fog conditions resulting in more closings of the Fairbanks International Airport.

- To meet the higher costs of living in the Fairbanks area, more women will seek employment to supplement family income.

- With the increased employment of women, there will be more unsupervised children.

- The incidence of traffic accidents will increase in relation to the increase of vehicular traffic

and in direct proportion to the number of
persons driving for the first time under
Alaskan winter conditions.

- While the value of real property in the Borough
will double within two years from January 1,
1974, the assessed value of real property in
the Borough will increase only 50 percent in
two years. The limiting factor will be the
number of tax assessors available for re-
appraisals.

Assumptions based upon personal experience were similar to assumptions based on recent history because they also
assumed that the processes by which events occurred would be
the same in the future as in the past. Thus, one assumed
that more ice fog would cause more airport closings or that
the assessors would continue to fall behind in their work,
based upon personal experience. New factors, such as a new
instrument landing system at the airport or a computerized
approach to assessing, were not incorporated into the assumption. When there are no baseline data nor published historical examples, personal experience can be useful, however.
Personal experience can help broaden the scope of the impacts
considered. For example, if there were more women in planning
or government, perhaps there would be greater consideration
of the effects of construction projects on women and children.
Similarly, a consultant hired outside Alaska would probably
not consider the local driving conditions in developing assumptions about traffic, accidents, and emergency medical care
as readily as one who could draw upon personal experience.

A third approach to making assumptions was to use
standard formulas or formulas derived from the best available
data. For example, the national average for the number of
persons per family has been used to predict population change.
Such formulas are used most commonly in making population projections and in economic modeling. Unfortunately, there are
not many formulas for predicting social impacts. Furthermore,

as discussed in Chapter 6, standard formulas did not always behave properly under unusual conditions, such as pipeline construction in Fairbanks.

In the absence of other people's assumptions, historical examples, and standard formulas, assumptions were often made on the basis of imagination and logic. Persons making such assumptions tried to project themselves into unfamiliar positions and then imagined how they would behave logically. The assumption was then made that others in the same positions would behave in the same manner. Using this approach, local planners made the following assumptions about how the pipeline would affect Fairbanks:[7]

- Regulations concerning camp residency and other restraints will not discourage the typical worker from bringing his family.

- Family immigration will begin after workers have gained some familiarity with the area and its conditions.

- Most relocations of families of workers stationed in camps between Mile 0 and Mile 602 will be to the Fairbanks urban area; workers stationed south of Mile 602 will be oriented toward Valdez and Anchorage.

- The rate of family relocations will be inversely proportional to the distance between camps and Fairbanks.

- The habits of pipeline workers regarding visits to Fairbanks, spending and services will also be influenced by access (distance) to Fairbanks.

- The direct relationship between distance and impact has continuity for the entire project from Prudhoe to Paxson with no change for break in mode of transportation. (In other words, people equal distance from Fairbanks will travel to Fairbanks the same number of times regardless of whether they must travel by air or highway.)

- Fairbanks will receive the major share of impact from employees on leave. Fairbanks will receive diminished impact relative to Anchorage, other Alaska points, and out-of-state points for longer furloughs.

All of the above assumptions were made by planners who had
not worked on pipelines and did not know very much about pipeline workers. They assumed that pipeline workers would be
like themselves--that they would have families and that their
families would want to be close to them, and when not working
they would want to go to the nearest town to entertain themselves. Persons who came to work on the pipeline did not have
the same values and lifestyles as the planners, however, and
they did not behave in the same ways that planners would have
behaved if they had been in a pipeline work situation. Apparently, professional pipeline and other construction workers
do not move their families every time they change jobs. While
employed, most construction workers want to work the maximum
hours in each day to accumulate as much overtime pay as possible. The combination of long working hours, recreational
activities in the construction camps and the lengthy amount
of time it takes to travel from the more remote camps to Fairbanks were disincentives for persons to visit Fairbanks
during their periods of employment.

Local planners were not the only ones to use a combination of imagination and logic in developing assumptions.
Some of the assumptions used by consultants to the oil companies were also apparently derived in this manner. Two examples are given below:

> It is doubtful that migrating welfare recipients
> will come to Alaska from the "lower 48" intending
> to retire on welfare payments in Alaska. Grants-
> in-aid are too low and living costs are too high.[8]

> It can be expected that increased prosperity will
> increase the rate of family break-up, thus in-
> creasing the number of claims for aid to dependent
> children.[9]

In each of these examples, the consultant was trying to project himself into the position of being a welfare recipient.

Trying to imagine how one would behave as a pipeline worker or a welfare recipient may have been an expedient way to develop assumptions which could be used to predict impacts, but it is no substitute for empiricism. A scientific approach to predicting impacts requires studying the lifestyles of pipeline construction workers, for example, before developing assumptions about their behavior.

Empirical approaches to developing assumptions about the impact of proposed projects are rarely used. This may be attributed to a lack of theory, data, and case studies upon which to base assumptions. Planners and consultants are often forced into producing environmental impact statements or other impact assessment reports without the adequate time or resources to perform necessary studies. The pressure to plug a figure into a model often results in pulling numbers out of the air, sometimes called "relying on intuition," rather than using a scientific approach.

In predicting impacts, the need for accurate assumptions is critical for two reasons. Not only do assumptions become the "input" for models which predict impact, but the models themselves are based upon assumptions about the way the world operates. The current model used for predicting social impacts is based upon two assumptions that the Fairbanks experience has not validated. First, it assumes that impact is a linear, quantitative function of the existing situation. Second, it assumes that communities are passive recipients of change. These two underlying assumptions must be reconsidered in light of the Fairbanks experience.

The most popular method used by consultants, planners, social scientists, and agency people for predicting impacts of proposed projects involves three steps:

Step 1. Describe the existing community.

Step 2. Describe the proposed project and the demands the proposed project will create in the community.

Step 3.   Sum Step 1 and Step 2 to determine the anticipated impacts.

Using hospital beds for an example, one would predict the
impact of a proposed project in the following manner:

Step 1.   Give the number of hospital beds in the
community and the current percentage of
hospital beds which are being used.

Step 2.   Make assumptions to determine the average
number of hospital beds which would be required daily to meet the medical emergencies
generated by the proposed project and the
number of hospital beds needed to serve the
additional population expected to result
from the proposed project.

Step 3.   Add the current number of hospital beds being
used (from Step 1) to the number of additional beds which would be used if the proposed project were to occur (from Step 2)
and compare this sum to the total number of
hospital beds available in the community to
determine whether there are enough hospital
beds to meet both the current and projected
needs, yielding how many beds will be required.

This traditional model for predicting impacts is basically
linear in that it assumes a direct relationship between the
needs generated by a proposed project and the demands on community services. It is also basically a quantitative model
because it relies on numbers and assumes that the numerical
relationships adequately represent the current and anticipated
situations. Linear relationships in this model can be expressed quantitatively using the formula

$$a + b = c$$

where $\underline{a}$ is the current situation, $\underline{b}$ is the demands of the proposed project, and $\underline{c}$ is the resultant impacts.

Two variations on this model have emerged. To some who employ a "more-is-better" philosophy, a better impact assessment involves more detailed descriptions. While this produces more massive environmental impact statements in numbers of pages, the model used is basically the same as before. It may be described by the following formula:

$$A + B = C$$

where

$$A = a_1 + a_2 + a_3 + \ldots a_x$$

and

$$B = b_1 + b_2 + b_3 + \ldots b_x$$

Thus, the formula remains the same, but the variables become more complex. The second variation on this model has been hailed as a newer, more sophisticated approach to predicting impacts. While it incorporates the linear and quantitative aspects of the "traditional" model, this "modern" model offers alternative impact packages, usually called "scenarios." Different scenarios are presented based on different assumptions, such as "low," "medium," and "high" development situations. This approach can be described as

$$a + b_x = c_x$$

which looks suspiciously like the original linear formula, except that different quantities can be plugged into the $\underline{b}$ slot to get different $\underline{c}$'s.

The Fairbanks experience suggests that the changes induced by the trans Alaska pipeline could not always be expressed in quantitative terms. Changes in community structure affected community needs and demands for community services. Using the traditional model according to the example cited, it was predicted that the new Fairbanks Memorial Hospital would be more than adequate for accommodating community needs during the pipeline period. Only eight months after pipeline construction officially began, the hospital was filled to capacity and faced with a growing demand. One reason for this unexpected impact was the changing structure of the health care delivery system and the resultant change in hospital utilization. Other changes in the Fairbanks community which could not have been accounted for in a strictly quantitative model included changes in political structure, social structure, residence patterns, and family life. The significance of structural changes is that the community does not behave in the same way that it did previously. Hence assumptions based upon history may not hold and the type of logic needed to make assumptions may change.

In addition to changes in community structure, other aspects of impact were not accurately assessed using the linear model. The Fairbanks experience suggests that instead of a linear relationship between increased demands and community impacts, some type of threshhold effects were operating. After a threshhold value was exceeded, the effects became considerably worse and the systems affected began to deteriorate. For example, it would not have sufficed to predict that without providing 3,000 more telephones to meet rising demands, 3,000 potential customers would have been deprived of telephone service. The Fairbanks telephone system became so overloaded that the quality of existing service diminished to the point that the system was malfunctioning much of the time during the pipeline period.

The linear model is problematic not only because it accounts for neither non-quantitative changes nor threshhold effects, but also because it does not contain enough variables. The model does not encompass the decisions by the local community. Communities are not necessarily passive recipients of change; they may make decisions which affect the quality and quantities of impacts. Some examples from the Fairbanks experience were the media campaign to discourage people without jobs from coming to Fairbanks, changing the downtown traffic patterns to reduce carbon monoxide in the core area in spite of traffic increases, installing a better instrument landing system at the airport to reduce the disabling effects of ice fog on airport activities, and instituting a computerized tax assessing to maximize local revenues.

In addition to the scenarios which reflect "high," "medium," and "low" development on the part of indistry, predicting impacts ought to include scenarios which reflect "high," "medium," and "low" levels of planning and response by the local community. Rather than using a linear approach, a matrix is needed which gives both industry and community alternatives and the impacts of each combination of alternatives.

Failure to consider community alternatives reinforces a sense of powerlessness on the part of the local community. That sense of powerlessness can lead to failure to respond, which in turn exacerbates the impacts. A more positive and productive approach is developing various strategies to avert, ameliorate, cope with, or respond to potential or real impacts of resource development. Aversion requires planning and preventive action. Amelioration requires some types of intervention to improve the situation. Coping is basically a maintenance posture. Responding to impacts after they occur is usually a matter of crisis intervention. These strategies may be developed by private concerns, such as oil companies, though ideally they would evolve through cooperative efforts between local communities, state and federal governments, and industry. Most of the strategies require goal definition, planning, policy-making, funding, and administration.

In the case of Fairbanks and the trans Alaska oil pipeline, the federal government played a minimal role in addressing impact situations. The state government provided impact funds and increased its services related to anticipated impact problems. In many cases, however, the state developed its programs too late to avert or ameliorate problems. One type of assistance that the state did provide to local areas was the implementation of Emergency Rent Review Boards to moderate problems of exorbitant rents during critical rental housing shortages. While this helped to control rent gouging, it did not help to provide the additional housing needed.

In general, the oil industry in Fairbanks assumed the attitude that it was responsible for paying taxes, but had no further responsibility to mitigate pipeline project impacts. In accord with stipulations in the pipeline permit, the oil companies did help to finance job training programs for Alaskan Natives. Alyeska Pipeline Service Company announced a program to minimize its contribution to the carbon monoxide level in Fairbanks; and, in times of electricity shortage, it generated its own electricity. As part of its public relations campaign, Alyeska also donated some money to charitable causes.

For the most part, the responsibilities for addressing impacts of the trans Alaska oil pipeline on Fairbanks rested with the local community. It is possible that Fairbanks could have fared better during the pipeline period if better strategies had been planned. Better planning, however, requires greater ability to predict the future based upon more viable models. Developing better models requires a more empirical approach to making assumptions and better understanding of the processes of community change--monumental challenges for social science.

Chapter 15
A MODEL FOR SOCIAL SCIENTISTS

In academic circles, the concept of "impact" is usually associated with the theoretical framework of "development"
in economics and sociology, and "culture change" in anthropology. Although the social sciences have not refined a
theoretical model to integrate the information needed to predict impacts of resource development, several disciplines use
similar concepts which incorporate environmental factors and
human behavior into a systems approach. Anthropologists call
it "cultural ecology," sociologists call it "human ecology,"
and psychologists call it "community mental health." In
general, this approach regards individuals or groups of individuals as components of a larger system which includes both
natural (non-human) and social (man-made) environments.

It appears that anthropology has gone the furthest
toward developing a tradition of holistic model-building related to culture change. However, most of the emphasis on
predictive models and most of the theoretical developments
have come from archeologists and prehistorians whose work
usually has been restricted to subsistence and agrarian societies. If complex culture is considered to be one end of a
conceptual continuum with subsistence-based culture at the
other end, a viable holistic model must fit all points of that
continuum. Theories about culture which have been defined by
anthropologists in relation to non-Western cultures are no
less applicable to Western culture. Following J.A. Barnes,[1]
R. Redfield,[2] J.W. Bennett,[3] and C.O. Frake,[4] one may view
the differences between points on the continuum from subsistence-based to complex culture as differences in effective
environments. Complex cultures may be defined as those in
which the social environment is an extensive network exerting

the dominant pressures which shape changes in the culture.
By contrast, in subsistence-based cultures the social environment is somewhat more limited and the natural environment
contains the dominant forces which shape changes in the local
group.

The impact of trans Alaska oil pipeline construction
on Fairbanks is a case of culture change in a complex society.
As such, this study ought to contribute to the development
of a cultural ecology paradigm by answering these questions:
What is the relationship between population and resources in
a complex culture? How does a culture evolve toward greater
complexity? How does a complex society adapt to changes in
its social environment? This chapter explores these questions
drawing upon the Fairbanks experience.

Carrying Capacity: A Concept for Explaining the Relationship
between Population and Resources in Complex Culture

Cultural ecologists have employed the concept of
carrying capacity to explain population dynamics, settlement
patterns, and other aspects of the relationships between
groups and their environments primarily among hunters/gather-
ers and agrarian cultures. However, the Fairbanks experience
suggests that the definition of carrying capacity must be
broadened and refined to encompass complex culture, such that
carrying capacity can be used nomothetically, integrating
theory at different levels of social complexity.

In his brief history of demography, LaMont Cole attri-
butes the concept of carrying capacity as a regulatory mechanism to an essay by Botero in 1588 entitled, "A Treatise Concerning the Causes of the Magnificency and Greatness of Cities,"
and to a later essay by Sir Walter Raleigh in 1650 entitled,
"A Discourse on the Original and Fundamental Cause of Natural,
Arbitrary, Necessary, and Unnatural War."[5] However, it was

not until Charles Darwin published <u>Origin of the Species</u> in
1859 that the relationship between environment and population
density became an accepted biological concept.[6] For biolo-
gists and botanists, carrying capacity is defined in terms of
the number of individuals of a species which can survive in
equilibrium on a given area of land.

Social scientists have extended the biological concept of carrying capacity. Beginning with Thomas Malthus,[7]
most social theorists have tended to view carrying capacity
as a function of resource availability and hence a limiting
factor in determining the density and size of human populations.
Ezra Zubrow, for example, defines carrying capacity as "the
maximum number of organisms or amounts of biomass which can
maintain itself indefinitely in an area."[8] Anthropologists
who have used this concept have tended to restrict their consideration of the dynamics of carrying capacity to the dynamics of homeostasis. Some independent variables have been
suggested for the homeostatic limit including changes in
available food supply,[9, 10, 11, 12] changes in the supply of energy,[13] efficiency in obtaining or extracting energy-providing
materials,[14] manner in which the population is organized to
produce and use resources,[15, 16] land use,[17] facilities for
transporting people to the source of supply or goods
to the people,[18] technology,[19, 20, 21] and creative altering of
the environment.[22]

The concept of carrying capacity as a limit and as a
homeostatic regulatory mechanism proved untenable when Joseph
Birdsell calculated that parts of populations tend to out-
migrate before the group reaches the "carrying capacity" of
the occupied area.[23] Birdsell estimated that the "budding-
off point" occurred when the population reached 60 percent
of the maximum density the local resources could support.[24]
Lewis Binford argues that because population density is

regulated well below the carrying capacity of the local food supply, carrying capacity does not limit population size.[25] Binford was seeking to use carrying capacity as a mechanism for explaining technological change, and in doing so he devised special demographic situations in which population density might hypothetically reach carrying capacity and thus stimulate technological change.[26]

For the most part, the concept of carrying capacity has not been applied to modern complex societies except in a global sense.[27, 28] Perhaps this may be attributed to a general belief that archeology is in the best position to test neo-Malthusian models because, "Modern technology with its concomitant diversity of resources, complex trade patterns, and ease of mobility complicate the data."[29] One might argue that the concept of carrying capacity used by anthropologists to date has been overly simplistic and that by studying modern complex culture a more realistic concept may be defined.

In subsistence and agrarian economies, the population is directly engaged in procuring natural resources; while in industrial economies, food production occurs outside urban areas and is traded for the production of goods and services. The carrying capacity of urban areas is, therefore, indirectly linked with the availability of food resources. The cultural ecology paradigm in this context must include the social environment as well as the natural environment, and "resources" extended beyond food. The following resources have been included in the proposed model:

1. Food
2. Cultural constructs for survival (shelter, clothing, medicine);
3. Means for distributing resources which are not immediately procured by the local population

(transportation, communication, market system);

4. Cultural constructs which provide social integration through which large numbers of persons can live together (government, law enforcement, socializing institutions such as schools and churches, etc.);

5. Knowledge which enables persons to function and survive in the cultural-ecological setting (science, leadership).

In urban areas, as well as in subsistence and agrarian economies, intensified or improved technology can increase the amount of resources available to a population at a given time.

Natural selection as a mechanism for achieving a homeostatic relationship between population and resources can be applied either by analogy or by extension to the urban situation. Whereas a subsistence economy selects for those persons most able to exploit the natural environment, the urban environment selects for those most able to exploit the cash economy. In both cases, however, it appears that the very young, the very old, and the physically and socially disabled are most likely to be eliminated when population size exceeds the amount of resources necessary to sustain it. Similar to experiments in overcrowding with rats, it appears that social and psychological disintegration occurs in human populations when the population exceeds the amount of needed resources available in the environment.[30, 31]

The finding that human populations are regulated below carrying capacity suggests that human existence does not hover precariously on the brink of crisis, and that carrying capacity is not a homeostatic regulatory mechanism for human population size under most conditions. Instead of being regulated by the threat of extinction, human population appears to be regulated by either a conscious or an unconscious attempt

to improve the human condition, or an individual's condition.
This concept has been labeled "welfare," "optimum," "quality
of life," "life chances," "standard of living," or "well-
being." The concept welfare/optimum has been related to the
environment by John B. Calhoun and A. H. Hawley:

> Individuals or assemblies of individuals
> have the genetically endowed or culturally
> acquired potentiality to profit from certain
> conditions which might exist in their en-
> vironment. Welfare is increased in pro-
> portion to the extent that the environment
> permits realization of these potentialities.[32]

> The optimum, for any species of life, is
> simply the number above and below which the
> chances of the survival of the species in a
> given area are considerably lessened, the
> number without which necessary forms of
> behavior cannot be maintained.[33]

The "optimum" which Hawley refers to is the point of maximum
welfare according to Calhoun. Calhoun explains the relationship between this point and the limit suggested by the concept
of carrying capacity:

> The concept of carrying capacity implies
> maximizing numbers alone. . . .maximizing
> numbers reduces the extent to which other
> aspects of welfare are realized. This suggests
> that the most favorable state of welfare is
> achieved when no one aspect is maximized,
> but rather when there is some over-all
> simultaneous optimizing of all the aspects.[34]

Population density in relation to well-being for a given amount
of resources may be viewed as a continuum, as illustrated in
Figure 35. Three points on that continuum are: (1) a minimum,
below which it would be difficult for the population to carry
out its activities and to perpetuate itself; (2) a midpoint,
representing the optimum level of the population for maxi-
mizing welfare; and (3) a high point, representing the limit

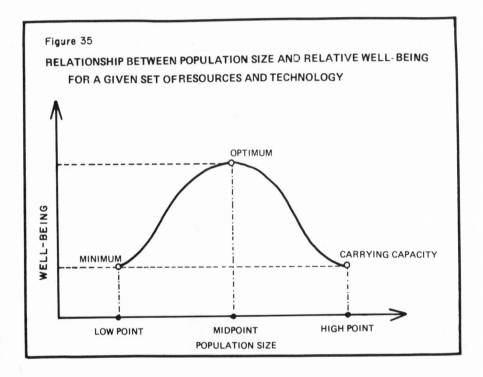

Figure 35

RELATIONSHIP BETWEEN POPULATION SIZE AND RELATIVE WELL-BEING
FOR A GIVEN SET OF RESOURCES AND TECHNOLOGY

or the carrying capacity of that environment, above which it
is difficult for the population to carry out its activities
and social and psychological disintegration occur. The "quality of life," or "life chances," or "standard of living," or
"welfare," increases as the population level moves from the
low point to the optimum point and decreases as the population
grows to the carrying capacity.

Changes in the amount or type of technology can change
the amount or type of resources available to a group at a
given time. This in turn may alter the shape or position of
the curve in Figure 35. The points of minimum, optimum, and
carrying capacity may change locus, but they will retain
their relationship to one another on the continuum, as illustrated in Figure 36. According to this model, carrying
capacity is not so much a cause of technological change,[37]
but a result of technological change.

The mechanism which appears to cause adjustments in
human populations through out-migration is the lowering of
the welfare or quality of life which occurs as the population
exceeds the optimum and approaches carrying capacity. Because
these adjustments take place prior to reaching carrying capacity, it is only under unusual, catastrophic, or artificial
conditions that the carrying capacity is exceeded. When this
happens, social and psychological disintegration may serve to
radically reduce welfare and thus hasten population regulation
through such means as death, disease, and warfare.

In considering several resources in addition to food,
ascertaining the overall carrying capacity for a given area
becomes problematic. The carrying capacity for each of the
component resources can be measured by determining the population size and density at which the demand for that resource
exceeds the capacity of that resource at its current level of
technological intensity and thus results in disintegration,

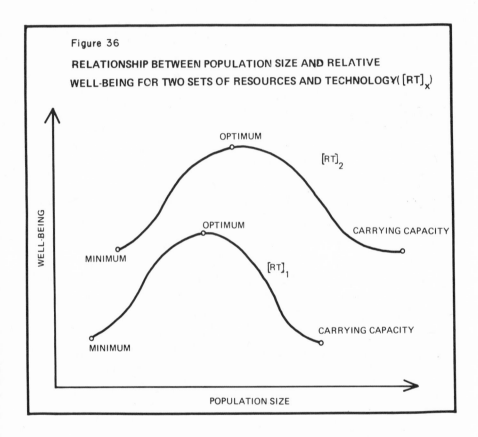

Figure 36

**RELATIONSHIP BETWEEN POPULATION SIZE AND RELATIVE
WELL-BEING FOR TWO SETS OF RESOURCES AND TECHNOLOGY($[RT]_x$)**

or an inability of that resource to function in its designated
role. The overall carrying capacity is a function of the
capacities of the component resources. The equation for that
function is a problem which requires much additional research.
It appears, however, that when carrying capacities have been
exceeded and resources disintegrate, to some extent the community collectively experiences disintegration and reintegrates
into a new, or changed community. By measuring the carrying
capacity of various resources, it may be possible to predict
the levels at which disintegration would occur from additional
demands created by introducing projects such as the trans
Alaska oil pipeline into the microenvironment.

Initial findings suggest that demands created by the
population increase in Fairbanks exceeded limits in the
amounts of some resources: the housing shortage was critical;
the hospital was filled to capacity; the telephone system was
dysfunctional and persons were unable to procure telephones;
there were shortages of goods due to inadequate availability
of transportation; personal transportation was inhibited by
lengthy automobile repair processes; schools were overcrowded;
and so forth. Thus, the population exceeded the carrying
capacity of many of Fairbanks' resources.

Under these conditions, competition for resources was
determined by personal income. Persons with the greatest
amount of cash were most likely to procure the limited resources. Because of the high wages and long working hours,
persons employed on pipeline-related jobs were most likely
to have the greatest personal income and, therefore, to obtain
limited resources. Financial pressures forced many persons
who previously held other jobs in the community to adapt to
the new situation by taking pipeline-related jobs. Pipeline
jobs appeared to select for single males with previous experience in construction or management; married males with

similar experience; and minority persons and women with job skills. Pipeline jobs selected against the unemployable or the marginally employable, such as the very old, the very young, persons who were physically, psychologically or socially handicapped, and persons without skills. It also selected against those who, for personal, moral, or professional reasons did not want pipeline jobs. Because there was a very limited amount of child care in the community and the limits of that resource were exceeded, and because of cultural attitudes toward parenting, many women with young children were unable to work at pipeline-related jobs.

The selection process may best be illustrated through the housing situation. As rents increased, persons unable to pay were evicted from their homes or left voluntarily and were replaced by persons with higher incomes. Those evicted had few alternatives. Little additional housing was available and rents on those places were most likely higher than the family income. Most low-income persons were unable to obtain mortgages to purchase trailers or houses. Persons who may have camped outside during the summer were unable to do so during the winter. The remaining alternatives were to live with friends or relatives, to sleep at the Rescue Mission or the Salvation Army, or to out-migrate to places where the cost of living was lower.

A major exogenous factor in this analysis is that, concurrent with pipeline construction in Fairbanks, the rest of the nation and much of the world was experiencing an economic recession accompanied by high unemployment rates. Thus, while some persons residing in Fairbanks may have perceived a decline in their well-being, the alternative of out-migration may have been perceived as not necessarily improving the individual's quality of life. This somewhat extraordinary situation in the macroenvironment may have accounted for population at a level beyond the carrying capacity of the existing technology for some resources.

Conversely, many newcomers to Fairbanks came to seek pipeline jobs as a way of improving their well-being in other settings. The situation resulted in a competition for resources, in this case cash income, between the resident population and populations from "neighboring territories." The State of Alaska attempted to "defend" the resources for its residents by legislating that Alaskans be given preferential status in hiring for pipeline jobs. However, the competition for the cash income was resolved in favor or those who had the necessary skills or connections, many of whom previously resided outside the Fairbanks microenvironment.

While the dynamics of migration are not well understood with regard to Fairbanks and the pipeline, it appears that there are some qualitative differences between migration patterns in complex society and in less complex societies. The extensive social networks of complex societies involve communication structures enabling people to gain access to information about conditions in other environmental settings. Hence, decisions to migrate are not based solely upon conditions in the immediate environment, but also a knowledge of alternatives with regard to other environmental settings. Furthermore, the failure of Fairbanksans to out-migrate may be attributed to their perception that the conditions which created their loss of well-being were limited in duration-- unlike natural events, such as droughts, for which there is no certainty about the length of the event and the subsequent duration of loss of welfare.

Preliminary findings indicate that the results of maintaining the population beyond the carrying capacity of some Fairbanks' resources have included psychological disintegration only among those who were least stable prior to the events related to pipeline construction. The reason that the population as a whole did not experience the types of social and psychological disintegration associated with exceeding resource limits [35, 36] may be that there was not a shortage of certain critical resources, such as food. Another plausible explanation is that the stress resulting from changes in the community was balanced by satisfactions to many individuals. Or, perhaps Fairbanks was able to avoid the thresholds at which social and psychological disintegration occur by improving and intensifying technology and thereby increasing resources.

It is anticipated that upon completion of the pipeline, unless another factor is introduced, such as a second pipeline, there will be a radical reduction in well-being resulting in an out-migration of people who came to Fairbanks to acquire cash income. These highly skilled and mobile people will seek other territories offering greater income and, thereby, greater well-being than Fairbanks can offer in the post-pipeline period. Since the pipeline construction brought Fairbanks a higher level of technology and technological intensity which expanded the resource base for such things as food, shelter, transportation, communication, government, schools, churches, and leadership, the community can support a greater population at an optimum level than previous to the pipeline construction.

How Does a Culture Evolve Toward Greater Complexity?

J.W. Bennett has defined complex society as one in which there is interplay between local and external, microcosm and macrocosm.[38] J. A. Barnes used a similar concept when he stated that "the principle formal differences between simple, primitive, rural or small scale societies as against modern, civilized, urban or mass societies is that in the former the mesh of the social network is small, in the latter it is large."[39] Other formal differences have also been suggested, such as the process of resource allocation[40] and the mental environment.[41,42] Assuming that a cultural system exists in a microenvironment (together forming a microcosm) which in turn exists in a macrocosm (together forming a macrocosm), the evolution of a culture toward complexity may be regarded as a process of strengthening the relationship between the culture and its macroenvironment.

Trans Alaska oil pipeline construction and its effects on Fairbanks may serve to illuminate these concepts. Because of its remoteness and relatively undeveloped transportation and communications networks to the "Outside," Fairbanks is a fairly well-defined microcosm in terms of political boundaries, demography, institutions and social structure. If one regards Fairbanks as the locus of both a society and its microenvironment, then its macroenvironment may be defined by the forces outside this microcosm which affect Fairbanks.

The concept of nesting, or nested relationships, may be useful in conceptualizing the macroenvironment. Fairbanks exists within the State of Alaska which exists within the United States, which exists in an international sphere. As a macroenvironment for Fairbanks, the State of Alaska encompasses the state government, the natural resources within the state including the oil at Prudhoe Bay, the transportation and communications networks within the state, and a multitide of other factors affecting Fairbanks. The United States influences Fairbanks both through the decisions and actions of the federal government and through the activities of urban centers outside Alaska, such as Washington, D.C., Seattle, Houston and Los Angeles. The international sphere includes both multinational corporations, such as oil companies, and nations other than the United States. Economic and political decisions made by other nations affect the world economy with regard to supply, demand and prices of resources, which in

turn influence the development of resources in Alaska, in
turn affecting Fairbanks.

Types of relationships between microcosm and macrocosm may be defined in terms of both structure and content.
Structures through which the microcosm and macrocosm relate
may be characterized as movements which have both direction
and strength. The direction of the movement may be unidirectional either from the macrocosm to the microcosm, or
from the microcosm to the macrocosm; or, it may be reciprocal. The strength of the movement may vary from controlling
events, to influencing events, to being the recipient of
events. In the case of a reciprocal relationship, there may
be a partnership, with equal strength of movement in each
direction, or there may be asymmetry of dominance and sub-
ordination.

A variety of contents flow between the microcosm and
macrocosm within the structures described in terms of direction and strength of movement. These contents may be classified into four types:

1. Information, including technology, information
    about conditions in a given microenvironment,
    and information about the ways that various sys-
    tems function;
2. Resources, including natural resources, manufac-
    tured goods, and money;
3. People, both consumers and producers of resources;
4. Power to make decisions.

The flow of information, resources, people and power between
the microcosm and the macrocosm may occur within the various
combinations of direction and strength of movement described
above.

Applying this typology, one may analyze pipeline impact to determine the ways in which relationships between

microcosm and macrocosm changed as Fairbanks evolved to greater complexity. What are the changes in movement, strength, and content of relationships and is there a sequence or pattern in these changes?

The pipeline may be considered the event which precipitated evolution toward greater complexity. Prior to the pipeline, the Fairbanks microcosm was influenced significantly by its macroenvironment, but the reverse was not true. Decisions made in the macroenvironment which directly controlled events in Fairbanks included whether to build the pipeline, where to build it, and what role Fairbanks would play in the construction. The decision of the federal government to lease Ft. Wainwright to Alyeska Pipeline Service Company was also made in the macroenvironment. Many of these decisions were unilateral with the decision-making power resting in the macroenvironment. Fairbanks did influence some decisions made at the state level, such as implementing an Alaska hire law and allocating a portion of the state's oil lease revenues to impact funds for local communities. But few decisions were made in the microenvironment which controlled or influenced events in the macroenvironment.

During pipeline construction the flows became more reciprocal. Flows of resources and people were most easily observed: manufactured goods, money, and labor came into Fairbanks from the macroenvironment. At the same time there was a flow of cash from Fairbanks to its macroenvironment in the form of wages to non-resident pipeline workers, and profits to and purchases from businesses headquartered Outside. Fairbanks acquired technology from the macroenvironment and a greater knowledge of the systems related to oil development and pipeline construction; and there was a flow of information about Fairbanks to the rest of the world.

Reciprocity seems to be the type of relationship between the community and its macroenvironment which strengthens

the ties and thereby creates a more complex social network.
However, it appears that as a community grows in size and
complexity, its relationship with the macroenvironment changes
from a unidirectional one with the macroenvironment controlling, to reciprocal with greater control in the microcosm,
to reciprocal with the microcosm controlling the macrocosm.

Fairbanks will probably never evolve to be a major
metropolitan center--like New York, Washington, or Los Ange-
les--from which flow the information, power and resources
which influence the macroenvironment. Ultimately, there will
be a flow of natural resources, namely oil, from Alaska to
the Outside. But it is likely that decisions made in the
macroenvironments will continue to affect Fairbanks and decisions made in Fairbanks will probably have little effect
on the world outside its tiny shpere of influence. Hence,
Fairbanks can probably only exemplify the early stages of
evolution toward greater complexity in which its relationship
with the macroenvironment became stronger and more reciprocal.

How Does a Culture Adapt to Changes in its Relationship
with the Macroenvironment?

Many events occurring in the microcosm of complex
cultures result from decisions made in the macroenvironment.
The culture affected by these events must adapt to changes in
its environment. This process of adaptation may occur through
adjustments in the relationship between population and resources described in conjunction with the concept of carrying
capacity. In addition, the culture adapts through internal
structural changes.

Changes in structure are dependent upon the structure
of the community when the new force is introduced into the
microenvironment. In the period before pipeline construction
began, Fairbanks was a relatively isolated small town with a

fairly stable social, political, and economic structure.
Anchorage, by comparison, was a fast-growing, rapidly changing town prior to the pipeline. Anchorage was more flexible
and able to absorb pipeline impact with less trauma than Fairbanks. Some evidence suggests that the size of a community
may determine the types of businesses and professional persons it can support which in turn affects the type of leadership and community decisions.

As a result of changes in its macroenvironment through
the event of pipeline construction, Fairbanks changed its political structure, social structure, residence patterns, and
family structure. Changes in the political structure included the formation of new interest groups, such as the Social Concerns Committee of the Fairbanks Council of Churches.
In addition, new individuals within old groups changed the
power structure of those groups--for example, the medical
profession. By acquiring more members, groups such as labor
unions achieved greater potential power. New problems and
goals resulting from pipeline construction redefined alliance
networks. Potential and real changes in land use, for example, created or changed alliances with regard to zoning.
To some extent, the neighborhood as an alliance network was
rejuvenated in response to rapid changes in the community as
a whole. Neighborhoods organized themselves to create formal
service districts for road maintenance and fire protection,
to present opposition to proposed zoning or zoning variances,
and to lobby for common goals, such as telephone service.

Social structure of the community was altered in
several ways. Patterns of participation in voluntary groups
changed, particularly with regard to membership in labor unions. Greater employment opportunities increased socioeconomic
mobility for some groups, especially teenagers, racial and
ethnic minorities, and women. Roles of social service organizations changed to reduce dependence upon government and

expand the role of religious organizations in providing social services.

Changes in residence patterns may be directly attributed to the organization of the pipeline workforce and the housing shortage in Fairbanks. More families had persons living with them who were not members of the nuclear family. There was a proliferation of institutionalized communal living arrangements, such as rooming houses and residential hotels. Many people built or purchased new homes during this period and others resorted to non-conventional housing, including mobile homes, trailers, tents, cars, shacks, and other dwellings. Pipeline construction camps created new residence patterns, with persons working on the pipeline residing away from their families for 9 to 13 weeks and with their families for one to two weeks at a time. Most of these changes in residence patterns appear temporary; however, they may have long-term ramifications for the types of housing available in Fairbanks in the future for family and social structure.

Changes in family structure observed in Fairbanks as a result of pipeline construction included new roles for family members. Extended absences of pipeline workers from their families might have forced their spouses and children to assume different roles. Teenagers and women entering the workforce also created changes in family structure. Patterns of child care changed as a result of double-shifting in the schools, a shortage of institutionalized child care, and longer working hours. A significant long-term effect of the pipeline construction period on family structure may be the increase in divorces.

Logically, it would seem that a community has many alternative strategies for adapting to changes in its relationship with the macroenvironment. While the logical alternatives may seem limitless, there are pragmatic limitations on

community decisions to select strategies. A community may
not be aware of or receptive to various alternatives. Decision-making may be affected by perceived power to affect
change and the degree to which there are common goals for the
future of the community. Some alternatives may not be viable
in a given situation because of cultural factors or problems
specific to the microenvironment. Even when a strategy is
acceptable and well-suited to local conditions , the community
may not have access to the resources or power to adapt that
strategy. To some extent, the relationship between the macrocosm and the microcosm determines the choices of adaptive
strategies made by communities.

As a culture evolves toward greater complexity, it
has greater access to information, resources, people, and
power in the macroenvironment. It would seem that as the relationship between microcosm and macrocosm becomes stronger
and more reciprocal, a culture has greater power to exercise
its logical alternatives for adapting internally to the environmental changes which result from the evolution toward
complexity. While the power to select alternative adaptive
strategies may increase with an evolution toward greater complexity, stronger and more reciprocal flows between macrocosm
and microcosm may create a desire to emulate other more complex systems and thereby restrict the perceptions of desir-
ability of various alternatives. The paradox which emerges
is that the evolution of a culture toward greater complexity
empowers it with the potential for greater diversity and at
the same time imbues it with the desire for greater homogene-
ity.

Chapter 16
LEARNING FROM
THE FAIRBANKS EXPERIENCE

Effects of the trans Alaska oil pipeline construction on Fairbanks may be regarded as an example of the social, cultural, and economic impacts of rapid resource development on a community, or it may be regarded as a unique event in the history of a small town in Interior Alaska. The Fairbanks experience probably ought to be regarded as both.

To the extent that Fairbanks has some fairly unique characteristics, the processes and results of pipeline impact may not be applicable to other situations of rapid resource development. For this reason, it is important to identify characteristics of Fairbanks which may have uniquely determined the course of events associated with pipeline impact. An obvious characteristic is city size; larger or smaller cities might have reacted differently to similar situations. Presumably, a larger city would have greater resources and be better able to absorb impacts. Smaller cities might have more difficulty making public investments, but might also have greater concensus about goals for the future of the community which could lead to more decisive leadership. Not only is the size of Fairbanks important, but also the types of resources available. For example, the presence of a military base for construction project headquarters probably precipitated a very different course of events than had there been no such facility. The university is another community resource not found in every city the size of Fairbanks.

Other characteristics which may have made the Fairbanks experience unique are a history of boom/bust cycles, a tertiary economy with no strong industrial or agricultural base, traditionally high rates of unemployment, a high cost

of living, a historically highly transient population, cultural heterogeneity, and the presence of powerful labor unions. Unlike many towns of similar size, Fairbanks has no
larger cities within a 200-mile radius. The remoteness,
accentuated by geographical barriers and a harsh climate,
may make patterns of migration to Fairbanks during the boom
period atypical. The remoteness was partially responsible
for the physical infrastructure, particularly relating to
communications and transportation, remaining relatively undeveloped prior to and during the pipeline construction period.

Despite these seemingly unique characteristics, Fairbanks may be representative of American towns of similar size,
with regard to social, political, and economic structure.
Strong representation of business persons in community decision-making and an inherent conservatism in those leaders
may be typical of towns similar to Fairbanks. A desire by
the leadership for economic development coupled with little
understanding of the potential power to control and guide
development and a lack of sophistication in dealing with
forces outside the community, may lead to being easily inti-
midated by big business and big government. Since Fairbanks
had little control over decisions in the macroenvironment
affecting it and little access to information which could
have enhanced the planning process, there was much uncertainty
about the future. This uncertainty, combined with limitations
on planning and sources of capital, prohibited the community
from expanding its infrastructure adequately to meet the needs
created by a boom situation. Because these characteristics
were inherent in the structure of the community, Fairbanks
could not avert or ameliorate many impacts, and was often inhibited from effectively coping with others. Fairbanks jumped
from crisis to crisis as it tried to respond to impacts after
they occurred.

Perhaps the most important lesson that can be learned

from the Fairbanks experience is that unjust and unrealistic expectations were placed on the community. Decisions about projects were made outside the community, but the community had to bear the responsibilities for coping with the consequences of those decisions. The inherent structure of the community meant that it could not cope effectively in many situations.

Solutions to this problem can come from two directions. First, communities could have more significant input into decision-making about projects which affect them. Given both the world power structure and the power structure of communities like Fairbanks, this alternative is not likely to succeed in reducing the negative impacts of resource development projects. The second approach is to distribute more equitably the responsibilities for solving impact problems. This means that federal and state governments and private industry would assume greater responsibilities in developing and implementing strategies responding to potential and real impacts of resource development. In this context, it may be helpful to understand why federal and state governments and private industry did not assume greater roles in averting or ameliorating the impacts of the trans Alaska oil pipeline on Fairbanks.

The minimal role of the oil industry may be attributed to several factors. First, the oil companies were not required by law to address social problems resulting from their activities. Although federal and state permits to build the pipeline contained many stipulations relating to the natural environment, few stipulations relating to the social environment were included in the legal documents giving the oil companies permission to build the pipeline. Second, in the context of the economic, social and political systems of the Unites States, the oil industry is viewed as a business and not as an institution for solving social problems. With this cognitive orientation, the oil industry was not expected to

address the social problems it may have created directly or
indirectly. Finally, the oil industry did consult with Fairbanks business leaders to determine what resources the community wanted to provide and what resources should be provided "in-house" by the oil companies. The Chamber of Commerce was eager for the community to acquire additional business and discouraged the oil companies from accepting more
responsibility in such areas as housing, office space, and
procurement of supplies. In the case of Fairbanks and pipeline impact, the oil industry did not accept more responsibility for social impacts because it was not required to do
so, it was not expected to do so, and it was, to some extent,
discouraged from doing so.

A major reason the federal government did not take
a more active role was that the environmental impact statement and hearing processes associated with the decision to
grant the trans Alaska right-of-way permit did not elucidate
any clear need for federal participation in addressing social
impacts, aside from those associated with Alaska Natives.
Testimony from Fairbanksans suggested that all of the social
and economic impacts of the pipeline construction would benefit the local community and its residents. No clear need for
a federal role with regard to social impacts was defined prior
to pipeline construction and no mechanism was established to
involve the federal government to any significant extent in
addressing social impacts after pipeline construction began.
Furthermore, the goal of achieving greater energy independence
for the nation cast the pipeline construction into a context
of positive social and economic impact on a national level,
transcending any of the smaller-scale problems experienced by
such remote and seemingly insignificant towns as Fairbanks,
Alaska.

While state government was more willing to assume responsibility for pipeline construction impacts, it was less

able to do so. State oil revenues do not accrue until after
pipeline completion, imposing financial restraints on the
state's ability to provide financial assistance to local
communities. Local communities needed more than financial
assistance, however; they also needed technical assistance.
At the beginning of trans Alaska oil pipeline construction,
the state government had very little experience with this kind
of massive development and was limited in the kinds of technical assistance it could provide. Both politics and lack
of experience made it difficult and time-consuming for the
state to develop programs for taxing the oil industry, job
training, enforcing the Alaska hire laws, emergency rent review boards, day care assistance, and other problems created
directly or indirectly by the pipeline. For the state government, the trans Alaska oil pipeline construction period was
a time of trial and error, learning, and acquiring greater
sophistication.

Failure of federal and state government and private
industry to assume greater responsibility for social and
cultural impacts of the trans Alaska oil pipeline need not
be repeated in other resource development situations. To
ensure more equitable distribution of responsibilities, environmental impact statements need to be more effective as
planning tools for local, state, and federal governments to
avert or ameliorate potentially negative social impacts of
projects and promote potentially positive impacts. In issuing
permits, federal and state governments need to include stipulations which define the role of the oil companies, or other
industries, in avoiding or otherwise mitigating the impact
situations which their projects create.

Some types of stipulations which could be conditions
of permits include requiring industry to provide the following:

Housing: Stipulations regarding the percentage of

housing which industry is to supply to its employees
and the disposition of that housing after the construction period has terminated may help to avert a
housing shortage and give the local community greater
certainty about the future housing market.

Highway repairs: Industry could be required to reim-
burse state and local governments for the cost of
repairing roads and highways which experience inordinate deterioration due to industry traffic.

Infrastructure cost sharing: Industry could be required to bear some of the costs of expanding the
infrastructure to meet its additional demands for
communications, electricity, water, etc.

Employment regulations: Stipulations with regard to
employment of minorities, women and local residents,
as well as forbidding discrimination, were included
in the trans Alaska oil pipeline right-of-way agreements.

Industrial alcoholism: Industrial alcoholism programs
associated with massive construction projects may help
improve safety records, as well as avoiding putting
the responsibility for these problems on the local
community.

Employee child care: A day care program for children
of employees could attract more female employees, relieve stress on community resources, and minimize
disruptions to children and families.

Car-pooling: Industry-initiated car-pooling or other
transportation programs may reduce traffic congestion
and air pollution.

Use of Local Volunteer Organizations: Industry should
be discouraged from using local volunteer organizations.
When the services of these organizations are used, they
should be compensated through donations of money or

other types of contributions. In Fairbanks, for example, most foremen on the pipeline received required
first-aid training from American Red Cross volunteers
at a considerable burden to the local Red Cross.
Information sharing: A stipulation forcing industry
to gather and disclose information would assist in
averting, ameliorating, or coping with social impacts.
This could include information about the characteristics of the labor force, expenditure patterns in
the local community, and industry plans and requirements which affect the local community.
Both federal and state governments need to establish mechanisms
for enforcing these stipulations, as they have done with regard to stipulations designed to protect the natural environment.

  To give communities a better opportunity to minimize
the negative impacts of large construction projects and maximize the potential benefits, there needs to be a delay between the time a decision is made by a federal or state agency
with regard to resource development and the time that a permit is issued. A delay of at least a year would give local
governments and business persons both certainty about the
impending project and time to plan for it. A delay may also
facilitate the initiation of job training activities and other
programs prior to construction so that local persons could
benefit from employment opportunities over the entire duration
of the project. Preferably, a more rapid decision-making
process would compensate for the delay between making the
decision and implementing it.

  Long-range planning for resource utilization in a
given area would be much more useful to communities than a
series of short-term plans for specific projects. If a community could know what to expect in the future, it would be
able to make better investment decisions. Long-range planning

could also help the community achieve more cohesive goals
for the future and develop the leadership to achieve these
goals.

Resource development industries could minimize impacts on communities if construction projects were planned
for longer periods of time. This would reduce the labor
force at any given time and the amount of overtime paid,
which in turn, would reduce the disparities between people
who did and did not work on the project, providing greater
stability in local conditions.

In addition to these general approaches to redistri-
buting more equitably the responsibilities for addressing
social impacts, the Fairbanks experience suggests some specific types of responsibilities which could be assumed by
federal government and private industry. Local governments
need financial assistance in expanding their infrastructures
to accommodate the increased demands generated by rapid resource development. Two suggestions for such assistance are
a federal bond guarantee program for local governments, and
a program by which the federal government holds local bonds
until the community grows to a population size or real property valuation which can support the bonds. Private businesses in the community need some assurances about their roles
in supplying the needs of the community and the resource development industry. These assurances must be meaningful to
lending institutions. Some form of federal or resource-
industry loan guarantees or contract agreements for local
businesses would enable them to expand their operations to
accommodate the increased demands.

Another lesson to be learned from the Fairbanks experience relates to the importance of information. To plan,
to react, to respond appropriately requires information. Local
communities need to know about industry plans as soon as

possible. Wrong, or deliberately conservative or exaggerated, estimates about workforce, resource needs, and costs are detrimental to any efforts communities may make to address impact problems. Not only do local communities need to know more about the industry which is affecting them, but they also need to know more about themselves.

The Impact Information Center was a very successful and creative approach to community-directed research and feedback. Programs like the Impact Information Center are not enough, however; there needs to be a greater emphasis on information at both the state and federal levels. State agencies play such an active role in Fairbanks that monitoring their activities is necessary to assess changes in the community. Similarly, it would be helpful to have federal agencies monitor their activities in the community.

The two most important types of information needed for assessing impacts of pipeline construction on Fairbanks, planning and decision-making, were never ascertained. These were the number of people in Fairbanks and changes in cost of living. To obtain census data and cost of living information requires a tremendous amount of technical expertise and economic resources which were simply not available to the community. The U.S. Bureau of the Census and the Bureau of Labor Statistics have specialized in gathering and analyzing this type of information, but their resources were not mobilized in the Fairbanks situation. A major contribution could be made by the federal government to help communities attain more autonomy and control over the impacts of massive development projects, if the appropriate federal agencies would assist in ascertaining changes in population and cost of living.

Information is also needed in a more generic sense. Relatively little is known about the dynamics of the impact of massive construction projects on communities. To better prepare for such impacts, it is imperative to understand them better and to develop better predictive models. To facilitate the development of social science in this area, there needs to be greater support for research on the impact of projects and the development of training programs for specialists in social impact assessment.

Finally, the Fairbanks experience poses an ethical dilemma to community leaders, planners, decision-makers, social scientists and citizens. Suppose for a minute that the purpose of environmental impact statements and case studies such as this is to optimize the well-being of a community in a time of rapid change, rather than merely avoiding negative impacts by keeping one jump ahead of the carrying capacity. Now, let us assume that the people of Fairbanks could have the benefit of learning from the trans Alaska oil pipeline experience and could bring their insights from that experience to start anew making decisions about their future. What if the community decided to do everything the same way again? Would that mean that community leaders, planners, decision-makers, social scientists, and citizens had failed? Or, would it mean that the local community had optimized its well-being under the circumstances and desired to maintain that optimum? Or, would it mean that the structure of a community is such a potent force in determining the decisions a community makes that no amount of information, experience, or insight is going to change the direction of community decisions?

Epilogue

September 1976. Construction of the trans Alaska oil pipeline has not yet been completed. A new high school is open, so teenagers are no longer on double-shifts. Senior Citizen housing is nearly ready for occupancy. The Borough

has just begun its public transportation program. The City
Manager announces that the city water supply is too short to
expand water lines according to the plans that voters approved
in the last bond election。 A 22-year-old is convicted of
murdering a cab driver--no motive, just confusion from drugs.
Police are investigating the disappearance of two Teamsters
who worked at the Alyeska warehouse in Fairbanks。 The slain
body of one has been found。 The Governor of Alaska has offered Fairbanks state assistance to combat problems of lawlessness and to help clean up Second Avenue. Results of the
recent primary election reveal that the most popular candi-
date for representative to the state legislature from Fairbanks is the local public relations representative for Alyeska
Pipeline Service COmpany。 Fairbanksans overwhelmingly support
construction of a trans Alaska gas pipeline。

NOTES

Chapter 1:   What Happened to Fairbanks

1. PL 91-190. Sec. 101(a).

2. Information about this document, as well as a wealth of
   information about the entire political process involved
   in issuing the trans Alaska pipeline right-of-way permit
   is contained in Mary Clay Berry's The Alaska Pipeline:
   The Politics of Oil and Native Land Claims, Bloomington:
   Indiana University Press, 1975.

3. Henry M. Jackson, preface to Congress and the Nation's
   Environment: Environmental and Natural Resources Affairs
   of the 92nd Congress, prepared by the Environmental Policy
   Division, Congressional Research Service, Library of Congress, U.S. Government Printing Office, Washington, D.C.,
   1973.

4. Joel Darmstadter and Hans H. Landsberg, "The Economic
   Background," in The Oil Crisis: In Perspective, Daedalus,
   (Fall 1975), p. 26.

5. Ibid., p. 31.

6. Berry, op. cit., p. 274.

7. Ibid.

8. PL 91-190, Sec. 101(b)(2).

9. Charles Edwardson, Jr., testimony before the Department
   of the Interior hearing on the draft environmental impact
   statement for the Trans Alaska Oil Pipeline, Washington,
   D.C., February 17, 1971.

10. Bryon Mallot, testomony before the Department of the Inter-
    ior hearing on the draft environmental impact statement
    for the Trans Alaska Oil Pipeline, Washington, D.C.,
    February 16, 1971.

11. Charles J. Cicchetti, Alaskan Oil: Alternative Routes and
    Markets, Baltimore: Johns Hopkins University Press,
    1972, p. 133.

12. Arlon K. Tussing, George W. Rogers, and Victor Fisher,
    Alaska Pipeline Report, Institute of Social, Economic and
    Government Research, University of Alaska, Fairbanks, 1971.

13. James Lundgren, testimony at the Department of the Interior hearings on the draft environmental impact statement for the Trans Alaska Oil Pipeline, Anchorage, Alaska, February 24, 1971.

14. Julian Rice, testimony at the Department of the Interior hearings on the draft environmental impact statement for the Trans Alaska Oil Pipeline, Anchorage, Alaska, February 24, 1971.

15. U.S. Census, 1970.

16. Robert Engler, The Politics of Oil: Private Power and Democratic Directions, Chicago: University of Chicago Press, 1961.

17. Ibid., p. 17.

18. Charles H. Parr, "Impact Information Center Schematic," paper presented to the Borough Assembly, Fairbanks North Star Borough, 1974.

19. Winthrop Griffith, "How boomtown greed is changing Alaska--blood, toil, tears and oil," New York Times Magazine, July 27, 1975.

20. Mike Goodman, William Endicott and Larry Pryor, "The troubled pipeline," series of articles from The Los Angeles Times, November 18, 19, 28, 1975.

21. Gorde Sinclair, "Demon greed invades Alaska," Edmonton Journal, July 5, 1975.

22. Pamela L. Baldwin and Malcolm F. Baldwin, Onshore Planning for Offshore Oil: Lessons from Scotland, Conservation Foundation, Washington, D.C., 1975.

Chapter 2: Gold in the Streets

1. Joseph G. Holtry, "Air quality in a subarctic community: Fairbanks, Alaska," Arctic, 26(4):297.

2. Carl Benson (personal communication, 1974).

3. Carl Benson, "The role of air pollution in arctic planning and development," The Polar Record, 14(93):788 (1969).

4. Anonymous, "Parker is pessimistic," Anchorage Daily Times, May 6, 1975.

5. Ibid.

6. Anonymous, "Teamsters ratify safety pact calling for flagmen in Elliott," Fairbanks Daily News-Miner, February 20, 1975.

7. Anonymous, "Fairbanks man survives Elliott truck accident," Fairbanks Daily News-Miner, April 9, 1975.

8. Anonymous, "Some loads moving as drivers await solution on road troubles." Fairbanks Daily-News Miner, February 20, 1975.

9. Advertisement in Fairbanks Daily News-Miner, August 14, 1975.

10. Anonymous, "Alyeska pulls Elliott ads after ridicule campaign," Fairbanks Daily News-Miner, August 12, 1975.

11. Anonymous, "Double-wide insulation loads unsafe, say Teamster drivers," Fairbanks Daily News-Miner, February 25, 1976.

12. Ibid.

13. Ibid.

14. Flip Todd, "Truckers putting on brakes after record run," Alaska Industry, January 1976, p. 51.

15. Edmund Orbeck, personal communication, letter of October 18, 1976.

16. Mike Goodman and William Endicott, "Alaska Today--runaway crime and union violence," The Los Angeles Times, November 18, 1975.

17. Craig Smith, "Power of the Teamsters," Fairbanks Daily News-Miner, October 25, 1975.

18. Flip Todd, op. cit.

19. Craig Smith, op. cit.

20. Mike Goodman and William Endicott, op. cit.

21. Howard Weaver and Bob Porterfield, "Union fiefdom rules Fairbanks warehouse," Anchorage Daily News, December 18, 1975.

22. Flip Todd, op. cit., p. 49.

23. Ibid., p. 32.

Chapter 3: $$$

1. Arlon Tussing and Monica Thomas, "Consumer prices, personal income and earnings in Alaska," Alaska Review of Business and Economic Conditions, 11(3) (October 1974).

2. Ibid.

3. Ibid.

4. Northern Heating, a Texaco distributor, raised the price per gallon of 100 gallons of #2 heating oil from .494 to .594; Kobuk Oil Company, a distributor of Tesoro petroleum products, raised the price per gallon of #1 heating oil from .454 to .559, and the price per gallon for 500 gallons of #1 heating oil from .454 to .549.

5. The dollar cost increase of automobile repairs was based upon estimates on accident forms filed with the Fairbanks Police Department and actual payments made by a State Farm Insurance Company agent as reimbursement for automobile repair expense.

6. Letter to the Editor from Mrs. William W. Willson, Fairbanks Daily News-Miner, February 27, 1976.

7. Food price increase for U.S. and Anchorage are taken from the Bureau of Labor Statistics Consumer Price Index. From January 1975 to January 1976, Anchorage experienced a 4.2% increase in prices of food at home, a 16.5% increase in prices of food away from home, and a total increase of 6.8% for all food purchased.

8. Budget and Audit Committee, Alaska State Legislature, "Summary of: A Review of Construction of State Owned Parking Garages in Anchorage, Juneau and Fairbanks," September 16, 1975.

9. Letter from Borough Mayor John A. Carlson to Alaska Governor Jay Hammond, October 28, 1975.

10. Figures provided by Alyeska Pipeline Service Company.

11. Figures from Alaska State Employment Center Daily Job Demand List.

12. Dave Little, Senior Cost Engineer for Alyeska Pipeline Service Company, personal communication, 1976.

13. Tom Russell, Manager of Nordstroms, as reported in Alaska Economic Trends, February 1976.

14. Unidentified official of Pay 'n' Save Company, as reported in Alaska Economic Trends, February 1976.

15. Fairbanks North Star Borough Financial Statement, February 1976. Table VIII, p. 12. Fiscal year references in this text cover the period from July 1 of the first year cited to June 30 of the second year cited.

16. Ibid.

17. Ibid., Table X, p. 14.

18. Statement by Earl Wyman, Director of the Fairbanks North Star Borough's Assessing Office, to the Impact Advisory Committee regular meeting, February 18, 1976.

19. Fairbanks North Star Borough Financial Statement, February 1976, Table XIV, p. 18.

20. Ibid.

21. Ibid.

22. This is made possible through the provisions of Alaska Statute 43, which stipulates that the State of Alaska assess oil and gas exploration, production, and pipeline transportation property and levy a 20 mills annual tax. Local governments may be reimbursed from the state fund for taxes on the same property at the rate that applies to other property taxed by the municipality. Since the state includes real property in its assessment, the borough benefits from this even though it does not levy taxes on the real property of other taxpayers in the borough.

23. In addition to grants to local governments in the Fairbanks area, Chapter 147, SLA1974, appropriated $1,894,000 to the City of Anchorage; $1,325,000 to the Anchorage Borough; $2,046,000 to the City of Valdez; $379,000 to Delta Junction; $379,000 to the North Slope Borough; and $189,000 to the City of Barrow.

24. Also granted under Chapter 8, SLA1974SSS, was $1,727,800 to the City of Anchorage; $1,583,000 to the Anchorage Borough; $1,416,500 to the City of Valdez; $312,500 to

Anchorage Community Hospital; $166,450 to the City of
Haines; $455,000 to the North Slope Borough; $100,300 to
Matanuska-Susitna Borough; $140,500 to the City of Cordova;
$123,000 to the City of Kenai; $56,500 to the City of
Seward; $84,000 to the City of Soldatna; and $53,900 to
the City of Yakutat.

25. U.S. Census, 1970: 14,771 in the City of Fairbanks plus
the populations of the subdivisions annexed that year,
including Graehl (349), Lemeta (1,318), Aurora-Johnson
(1,454), South Bjerremark (76), and two other areas total-
ling 75.

26. U.S. Census, 1970.

27. The figure $301,048 is derived from summing the following
appropriations: $59,298 for Impact Information Center;
$113,100 for Fairbanks Native Association recreation pro-
gram; $113,730 for the emergency sleep-off shelter;
and $14,920 for the emergency service patrol.

28. Tussing and Thomas, op. cit., p. 23.

Chapter 4: Alaska Hire and Minority Hire

1. Alaska Statutes, Title 38, Sec. 38.40.010.

2. Right of Way Lease for the Trans Alaska Pipeline between
the State of Alaska and Amerada Hess Corporation, ARCO
Pipe Line Company, Exxon Pipeline Company, Mobil Alaska
Pipeline Company, Phillips Petroleum Company, Sohio Pipe
Line Company, and Union Alaska Pipeline Company.

3. Alaska Statutes, Title 36, Sec. 36.10.010.

4. Alaska Statutes, Title 38, Sec. 38.40.020(b).

5. Alaska Statutes, Title 38, Sec. 38.40.050.

6. Alaska Statutes, Title 38, Sec. 38.40.090.

7. Regulations published in the Federal Register, 39(186)
(September 24, 1974), pp. 31285-31290.

8. Glen Ritt, "Pipeline job charges fly," Anchorage Daily
Times, October 11, 1974.

9. Anonymous, "Meet is set to discuss minority hire," Anchorage Daily Times, October 26, 1974.

10. Anonymous, "Minorities agree 'Alaskans First'," Anchorage Daily Times, November 15, 1974.

11. Anonymous, "Task Force of minority plans march," Anchorage Daily Times, January 22, 1975.

12. Anonymous, "Minority hire chief gives up job," Anchorage Daily Times, September 23, 1974.

13. Anonymous, "Outside job seekers pack license bureau," Anchorage Daily Times, August 14, 1974.

14. Anonymous, "Alyeska's Patton tells giant project's status," Alaska Industry Magazine, December 1974, pp. 45-46, 54-62.

15. Letter from Glenn H. Lundell, Manager of Alaska Manpower Resources Department of Alyeska Pipeline Service Company, to Joe LaRocca, Director of the Impact Information Center, April 13, 1975.

16. Letter from State Senator John Sackett to Mim Dixon, January 15, 1975.

17. Figures provided by Peter Reamey, Apprenticeship Outreach Program, personal communication, 1975.

18. Quotation from Frank Baily, "Minority hire chief gives up job," Anchorage Daily Times, September 23, 1974.

19. Quotation from State Pipeline Coordinator Chuck Champion in "Hiring investigators get $148,300 budget," Fairbanks Daily News-Miner, October 15, 1974.

20. Anonymous, "The anti-bias bottleneck," Wall Street Journal, October 22, 1974.

21. Trans-Alaska Pipeline System Project Agreement, May 7, 1974, Article VI, Part 6.

22. Letter from Kevin F. Kelly, legal counsel for Alaska State Department of Labor, to James A. Witt, general counsel for Teamsters Local 959, March 16, 1976.

23. Letter from Kevin F. Kelly, legal counsel for Alaska State Department of Labor, to John S. Irving, general counsel for National Labor Relations Board, March 18, 1976.

24. Laborers Local 341 Case No. 19-CB-2626.

25. Other cases cited by the NLRB in the summary report of their decision were Bricklayers, Local 28 (Plaza Builder,

Incorporated), 134 NLRB 751; Local Union No. 337 (Townsend
& Bottum, Inc.), 417 NLRB 929; J. Willis & Son Masonry,
191 NLRB 872, 873-874; Local 8, IBEW (Romanoff Electrical
Corp.), 221 NLRB No. 180; and Local 5420 Operating Engineers (Ralph A. Marino), 151 NLRB 497, 500.

26. Local 798 was not a party to the project labor agreement
and signed a separate agreement with the oil companies
which did not have an Alaska hire clause, thereby giving
the State of Alaska no leverage in promoting the participation of Alaska residents in the union.

27. Quotation from Bill Vaudrin, executive director of the
Alaska State Human Rights Commission, in "Human Rights
executive quits after threats, harrassment," in Fairbanks
Daily News-Miner, September 26, 1974.

28. Glenn Lundell, Manager, Alaska Manpower Resources, Alyeska Pipeline Service Company, personal communication,
1976.

29. Russell Molt, Director, Wage and Hour Division, Alaska
Department of Labor, personal communication, 1976.

30. Figure for First Quarter, 1976, "Fiscal '75 Pipeline
Resident Analysis by Quarterly Report," Alaska State
Department of Labor.

31. Alyeska Pipeline Service Company, "Plan of Action--
Native Utilization," p. 5.

32. Ibid., p. 6.

33. Glenn Lundell, Manager, Alaska Manpower Resources, Alyeska
Pipeline Service Company, personal communications, 1976.

34. Ibid.

35. Alyeska Pipeline Service Company, "Fact Book Insert--
Chronology," December 1975.

Chapter 6: Impact that Didn't

1. Fairbanks North Star Borough, "Fairbanks North Star Borough
Oil Pipeline Impact Statement," January 15, 1974, p. 30.

2. Figures are taken from a survey conducted by Alyeska Pipeline Service Company in conjunction with the Fairbanks
North Star Borough Impact Information Center. All newly-

hired non-resident pipeline workers were asked during
orientation to fill out a form which indicated whether
they had brought or planned to bring their families to
Fairbanks, the ages of their children, and when they
planned to relocate their families. Ratios were based
upon the number of people going through orientation in
relation to the information on the returned forms. The
ratios varied over time, with more people indicating that
they intended to bring their families to Fairbanks during
the first construction season, and fewer people planning
to bring families during the second construction season.
There was no follow-up to determine how many of the people
who intended to bring their families to Fairbanks actually
did so.

3. Alaska Statutes 34.06, Emergency Residential Rent Regu-
    lations and Control Act.

4. Jean Kizer, "Wanted: 45 roommates to share rent," Fair-
    banks Daily News-Miner, May 9, 1975.

5. Letter to the Editor, Fairbanks Daily News-Miner, May 11,
    1975.

6. Anonymous, "The Northern Light," Fairbanks Rescue Mission,
    March 1976.

7. Bureau of the Census, U.S. Department of Commerce, "Esti-
    mates of the Population of Alaska Census Divisions and
    Metropolitan Areas: July 1, 1973 and 1974," June 1975.

8. This approach, first developed by Mathematical Science
    Northwest, Inc., was used by many sources, including the
    Fairbanks North Star Borough in its "Fairbanks North Star
    Borough Oil Pipeline Impact Statement," January 15, 1974.

9. Marsha Bennett, Valdez Project research team member,
    personal communication, 1976.

Chapter 7:   Boom/Bust Dilemma

1. Joe LaRocca, Pipeline Impact Office Report No. One, Fair-
    banks North Star Borough, July 11, 1974, p. 5.

2. Department of Housing and Urban Development, Region X,
    "Housing and Urban Development Situation Report, Fairbanks,
    Alaska, as of April 1, 1975," Fairbanks, Alaska, June 1975.

3. "Housing Market," Pipeline Impact Information Center Re-
    port Number 26, Fairbanks North Star Borough, April 21, 1976

4. Ibid.

5. Mobile home figures compiled by the Fairbanks North Star Borough Impact Information Center, based upon records from the Borough Assessing Office.

6. Golden Valley Electric Association requested a 48.7 percent rate increase in 1976 over the base rate which applied since 1973; however, during the interim GVEA consumers paid a surcharge on their electric bills which was equivalent to the proportional increase in costs.

7. Richard A. Cooley, Fairbanks, Alaska: A Survey of Progress, Juneau: (Territorial) Development Board, 1954, p. 5.

8. Ibid.

9. Ibid.

10. Donald L. Quandt, Fort Wainwright's Contribution to the Fairbanks Economy. Unpublished Master's thesis, Fairbanks: University of Alaska, 1974, p. 25.

11. Cooley, op. cit., p. 6.

12. Ibid., p. 22.

13. Ibid., p. 11.

14. James H. Shoemaker, Fairbanks and the Interior of Alaska: Potentials for Growth, 1970-1980, College: University of Alaska, 1970, preface.

15. Alaska State Housing Authority, Community Impacts of the Trans Alaska Pipeline, Juneau, Alaska, 1971, p. 15.

16. John Carlson, speech given at "Fairbanks and Interior ALaska" A One Day Community Forum on Growth," Fairbanks, Alaska, April 26, 1975.

Chapter 8: The Chamber and the Churches

1. "Fairbanks, Alaska," Fairbanks Commercial Club, 1916.

2. Berry, 1971, p. 91.

3. Celia B. Hunter, testimony at the Department of the Interior hearings on the draft environmental impact statement for the Trans Alaska Oil Pipeline, Anchorage, Alaska, February 24, 1971.

4. Craig Smith, "Gilmer's swan song: greed?" Fairbanks
   Daily News-Miner, October 13, 1975.

5. According to Alaska Department of Labor figures, in 1974
   the total employment in the Fairbanks Election District
   was 18,963, of which 6,823 were employed in federal,
   state and local government jobs.

6. Gene Straatmeyer and others, "Social Concerns Task Force--
   Alaska Christian Conference," February 1, 1975, p. 1.

7. Anonymous, "Legalized prostitution, gambling is proposed:
   Church Council Committee plans public forum," All-Alaska
   Weekly, October 8, 1974.

8. Anonymous, "Businessmen chided for skipping forum," Fairbanks Daily News-Miner, April 29, 1975.

9. Ibid.

10. Ibid.

11. "Fairbanks and Interior Alaska: A One Day Community Forum
    on Growth," published by the Social Concerns Committee of
    the Fairbanks Council of Churches in cooperation with the
    Fairbanks Town and Village Association for Economic De-
    velopment, Incorporated, July 1975.

12. Jean Straatmeyer, "Theology and Social Involvement,"
    paper presented to Alaskan Anthropology Conference,
    Fairbanks, Alaska, March 14-15, 1975.

13. In-depth interviews with 10 local ministers were conducted
    by Jean Straatmeyer and another interview was conducted
    by Bob Clemens in 1975. Quotations are taken from the
    written accounts of those interviews.

14. Questionnaire survey of local churches was conducted by
    the Impact Information Center in March 1976, and reported
    in Pipeline Impact Information Center Report Number 26,
    April 26, 1976.

15. Ibid.

16. Ibid.

17. Ibid.

Chapter 9: Unexpected Impacts

1. Impact Information Center Report No. 27.

2. Ibid.

3. Ibid.

4. Ibid.

5. Ibid.

6. Ibid.

7. Ibid.

8. Ibid.

9. Figures derived from monthly reports of the Northern
    Regional Laboratory, Division of Public Health, Department
    of Health and Social Services, State of Alaska.

10. Julie Stuart, "Post Office is Fairbanks barometer," Fair-
    banks Daily News-Miner, October 20, 1975.

11. Ibid.

12. Impact Information Center Report No. 26.

13. Ibid.

14. Judy Blake, "It's not sunny Cuba but it is a better life,"
    Fairbanks Daily News-Miner, February 19, 1976.

Chapter 10: Teenagers are Running Fairbanks

1. Fairbanks Juvenile Intake Office, "Summary of Children's
    Delinquent Acts, 1973-1975," Juvenile Intake Office,
    Family Division, Fourth Judicial District, Superior Court
    of the State of Alaska, Fairbanks, Alaska, 1976.

2. Ibid.

3. Ibid.

4. Julie Stuart, "Boy sent to Alcantra," Fairbanks Daily
    News-Miner, March 31, 1976.

5. Anonymous, "Police scotch robbery wave, nab juveniles,"
    All-Alaska Weekly, February 20, 1976.

6. Julie Stuart, "Judge rules youth to be tried as adult," Fairbanks Daily News-Miner, March 4, 1976.

7. Anonymous, "Court roundup--Boys plead guilty to armed robbery," Fairbanks Daily News-Miner, February 28, 1976.

8. Fairbanks Police Department Activity Reports, December 1973 and December 1975.

9. Fairbanks Juvenile Intake Office, 1976.

10. Jean Kizer, "Local police 'crack' car theft operation," Fairbanks Daily News-Miner, February 25, 1976.

11. Anonymous, "Fairbanks youths 'collared' for four-wheel drive thefts," Fairbanks Daily News-Miner, April 8, 1976.

12. Julie Stuart, "Facts of case were sinple, but things grew complicated," Fairbanks Daily News-Miner, April 8, 1976.

13. Fairbanks Juvenile Intake Office, op. cit.

14. Alaska Department of Public Safety, "Pipeline Yearly Report, 1975," 1976.

15. Ibid.

16. Letter to the Editor, Fairbanks Daily News-Miner, March 19, 1976.

Chapter 11: The Newest Spectator Sport

1. Anonymous, "On the inside," Fairbanks Daily News-Miner, September 24, 1975.

2. Anonymous, "Council takes no action on bar license transfer," Fairbanks Daily News-Miner, November 4, 1975.

3. Ronald Crowe, Letter to the Editor, "A Happy Reunion," Fairbanks Daily News-Miner, February 23, 1976.

4. Nancy Doherty, "The prostitution question--views from a different world," Anchorage Daily News, April 19, 1976.

5. Anonymous, "Prostitution results in assault," Fairbanks Daily News-Miner, May 19, 1976.

6. Anonymous, "Troopers continue probe of local cab driver murder," Fairbanks Daily News-Miner, January 29, 1976.

315

7. Anonymous, "Checker Cab drivers riled up--many carry guns for protection," All-Alaska Weekly, January 30, 1976.

8. Julie Stuart, "Criminal element won't pack bags and leave," Fairbanks Daily News-Miner, April 1, 1976.

9. Ibid.

10. Mike Goodman and William Endicott, "Alaska today--runaway crime and union violence," The Los Angeles Times, November 18, 1975.

11. Howard Weaver and Robert Porterfield, "Union fiefdom rules Fairbanks warehouse," Anchorage Daily News, December 18, 1975.

12. Anonymous, "Specialist urges probe of crime," Anchorage Daily News, December 30, 1975.

13. Ibid.

14. Fairbanks Daily News-Miner, February 4, 1976.

15. Anonymous, "Troopers are 'snowed'," Fairbanks Daily News-Miner, October 22, 1975.

16. Ibid.

17. Steve Kline, "Don't call a cop in Fairbanks," Anchorage Daily News, March 7, 1975.

18. Anonymous, "Manpower shortage puts burden on law," Fairbanks Daily News-Miner, May 13, 1975.

19. Steve Kline, op. cit.

20. Anonymous, "New 'top' troopers move to Fairbanks detachment," Fairbanks Daily News-Miner, July 30, 1975.

21. Anonymous, "Troopers are 'snowed'," Fairbanks Daily News-Miner, October 22, 1975.

22. Jean Kizer, "Drug arrests sweep streets," Fairbanks Daily News-Miner, December 26, 1975.

23. Ibid.

24. Jean Kizer, "Nine arrested on heroin charges," Fairbanks Daily News-Miner, December 6, 1975.

Chapter 12:   Mental Health

1.   Francis T. Miller, et al., Experiences in Rural Mental
     Health Measuring and Monitoring Stress in Communities,
     Department of Psychiatry, Division of Community Psychia-
     try, Chapel Hill: University of North Carolina School of
     Medicine (1974), p. 3.

2.   Fairbanks Community Survey, conducted by the Institute of
     Social and Economic Research at the University of Alaska,
     Fairbanks, under the direction of John A. Kruse.   Dr.
     Kruse presented preliminary findings of the survey in a
     panel at the 27th Alaska Science Conference in Fairbanks,
     August 6, 1976.

3.   Marge Pentland, Social Worker with the Division of Social
     Services, Alaska State Department of Health and Social
     Services, personal communication, 1976.

4.   Robert Kraus and Patricia Buffler, "Intercultural varia-
     tions in mortality due to violence," paper presented at
     the Annual Meeting of the American Psychiatric Associa-
     tion, Miami, Florida, May 1976.

5.   Alaska Department of Health and Social Services, "Octo-
     ber Reports."

6.   Percentages are based on figures prepared by Sue Fison,
     Fairbanks North Star Borough Impact Information Center,
     in conjunction with the Alaska Department of Health and
     Social Services.

7.   Letter from W.W. Gray, Social Worker II, Division of
     Family and Children Services, Department of Health and
     Social Services, State of Alaska, to Mim Dixon, May 16,
     1975.

8.   Ibid.

9.   Fairbanks Community Survey, conducted by the Institute of
     Social and Economic Research at the University of Alaska,
     Fairbanks, under the direction of John A. Kruse.   Dr.
     Kruse presented preliminary findings of the survey in a
     panel at the 27th Alaska Science Conference in Fairbanks,
     August 6, 1976.

10. Miller et al., op. cit., p. 3.

Chapter 13:   People with the Most to Lose and the Least to Gain

1. A one-page questionnaire containing 10 questions was de-
    veloped by the Impact Information Center. A total of
    482 questionnaires were distributed by the Manpower Ser-
    vices Department of Bechtel Corporation, then-management
    contractor for Alyeska Pipeline Service Company. Sets of
    questionnaires were sent to secretaries of 26 departments
    within Bechtel and 21 other pipeline-related offices.
    The secretaries were requested to distribute the question-
    naires to employees within their offices, to collect the
    completed questionnaires, and to mail them to the Impact
    Information Center. Approximately one-half of the
    questionnaries were returned. Although the sampling was
    not done scientifically, a broad range of pipeline offices
    was sampled and the sample appears to approximate the
    workforce in distribution by sex.

2. Quotation taken from survey of Senior Citizens conducted
    by the Impact Information Center in conjunction with the
    North Star Council on Aging in March 1975.

3. Ibid.

4. Ibid.

5. Ibid.

6. Ibid.

7. A questionnaire survey of Senior Citizens residing in the
    Fairbanks area was conducted in March 1975 by the Impact
    Information Center in conjunction with the North Star
    Council on Aging. A survey form with 16 questions was de-
    veloped after talking with persons who work with Senior
    Citizens. The questionnaire was then pretested on several
    Senior Citizens and revised. It was then reproduced and
    attached to the front of the North Star Council on Aging
    monthly newsletter and distributed along with a self-
    addressed, stamped envelope, to approximately 600 persons.
    To explain the purpose of the questionnaire and to help
    persons fill out the form, an outreach program was initia-
    ted utilizing radio, television, the local newspaper, and
    direct contact. A total of 174 completed questionnaries
    was returned by April 1, 1975, representing a total of
    304 persons residing in households of the respondents.
    The sample includes roughly 17 to 30 percent of the Senior
    Citizens in the Fairbanks area. The age distribution of
    the survey respondents was:

7. (continued)

Age	Number
60-64	38
65-69	58
70-74	37
75-79	18
80-84	12
over 85	6

A more in-depth analysis of the survey results was published by the Impact Information Center as a special report entitled, "Senior Citizens: The Effects of the Pipeline Construction on Older Persons Living in Fairbanks," June 25, 1975.

8. Quotation taken from Senior Citizens survey conducted by the Impact Information Center in connunction with the North Star Council on Aging, March 1975.

9. Ibid.

0. Ibid.

11. Ibid.

12. Ibid.

13. Ibid.

14. Ibid.

15. Ibid.

16. Ibid.

17. Ibid.

18. Ibid.

19. Ibid.

Chapter 14: Reviewing Assumptions, A Model for Planners

1. Mathematical Sciences Northwest, Inc., A Study of the Economic and Sociological Impact of Construction and Initial Operation of the Trans Alaska Pipeline, MSNW Report 72-4d-4,5,6, Seattle, Wash.: Mathematical Sciences Northwest, Inc.

2. Department of the Interior, Final Environmental Impact Statement, Proposed Trans-Alaska Pipeline, Springfield, Va.: National Technical Information Service (1972).

3. Northwest Federal Regional Council, Attachment A: A Case Study, The Secondary Socioeconomic Impacts of the Trans Alaska Pipeline, appended to "Social and Economic Impact of Energy Developments," January 24, 1975.

4. Fairbanks North Star Borough, "Fairbanks North Star Borough Oil pipeline Impact Statement," January 15, 1974.

5. Mathematical Sciences Northwest, op. cit., Vol. 1, p. 3.

6. Ibid, Vol. II, p. 181.

7. Fairbanks North Star Borough, op. cit., p. 6-7.

8. Mathematican Sciences Northwest, op. cit., Vol. II, p.1975.

9. Ibid, p. 176.

Chapter 15: A Model for Social Scientists

1. J.A. Barnes, "Class and committees in a Norwegian parish island," Human Relations, 7: 1954, pp. 39-58.

2. R. Redfield, The Little Community: Viewpoints for the Study of a Human Whole, Chicago: University of Chicago Press, 1955.

3. J.W. Bennett, "Microcosm-macrocosm relationships in North American agrarian society," American Anthropologist, 69, 1967, pp. 441-454.

4. C.O. Frake, "Cultural ecology and ethnography," American Anthropologist, 64, 1952, pp. 54-59.

5. Lamont Cole, "Sketches of general and comparative demography," Cold Springs Harbor Symposia on Quantitative Biology, Vol. 22, New York: Long Island Biological Association, 1957, pp. 1-15.

6. Charles Darwin, The Origin of Species, New York: P.F. Collier & Son, 1859.

7. Thomas R. Malthus, An Essay on the Principle of Population, London: Ward, Lock, 1890.

320

8. Ezra Zubrow, "Carrying capacity and dynamic equilibrium in the prehistoric Southwest," American Antiquity, 36, 1971, p. 128.

9. Robert J. Braidwood, "Prehistoric Men," Chicago: Field Museum of Natural History, 1963, p. 121.

10. Gordon V. Childe, "The urban revolution," in Mark P. Leone (ed.), Contemporary Archeology, A Guide to Theory and Contributions, Carbondale: Southern Illinois University Press, 1972, p. 98.

11. D. E. Dumond, "Population growth and culture change," Southwestern Journal of Anthropology, 21, 1965, p. 310.

12. Zubrow, op. cit., p. 128.

13. Ibid.

14. Joseph B. Birdsell, "Some population problems involving Pleistocene man," Cold Spring Harbor Symposoa on Quantitative Biology, Vol. 22, New York: Long Island Biological Association, 1957, p. 61.

15. A. J. Hawley, Human Ecology: A Theory of Community Structure, New York: Ronald Press, 1950, p. 151.

16. J.H. Steward, Theory of Culture Change: The Methodology of Multilinear Evolution, Urband: Univeristy of Illinois Press, 1955, p. 41.

17. Ibid., p. 42.

18. Ibid., p. 41.

19. Childe, op. cit.

20. Hawley, op. cit., p. 151.

21. Steward, op. cit., p. 42.

22. R.C. Lewontin, "The adaptations of populations to varying environments," Cold Springs Harbor Symposia in Quantitative Biology, Vol. 22, New York: Long Island Biological Association, 1957, p. 397.

23. Birdsell, op. cit.

24. Ibid., p. 64.

25. Lewis R. Binford, "Post-Pleistocene adaptations," in S.R. Binford and L.R. Binford (eds.), New Perspectives in Archeology, Chicago: Aldine, 1968, p. 248.

26. Ibid.

27. Malthus, op. cit.

28. V.C. Wynne-Edwards, "Self-regulating systems in populations of animals," Science, 147, 1965, pp. 1543-1548.

29. Zubrow, op. cit., p. 128.

30. Cole, op. cit., p. 13.

31. Edward T. Hall, The Hidden Dimension, Garden City, N.Y.: Doubleday, 1966.

32. D.H. Scott, "Cultural and natural checks on population growth," in Andrew P. Vayda (ed.) Environment and Cultural Behavior, Garden City, N.Y.: Natural History Press, 1969.

33. John B. Calhoun, "Social welfare as a variable in population dynamics," Cold Spring Harbor Symposia in Quantitative Biology, Vol. 22, New York: Long Island Biological Asosciation, 1957, p. 339.

34. Hawley, op. cit., p. 171.

35. Calhoun, op. cit., p. 339.

36. Hall, op. cit.

37. Scott, op. cit.

38. This hypothesis is put forth by Lewis Binford, op. cit.

39. Bennett, op. cit., p. 452.

40. Barnes, op. cit., p. 44.

41. Bennett, op. cit., p. 444.

42. Redfield, op. cit., p. 29.

43. Frake, op. cit., p. 54.

BIBLIOGRAPHY

Alaska Department of Community and Regional Affairs
1974   Pipeline Corridor Community Conference, Fairbanks,
        Alaska, June 3-5, 1974. Photocopy.

1976   Report on trans-Alaska pipeline impact expenditures
        by state and local governments draft report, Febru-
        ary 1976, prepared by Community Planning Division,
        Alaska Department of Community and Regional Affairs,
        Juneau, Alaska.

Alaska Department of Labor
1976   Fiscal '75 pipeline resident analysis by quarterly
        report. Unpublished.

Alaska Department of Law
1976   An Impact Analysis of Construction of the Trans-
        Alaska Pipeline on the Administration of Criminal
        Justice in Alaska. Juneau: Criminal Division,
        Alaska Department of Law.

Alaska Department of Public Safety
1976   Pipeline yearly report, 1975. Juneau: Department
        of Public Safety, State of Alaska. Photocopy.

Alaska Division of Legislative Audit
1973   A study of food stamp recipients in Alaska, Decem-
        ber, 1973. Prepared for Department of Health and
        Social Services by the Division of Legislative Audit,
        Juneau, Alaska.

Alaska State Housing Authority
1971   Community impacts of the trans-Alaska pipeline.
        Juneau: Alaska State Housing Authority.

Alaska State Legislature
1975   Summary of: A review of construction of state owned
        parking garages in Anchorage, Juneau, and Fairbanks.
        A memorandum from the Budget and Audit Committee,
        Alaska State Legislature, September 16.

Alaska State Superior Court Juvenile Intake Office
1976   Summary of children's delinquent acts, 1972-1975.
        Fairbanks: Alaska State Superior Court Juvenile
        Intake Office, Family Division, Fourth Judicial
        District. Photocopy.

Alyeska Pipeline Service Company
1974   Trans-Alaska Pipeline System Project Agreement,
        May 7, 1974.

1974   Pipeline and roads monthly EEO compliance report by
        job classification, July 1974-December 1974. Sub-
        mitted to the Office for Equal Opportunity, U.S.
        Department of the Interior.

1975   Pipeline and roads monthly EEO compliance report by
        job classification, January 1975-August 1975. Sub-
        mitted to the Office for Equal Opportunity, U.S.
        Department of the Interior.

1975   Alyeska employer information report EEO-1, Septem-
        ber 1975-December 1975. Computer printouts sub-
        mitted to the Office for Equal Opportunity, U.S.
        Department of the Interior.

1976   Alyeska employer information report EEO-1, January
        1976-March 1976. Computer printouts submitted to
        the Office for Equal Opportunity, U.S. Department of
        the Interior.

n.d.   Plan of action--Native utilization. Photocopy.

Baldwin, Pamela L. and Malcom F. Baldwin
1975   Onshore Planning for Offshore Oil: Lessons from
        Scotland. Washington, D.C.: Conservation Foundation.

Barnes, J.A.
1954   Class and committees in a Norwegian parish island,
        Human Relations, 7:39-58.

Bennett, J.W.
1967   Microcosm-macrocosm relationships in North American
        agrarian society, American Anthropologist, 69:441-454.

Benson, Carl S.
1969   The role of air pollution in Arctic planning and
        development, Polar Record, 14(93).

1970   Ice fog--low temperature air pollution. Cold Regions
        Research and Engineering Laboratory (CRREL), Re-
        search Report 121. (This report may be obtained
        from the Geophysical Institute, University of Alaska,
        Fairbanks, or from the U.S. Army Corps of Engineers,
        Cold Regions Research and Engineering Laboratory,
        Hanover, New Hampshire.)

Benson, Carl S. (continued)
1970   Ice fog, Weather, 25(1).

n.d.   Ice fog. Engineering and Science, Los Angeles:
        California Institute of Technology.

Berry, Mary Clay
1975   The Alaska Pipeline--The Politics of Oil and Native
        Land Claims. Bloomington: Indiana University Press.

Binford, Lewis
1968   Post-Pleistocene adaptations, in Binford, S.R. and
        Binford, L.R. (eds.) New Perspectives in Archeology.
        Chicago: Aldine.

Birdsell, Joseph B.
1957   Some population problems involving Pleistocene Man,
        pp. 47-68 in Cold Spring Harbor Symposia on Quanti-
        tative Biology, Vol. 22. New York: Long Island
        Biological Association.

Braidwood, Robert J.
1963   Prehistoric Men. 6th ed. Popular Series, Anthro-
        pology, No. 37. Chicago: Field Museum of Natural
        History.

Calhoun, John B.
1957   Social welfare as a variable in population dynamics,
        pp. 339-355 in Cold Spring Harbor Symposia on Quanti-
        tative Biology, Vol. 22. New York: Long Island
        Biological Association.

Carlson, John
1975   Speech to Fairbanks and Interior Alaska: A one day
        community forum on growth. Fairbanks, Alaska,
        April 26.

Center for Political Research
1970   Federal policy on the trans-Alaska oil pipeline.
        Washington, D.C.: photocopy.

Childe, Gordon V.
1950   The urban revolution. Town Planning Review, Vol. 21,
        pp. 3-17.

Cicchetti, Charles J.
1972   Alaskan Oil: Alternative Routes and Markets.
        Baltimore: The Johns Hopkins Press.

City of Fairbanks
1973   Fairbanks Police Department activity report,
        December. Photocopy.

1974   Fairbanks Police Department activity report.
        December. Photocopy.

1975   Fairbanks Police Department activity report.
        December. Photocopy.

Clemen, Robert
1975   The Social Concerns Committee: Religion and Poli-
        tics. Paper presented to the Alaska Anthropological
        Conference, Fairbanks, Alaska, March 14-15, 1974.

Cole, LaMont, C.
1957   Sketches of general and comparative demography,
        pp. 1-15 in Cold Spring Harbor Symposia on Quanti-
        tative Biology, Vol. 22. New York: Long Island
        Biological Association.

Cooley, Richard A.
1954   Fairbanks, Alaska: A survey of progress. Juneau:
        (Territorial) Development Board.

Darnstadter, Joel and Hans H. Landsberg
1975   The economic background in the oil crisis: In per-
        spective, Daedalus, Fall, p. 26.

Darwin, Charles
1859   On the Origin of Species by Means of Natural Selec-
        tion. London: John Murray.

Despres, L.A.
1968   Anthropological theory, cultural pluralism, and the
        study of complex societies, Current Anthropology,
        9:3-26.

Dumond, D.E.
1965   Population growth and culture change, Southwestern
        Journal of Anthropology, 21:302-324.

Engler, Robert
1961   The Politics of Oil: A Study of Private Power and
        Democratic Directions. Chicago: University of
        Chicago Press.

Environmental Policy Division, Congressional Research Service,
     Library of Congress
1973   Congress and the Nation's Environment--Environmental
        and Natural Resources Affairs of the 92nd Congress.
        Washington, D.C.: U.S. Government Printing Office.

Fairbanks Commercial Club
1916   Fairbanks, Alaska.

Fairbanks North Star Borough
1974   Oil pipeline impact statement. Photocopy.

1974   Impact Information Center Regular Reports, Nos. 1-11.
        Fairbanks: Fairbanks North Star Borough Impact
        Information Center. Photocopy.

1975   Impact Information Center Regular Reports, Nos. 12-22.
        Fairbanks: Fairbanks North Star Borough Impact
        Information Center. Photocopy.

1975   Minority hire and Alaska hire on the pipeline. Im-
        pact Information Center Special Report No. 1, Febru-
        ary 1. Fairbanks: Fairbanks North Star Borough
        Impact Information Center. Photocopy.

1975   Senior citizens: The effects of pipeline construc-
        tion on older persons living in Fairbanks. Impact
        Information Center Report No. 2, June 25. Fairbanks:
        Fairbanks North Star Borough Impact Information
        Center. Photocopy.

1975   Questions and answers about the cost of living in
        Fairbanks. Impact Information Center Special Report
        No. 3, December 12. Fairbanks: Fairbanks North
        Star Borough Impact Information Center. Photocopy.

1976   Financial statement, February. Fairbanks: Fair-
        banks North Star Borough.

1976   Impact Information Center Regular Reports, Nos. 23-
        29. Fairbanks: Fairbanks North Star Borough Impact
        Information Center. Photocopy.

1976   Mobile home living in Fairbanks. Impact Information
        Center Special Report No. 4, September. Fairbanks:
        Fairbanks North Star Borough Impact Information
        Center. Photocopy.

Fairbanks Rescue Mission
1976   The Northern Light. Fairbanks: Fairbanks Rescue
        Mission.

Frake, C.O.
1962   Cultural ecology and ethnography, American Anthro-
        pologist, 64:54-59.

Hall, Edward T.
1966   The Hidden Dimension. Garden City, N.Y.: Doubleday.

Havelock, John E.
1973   Moving Alaskan Oil: Trans-Canada or Trans-Alaska?
        A Study of the Merits. Report of the Pipeline
        Coordinating Committee, State of Alaska. Photocopy.

Hawley, A.H.
1950   Human Ecology: A Theory of Community Structure.
        New York: Ronald.

Holty, Joseph G.
1973   Air quality in a subarctic community: Fairbanks,
        Alaska. Arctic, 26(4):229.

Jackson, Henry M.
1973   Preface to: Congress and the Nation's Environment:
        Environmental and Natural Resources Affairs of the
        92nd Congress. Prepared by the Environmental Policy
        Division, Congresional Research Service, Library of
        Congress. Washington, D.C.: U.S. Government
        Printing Office.

Kraus, Robert, and Patricia Buffler
1976   Intercultural variation in mortality due to violence.
        Paper read at the annual meeting, American Psychia-
        tric Association, Miami, Florida.

Kruse, John A.
1976   Fairbanks Community Survey. Institute of Social and
        Economic Research, University of Alaska, Fairbanks.
        Preliminary findings of the survey presented in a
        panel at the 27th Alaska Science Conference, Fair-
        banks, August 6.

LaRocca, Joe E.
1973   Anatomy of a pipeline, Countermedia, August.

Lewontin, R.C.
1957   The adaptations of populations to varying environ-
        ments. In Cold Spring Harbor Symposia on Quanti-
        tative Biology, Vol. 22. New York: Long Island
        Biological Association.

328

Malthus, Thomas Robert
  1890   An Essay on the Principle of Population. London:
          Word, Lock.

Mathematical Sciences Northwest, Inc.
  1972   A Study of the Economic and Sociological Impact of
          Construction and Initial Operation of the Trans
          Alaska Pipeline. Prepared for Alyeska Pipeline
          Service Company. Seattle: MSNW Report No. 72-4D-
          4,5,6.

Miller, Francis T., et al.
  1974   Experiences in Rural Mental Health Measuring and
          Monitoring Stress in Communities. Chapel Hill:
          University of North Carolina School of Medicine,
          Department of Psychiatry, Division of Community
          Psychiatry.

Nash, Roderick (ed.)
  1968   The American Environment: Readings in the History of
          Conservation. Readings, Mass.: Addison-Wesley.

North Pacific Consultants
  1959   Economic analysis of Fairbanks and contiguous areas,
          Alaska. Report prepared for Golden Valley Electric
          Association. Fairbanks: North Pacific Consultants.

Northwest Federal Regional Council
  1975   Social and economic impact of energy development.
          Draft report, January 24.

Parr, Charles H.
  1974   Impact Information Center schematic. Paper presented
          to the Fairbanks North Star Borough Assembly.

Pearson, Roger W. and Daniel W. Smith
  1975   Fairbanks: A study of environmental quality, Arctic,
          28(2).

Quandt, Donald L.
  1974   Fort Wainwright's Contribution to the Fairbanks
          Economy. Unpublished Masters thesis. Fairbanks:
          University of Alaska.

Redfield, R.
  1955   The Little Community: Viewpoints for the Study of a
          Human Whole. Chicago: University of Chicago Press.

Rogers, George (ed.)
  1970   Change in Alaska--People, Petroleum and Politics.
          College: University of Alaska.

329

Shoemaker, James H.
1970   Fairbanks and the Interior of Alaska: Potentials
        for Growth, 1970-1980. Fairbanks: University of
        Alaska.

Social Concerns Committee, Fairbanks Council of Churches
1975   Fairbanks and Interior Alaska: A One Day Community
        Forum on Growth. Published in cooperation with the
        Fairbanks Town and Village Association for Develop-
        ment, Inc.

Steward, J.H.
1955   Theory of Culture Change: The Methodology of Multi-
        linear Evolution. Urbana: University of Illinois
        Press.

Scott, D.H.
1969   Cultural and natural checks on population growth,
        in Andrew P. Vayda (ed.), Environmental and Cultural
        Behavior. Garden City, N.Y.: Natural History Press.

Straatmeyer, Jean
1975   Theology and social involvement. Paper presented to
        the Alaskan Anthropology Conference, Fairbanks,
        March 14-15.

Straatmeyer, Gene, et al.
1975   Social Concerns Task Force--Alaska Christian Confer-
        ence. Mimeographed report.

Tussing, Arlon R. et al.
1971   Alaska Pipeline Report. Fairbanks: Institute of
        Social, Economic and Government Research, University
        of Alaska.

Tussing, Arlon R. and Monica Thomas
1974   Consumer prices, personal income and earnings in
        Alaska, Alaska Review of Business and Economic
        Conditions, 11(3).

U.S. Bureau of the Census
1975   Estimates of the Population of Alaska Census Divi-
        sions and Metropolitan Areas: July, 1973 and 1974.

U.S. Department of Housing and Urban Development
1975   Housing and Urban Development Situation Report,
        Fairbanks, Alaska as of April 1, 1975. Photocopy.

U.S. Department of the Interior
1971   Trans Alaska Pipeline hearings: Proceedings, ex-
hibits, and supplemental testimony. Washington:
Hoover Reporting Company.

1972   Final Environmental Impact Statement for Proposed
Trans-Alaska Pipeline. Vols. 1-6. Springfield,
Virginia: National Technical Information Service.

Viereck, Eleanor C. (ed.)
1970   Proceeding of the Twentieth Alaska Science Conference, College, Alaska. Fairbanks: Alaska Division
of the American Association for the Advancement of
Science.

Wynne-Edwards, V.C.
1965   Self-regulating systems in populations of animals.
Science, 147.

Zubrow, Ezra B.W.
1971   Carrying capacity and dynamic equilibrium in the
prehistoric Southwest. American Antiquity, 36(2).

Miscellaneous

1974   Agreement and Grant of Right-of-Way for Trans-Alaska
Pipeline between the United States of America and
Amerada Hess Corporation, ARCO Pipe Line Company,
Exxon Pipeline Company, Mobil Alaska Pipeline Company,
Phillips Petroleum Company, Sohio Pipe Line Company,
and Union Alaska Pipeline Company. January 23, 1974.

1974   Right-of-Way Lease for the Trans-Alaska Pipeline be-
tween the State of Alaska and Amerada Hess Corporation
ARCO Pipeline Company, Exxon Pipeline Company, Mobil
Alaska Pipeline Company, Phillips Petroleum Company,
Sohio Pipe Line Company and Union Alaska Pipeline
Company. May 3, 1974.

Newspapers and Magazines

Alaska Industry Magazine   Fairbanks Daily News-Miner

All-Alaska Weekly   Federal Register

Anchorage Daily News   Los Angeles Times

Anchorage Daily Times   New York Times Magazine

Edmonton Journal   Wall Street Journal

INDEX